THE GOSPEL OF JOHN AND CHRISTIAN ORIGINS

JOHN ASHTON

Fortress Press
Minneapolis

THE GOSPEL OF JOHN AND CHRISTIAN ORIGINS

Cover image © Thinkstock

Cover design: Tory Herman

Library of Congress Cataloging-in-Publication Data

Ashton, John, 1931-

The gospel of John and Christian origins / John Ashton.

pages cm

Includes bibliographical references.

ISBN 978-1-4514-7214-1 (pbk. : alk. paper) — ISBN 978-1-4514-7982-9 (ebook)

1. Bible. John–Criticism, interpretation, etc. 2. Christianity and other religions–Judaism. 3. Judaism–Relations–Christianity, 4. Christianity–Origin. I. Title.

BS2615.52.A83 2014

226.5'06–dc23

2013034858

Manufactured in the U.S.A.

This book was produced using Pressbooks.com, and PDF rendering was done by PrinceXML.

For Philip and Patricia

The enquiry of truth, which is the lovemaking or wooing of it; the knowledge of truth, which is the presence of it; and the belief in truth, which is the enjoying of it—is the sovereign good of human nature.

——FRANCIS BACON

CONTENTS

Acknowledgements

First I want to thank Philip Esler for inviting me to St Mary's University College, Strawberry Hill, where he had recently taken up the post of Principal, for the purpose of giving the short series of lectures on which this book is based. The invitation was especially welcome because an offer to my own university, Oxford, to give the lectures there had recently been turned down.

A similar offer to Judith Lieu in Cambridge met with a similar, though very gracious answer: the lecture syllabus was already full. So I was especially grateful for Philip's immediate response to the expression of my disappointment, while I was entertaining him to breakfast along with his wife, Patricia, one bright summer morning in my Oxford flat: "Come and give your lectures at St Mary's, John. What's more, I'll pay you."

Like many storytellers, I have begun at the end. The true beginning was an offer by my very good friends Catrin Williams and Christopher Rowland to organize a colloquium on my work at the University of Bangor. A month before this took place, in July 2010, I had returned to Oxford after a long stay in France, convinced (having recently completed a second edition of my book *Understanding the Fourth Gospel*) that I had nothing left to say on the Gospel of John. But of course I was obliged to introduce the Bangor colloquium, and to write up my piece afterwards for the book that Catrin was editing. A spin-off from this work was an article on the Son of Man, published the following year in *New Testament Studies*. Meanwhile I had been asked to contribute something to a book celebrating the fiftieth anniversary of C. H. Dodd's *Historical Tradition in the Fourth Gospel*. What with one thing and another I felt I had accumulated enough material for a short series of lectures, and possibly, after that, for another book. Hence my offer to Oxford, and hence too my gratitude at Philip Esler's immediate response to my story of its rejection.

I must now name the five friends who have generously and unstintingly given me advice during the composition of this book. I have already mentioned Catrin Williams and Christopher Rowland, but it is to Chris especially that I owe many stimulating suggestions about how my work could be improved. Another old friend and colleague who has given me help is Robert Morgan, and I remember in particular one summer day last year in his Sandford garden, when we were hunting through a decidedly prolix book by F. C. Baur, the great nineteenth-century exegete and theologian whose work he knows so much better than I. The oldest friend of all, Robert Butterworth, has reviewed my work for many years with a clarity of perception and a refusal of fudge that only a true friend could supply. Lastly a newer and much younger friend whose opinion I have come to value, Ben Reynolds, whom I see somehow as picking up the baton of Johannine studies and carrying it for a long time to come.

To all these, and to many other friends who have helped me in different ways, I am very very grateful. And in adding a word of thanks to Fortress Press I want to record my delight and surprise when a submission made by email when the book was almost finished was greeted an hour later with a message from the editor, Neil Elliott, that included the words, "I know your work well."

April, 2013

Introduction

One day in early August 1942, when a German nun called Sister Benedicta was at prayer in the chapel of the Carmelite convent in the Dutch town of Echt, members of the German SS presented themselves at the convent door. They told the prioress to inform Sister Benedicta, whose original name was Edith Stein, that she had ten minutes to pack all that she needed for a journey to Germany. From Germany she was transported to Auschwitz, in Poland, where she was murdered. She was fifty years old. Ten years earlier she had entered the Carmelite order. Edith Stein was Jewish; but one day in 1921, at the age of thirty, she had picked up and read from cover to cover a copy of the autobiography of St. Teresa of Avila. She had been interested in Christianity for some time, but for her this book was the last step in her long search for truth. On finishing it she said to herself, "Das ist die Wahrheit!"—"That is the truth." Looking back, she realized that this was the moment both of her decision to become a Catholic and of her vocation to the Carmelite Order. She went to tell her mother, a fervent, practicing Jew, who was horrified, and wept. Edith was very close to her mother, but she had never seen her in tears before. Shortly afterwards, on Yom Kippur, the two women went together to the synagogue. When the rabbi intoned the words, "Höre O Israel, Dein Gott ist ein Einziger" ("Hear, O Israel, your God is One"), Edith's mother leaned over and whispered to her daughter, "Hörst Du? Dein Gott ist ein Einziger"—"Do you hear? Your God is One, and only One."

Here is the boundary line: one God. Christianity also proclaims one God, but its two central doctrines, Incarnation and Trinity, sharply differentiate it from the other "religions of the book," Judaism and Islam. These two doctrines are found in the Gospel of John, the first spelled out explicitly on its first page, the second clearly adumbrated in the part of the Gospel we call the Farewell Discourse (chs. 14–16). They situate it poles apart from Judaism, further away than any other writing in the New Testament, and consequently make it the hardest of all to explain. Even considered in isolation, with no consideration of its relation to Judaism, it is an astonishing, bewildering, mysterious work. So we should not be surprised that the great German scholar Adolf Harnack declared in 1886 that "the origin of the Johannine writings is, from the standpoint of a history of literature and dogma, the most extraordinary enigma which the early history of Christianity presents."[1] What Harnack actually wrote was "das wundervollste Rätsel," the most marvelous riddle, or a puzzle full of mysteries. The Gospel of John is indeed "a puzzle full of mysteries." How are we to explain it?

The Jewish religion as we see it today is far from uniform. But although there are considerable differences between the Ashkenaz and Sephardic traditions, and between the three main groupings, Orthodox, liberal, and Reform, the differences are not great enough to warrant our speaking of a plurality of Judaisms. Similar differences between the two great branches of Islam, the Sunni and the Shia, and between the various regions of the world where Islam has taken hold, are too small to justify our talking of a plurality of Islams.

The differences today between some branches of Christianity are great enough, in my opinion, to make them into different religions. Yet we never hear people speaking of different Christianities any more than we do of different Judaisms or Islams. No branch of Christianity could possibly have emerged from any of the modern varieties of Judaism. Why? Fundamentally because the two religions, though both profess belief in one God, have completely opposed conceptions of God's definitive revelation to humankind. For Jews this can be summed up as the Torah, the law revealed to Moses. For Christians it is summed up in the very person of Christ.

One of the best summaries of the ineradicable difference between the two religions comes in the Prologue to the Gospel of John: "For the law was given through Moses; grace and truth came through Jesus Christ" (1:17). This statement, bleak, blunt, uncompromising, illustrates more clearly than any other in the whole of the New Testament the incompatibility of Christianity and Judaism. It announces a new religion. Yet whoever wrote it (it comes towards the end of the Prologue of John's Gospel) had worshiped in a Jewish synagogue. This Gospel tells among other things of the decision of "the Jews" to expel from the synagogue anyone who confessed Jesus to be the Messiah. Yet, unlike the proclamation of a Jewish Messiah (which can only be made *from within* Judaism), the rejection of the law of Moses clearly implied in the statement above amounts to a rejection of Judaism itself. So how are these two related? How could someone who once claimed that Jesus was the long-awaited Jewish Messiah go on to abandon the traditional beliefs without which such a claim could have no meaning? How, within roughly half a century, was the move made from one religion to the other? The answer to this question lies hidden somewhere in the pages of John's Gospel, and one of my aims in this book is

1. Adolf Harnack, *History of Dogma* (7 vols.; New York: Russell & Russell, 1958), 1:96-97 (first German edition, 1886).

to tease it out. I will be arguing, in fact, that the Gospel represents a deliberate decision to supplant Moses and to replace him with Jesus, thereby substituting one revelation, and indeed one religion, for another.[2]

While I was writing this book, it was borne in on me that its central argument rests on three basic propositions, none of which can be taken for granted. My guess is (for I have made no attempt to verify this supposition by combing through the hundreds of books and articles that have been published on the Gospel of John within, say, the last five years) that the great majority of contemporary experts would either reject these propositions outright or feel themselves justified in ignoring them. So I have set out to prove in three excursuses that (1) the Gospels are not to be thought of simply as Lives of Christ; (2) that the Gospel of John was not written as a continuous composition over a short stretch of time but went through at least two editions; and (3) that it was composed by a member of a particular community for the benefit of his fellow members. Introducing a collection of essays published the same year as the second edition of *Understanding the Fourth Gospel*, Richard Bauckham takes issue with what he calls "the dominant approach in Johannine scholarship," which he associates in particular with Raymond E. Brown, J. Louis Martyn, and myself.[3] (Having seen many more references in the secondary literature to Bauckham's book than to my own, I rather doubt if my views on John could be said to represent the dominant approach.) Finally, I have added a fourth excursus to defend the proposition that the main theme of the Prologue is not creation (as is generally assumed), but God's plan for humankind.

Because Moses was so important in the experience of the evangelist, and therefore in his thinking too, I have prefaced my new book with some reflections on his changing role, taking my illustrations not in the order in

2. Garry Wills, reviewing a recent book on changing Catholic attitudes to Judaism (*New York Review of Books*, vol 60, no. 3, March 21–April 3, 2013, 36–37) does not disguise his abhorrence of what he calls *supersessionism* (ugly word), which he clearly associates with anti-Semitism. He ascribes this to the Letter to the Hebrews, which he contrasts with Paul's Letter to the Romans. But Paul too, like John, had to choose between Christ and the law. The root difficulty is the ambiguity of the word *Jewish*, which has both a religious and a racial reference, as it did at the turn of the era. If we blanket out the racial reference altogether, then of course Christianity is anti-Jewish, just as Judaism is anti-Christian. The two religions are incompatible. But it does not follow that Christians and Jews can't be friends. The adoption of a new religion by New Testament writers, most of whom were Jewish, did not turn them into anti-Semites. One reason for beginning this book with the story of Edith Stein is to illustrate what should in any case be an obvious truth.

3. Richard Bauckham, *The Testimony of the Beloved Disciple: Narrative, History, and Theology in the Gospel of John* (Grand Rapids: Baker Academic, 2007). Apart from the introduction only one chapter in the book directly attacks "the dominant approach," and I deal with this in Excursus II.

which they appear in the Gospel as we have it, but in the order in which the evangelist himself came to them. (The first two, I think, were present in sources he took over; the last two were added at a later stage of his work.)

In chapter 2, "Consciousness of Genre," I argue that the evangelist, fully aware of the problems inherent in the gospel genre that he had chosen for his work, reflected upon them and exploited them for his own purposes. In chapter 3 I attempt to explain the phrase "chief priests and Pharisees" as it is used in the Gospel. Both of these groups have been fully investigated by scholars, but there is no satisfactory short account available either of their history or of their essential nature. Since they both play a significant part in John's Gospel, a summary description of their history and nature furnishes a useful introduction. A secondary aim of this chapter is to indicate where I believe we should look if we wish to understand the great debates of the Gospel, mostly with "the Jews" but also with the Pharisees—namely, in first-century Palestine (Jamnia). Indirectly, therefore, I am taking issue with the views of two great scholars who have written extensively about the Fourth Gospel. Were we to follow Rudolf Bultmann we would be looking rather to Iraq (where, apparently, the Mandaean writings were composed, no earlier than the eighth century CE); and if instead we followed C. H. Dodd we would be looking to Egypt (where the *Hermetica* were written, in the second and third centuries CE). A third aim of the chapter is to explain the evangelist's puzzling use of the term Ἰουδαῖοι (Jews) to refer to Jesus' adversaries—puzzling not least because he and his disciples were Jews themselves.

The relevance of the fourth chapter, on the Essenes, is less immediately evident, because this sect is never mentioned in the Gospel (or, for that matter, anywhere else in the New Testament). But in the course of a more general discussion of the history of this sect, and of the scrolls that formed the library of the Qumran community, I shall argue that, besides writings that demonstrate their incontestable allegiance to the Mosaic law, there are others that show a surprising affinity to the Gospel of John.

Some may think that these two chapters (3 and 4) are of only marginal relevance to the book as a whole. But the third chapter anchors the Gospel in its historical setting and thus avoids the risk of allowing it to float free, and the fourth provides some useful and relatively accessible information about a sect that is still little known except to specialists.

In the fifth chapter, taking an historical approach, I inquire into the circumstances of the Gospel's composition and follow this by offering a radically altered version of a chapter of my earlier book entitled "Intimations of Apocalyptic."[4] I conclude this by asking in what sense if any the Gospel might be called "an apocalypse in reverse." The seventh chapter, one of two to deal with the evangelist's adaptation of Jewish traditions, is concerned with the claim that Jesus fulfilled the prediction of a Moses-like prophet, and the eighth ("Human or Divine?") deals with two other Jewish traditions, Wisdom and the Son of Man. In the final chapter I attempt to explain the difference between the Johannine portrait of Jesus and the much more readily comprehensible picture of the Synoptic Gospels.

4. John Ashton, *Understanding the Fourth Gospel* (Oxford: Clarendon, 1st ed. 1991; 2nd ed. 2007). Unless otherwise noted this work will be cited from the second edition.

1

Moses

Not everybody knows that besides the sublime frescoes of Michelangelo that adorn its ceiling the Sistine Chapel in Rome also contains frescoes painted between 1481 and 1483 by four other great Italian artists, including Domenico Ghirlandaio, to whom Michelangelo was for a time apprenticed, and Sandro Botticelli (not to mention several tapestries by Raphael). The paintings on the middle sections of the two side walls of the chapel portray a series of episodes from the Old Testament, opposite scenes from the New Testament they were thought to have prefigured. Moses, on the left (south) wall, confronts Christ, on the right. The original sequence began on the altar wall itself with the *Finding of Moses* and the *Birth of Christ* (events also associated in Matthew's Gospel), but both of these paintings were subsequently destroyed to make way for Michelangelo's *Last Judgment*, painted over a half-century later in the new mannerist style. (The two final paintings on the entrance wall, opposite the altar, deteriorated so badly that they had to be replaced.) The remaining dozen paintings of the sequence, six on each wall, have survived and can still be seen today, starting with two paintings of Perugino, the *Circumcision of the Son of Moses* and the *Baptism of Christ*. Next come two pictures of Botticelli, one depicting the *Temptation* (or *Trial*) *of Moses* in the desert, the other the *Temptation of Christ*, in which the three temptations of Jesus are placed in the upper register of the painting. Then comes Ghirlandaio's *Crossing of the Red Sea* opposite his *Calling of the Apostles*. After that the *Dispensation of the Ten Commandments*, by Cosimo Roselli, showing the handing over of the tablets of the law, is paralleled by the *Sermon on the Mount*. (Although Roselli was undoubtedly the weakest of the four, he was still an artist of considerable talent.) Another pair of pictures by Botticelli represents occasions of disarray or rebellion (*conturbatio*): one in the life of Moses, based on the story in Numbers 16 according to which the rebellious Korah ends up being swallowed up into the ground (while his sons, in accordance with Num. 26:11, are shown tucked away in the lower left corner, relieved and somewhat bemused to be still alive); and the other in the life of Christ (with the arch of Constantine in the background). In the last two surviving paintings the *Death of Moses* is shown opposite a painting of the *Last Supper*. Although four different artists were involved, the frescoes are broadly similar in conception: the scale of the figures is the same, and so are the range of colors and the style of the landscapes. Moses, a dignified and authoritative figure who appears in each of the paintings on the south wall (several times in some of them), is depicted throughout wearing a yellow robe and an olive-green cloak. There can be no doubt that the series was conceived from the outset as a unified whole.[1]

Sixtus's secretary, Andreas of Trebizond, who probably masterminded the whole series, summed it up as paintings of two legal systems, a summary borne out by the Latin inscriptions above the pictures: for five of the six captions on the south wall include the words *lex scripta*—the written law—and five of the six on the north wall contain the words *evangelica lex*—the law of the gospel. The caption above Roselli's picture of the Last Supper, for instance, reads, surprisingly, *Replicatio legis evangelicae a Christo*—Christ's repetition of the law of the gospel. The parallel picture, whose central scene shows Moses reciting the law to the assembled multitude on the eve of his death, bears the caption, *Replicatio legis scriptae a Moise.*[2] This makes the other title slightly more comprehensible; but it is still very strange.

It can hardly be doubted that had Martin Luther ever seen the paintings on the walls of this chapel (completed thirty-five years before he posted the famous ninety-five theses on the door of a church in Wittenberg in 1517) he would have been no less offended by the assumption that the gospel was a system of law matching the law of Moses than he was by the sale of indulgences that helped to pay for the paintings. Some justification for this way of looking at the moral teaching of Jesus can be found in the declaration attributed to him in Matthew's Gospel (5:17) that he had come not to abolish the law and the prophets but to fulfill them (although the Sermon of the Mount is more concerned with ideals and principles than with prescriptive legislation). Luther, of course, was to insist on the absolute opposition between law and gospel; and although he may have exaggerated the extent of Paul's rejection of the

---

1. Most of this information comes from a multi-authored work entitled *The Sistine Chapel: Michelangelo Rediscovered* (London: Muller, Blond & White, 1986). The title is misleading, for one chapter of the book deals (not always accurately) with the decorations of the walls. The author of this chapter is John Shearman.

2. The *Oxford Latin Dictionary* does not include *repetition* under *replicatio*, nor *rebellion* under *conturbatio*. But these are the meanings required by the context.

law, Christians of every denomination have accepted the general thrust of his arguments concerning the incompatibility of Christian teaching with the Jewish law. I cannot be alone in my astonishment when I first read the captions above the frescoes decorating the walls of the Sistine Chapel.

Toward the end of the fifteenth century, which was when the walls and ceiling of the Sistine Chapel were painted, the Church of Rome, having recovered from the forty-year schism arising from the squabble of the three popes, was beginning to regain its authority. The prominence given to Moses in these paintings, whose every action in the frescoes on the south wall is positive, and often heroic, shows that Judaism was no longer thought of as a rival to Christianity, but simply as a precursor. In one obvious sense Jesus was now seen (as he had been by Matthew) as a second Moses.

Moses in the Fourth Gospel

Where does the Gospel of John, I now want to ask, stand in relation to the portrayal of Moses in the Sistine Chapel? It would be a mistake to assume that the positive, generally sympathetic attitude to Moses evident in these frescoes must also have characterized the very earliest Christian movement. Running throughout the present book will be the thesis that before, during, and after the painful break between the advocates of Jesus and their more traditional rivals in the synagogue around the end of the first century CE , the opposition between Moses and Jesus was at the heart of the conflict between these two groups. Commentators often speak of the Jesus group in the synagogue as Christians, and although they are not altogether wrong, the easy, anachronistic use of a name that had not yet been coined (or at any rate was not yet current) can be misleading, for it appears to suggest that the new religion had already made its mark even while the struggle for independence was still going on. It is true, I think, that in ousting Moses from his central place as God's representative in his dealings with his people, the fourth evangelist (along with those on whose behalf he spoke and wrote) was effectively establishing a new religion. But this needs to be demonstrated and should not simply be assumed. In the remainder of this chapter I will appeal to the Gospel itself for evidence that at the same time as promoting Jesus' new revelation the evangelist was deliberately repudiating traditional Judaism.

Written as it was by someone who worshiped in a Jewish synagogue, the account in John's Gospel of a complete and comprehensive religious revolution is truly astonishing. Its extraordinary nature is veiled from us largely because, reading the Gospel as a proclamation of the new religion, we are understandably more interested in how its author concluded his religious conversion than in how he began it. Moreover, this is one document of which it can truly be said that its end is its beginning, insofar as the choice of one religion to replace another is tersely announced on its very first page. Since the uncompromising rejection of Moses and the law in favor of the grace and truth brought by Christ is stated in the Prologue, it is hard not to read all that follows in the light of this new revelation. But from the historian's point of view the Prologue should be seen as a conclusion rather than as a commencement. We should start our inquiry at a point where the evangelist and the group he represents are still "disciples of Moses," worshiping in the synagogue alongside people convinced that God's last word had already been uttered in the foundation document of the people of Israel that we call the Torah. Or, even better, we should go back to the source, namely, to a section of the Gospel that was taken over by the evangelist and adapted to form the beginning of his story—the sudden appearance of the man we call John the Baptist, whose dramatic gesture in pointing to the one of whom he said "he ranks before me" has been recorded thousands of times in Christian art.

Accordingly I propose in what follows to discuss the Moses passages in the Gospel in some sort of chronological order, starting from the missionary document generally known as the Signs Source, followed by what I believe to have been a second missionary document directed to the Samaritans. After that I will deal with some passages from the first edition of the Gospel, add a short comment about the Farewell Discourse, and conclude with two texts from the second edition,[3] first a few verses from chapter 6 and, second, the Prologue.[4]

---

3. That the Gospel underwent (at least) two editions will be fully argued in Excursus III.

4. I will treat of most of the passages discussed in chapter 6 of J. Louis Martyn's *History and Theology in the Fourth Gospel*, 3rd ed. (Louisville/London: Westminster John Knox, 2003), 101–24 ("From the Expectation of the Prophet-Messiah like Moses . . .") along with most of Martyn's primary sources. I differ with him insofar as I attempt to trace some sort of chronological development in the evangelist's thinking about Moses, and also (more importantly) in that I hold the titles of Messiah and Prophet apart. The Mosaic prophet unquestionably has a major role to play throughout the Gospel, but what Martyn calls "the Moses-Messiah typology" is largely his own invention. It is true that the Samaritan woman uses the term *Messiah* when referring to the Taheb (4:25; see below), but the evidence from Jewish sources is restricted to a saying ascribed to Rabbi Akiba in a late midrash (*Tanḥuma 'Ekeb* 7), predicting that the Messiah will condemn his people to another forty-year sojourn in the desert, and a fuller but even later reference in *Qoheleth Rabba* 1.8 (both texts quoted by Martyn on p. 107). But John's Messiah is Davidic. The Messiah and the prophet appear not far apart in a number of passages in the Gospel but are never identified. In John 1 they are named separately by John the Baptist and discovered independently by two different disciples, Andrew and Philip. The questions concerning the two in John 7 come from different voices in the crowd, and *contra* Martyn (p. 111) there is no "easy modulation from the Mosaic Prophet to the Mosaic Prophet-Messiah." Nor are they directly associated in John 9. Yet despite the weakness of his "Messiah like Moses" thesis, Martyn's discussion is always illuminating and illustrates how the Johannine

Some of these passages will receive a rather summary treatment here, but I shall be focusing on them more intently later in the book.

It is not easy to stick to this program, because what may plausibly be regarded as the first edition of the Gospel already belongs to a period following the dramatic breakup of the opposing parties in the synagogue. In particular it includes the three great challenges to Jesus that figure prominently in chapters 5, 8, and 10. Not surprisingly, then, the first edition already contains many indications of the radical rejection of the authority of Moses expressed most clearly in the Prologue.

JOHN 1:19—2:11

Nevertheless there are two passages in the Gospel that were probably drawn from, or at least based on, missionary manifestos designed to promote faith in Jesus as the Messiah and the prophet like Moses foretold in Deut. 18:15, 18, verses of such importance that they should be quoted here:

[And Moses summoned the people of Israel and said to them:]
"The Lord your God will raise up for you a prophet like me from among you, from your brethren—him you shall heed.". . . And the Lord said to me, "They have rightly spoken. I will raise up for them a prophet like you from among their brethren; and I will put my words in his mouth, and he shall speak to them all that I command him."

The first of these passages (1:19—2:11), the commencement of what is commonly designated "the Signs Source," begins with a denial on the part of John the Baptist that he was either the Messiah, or Elijah, or "the prophet" (1:20-22). John pointed instead to Jesus, who was soon discovered—by those who became his first disciples—to be both the Messiah and the one "of whom Moses in the law and also the prophets wrote" (1:45). The role of Moses in this early source was simply and solely that of a prophet who predicted the coming of another prophet like himself. So far there is no controversy and no conflict.[5]

JOHN 4:1-42

The second passage is the story of the woman at the well. A well is in any case an obvious location for a dialogue about water; but this particular well was

group in the synagogue may have been constantly subjected to a series of probing questions concerning the claims they made for Jesus.

5. I will discuss this passage much more fully below in chapter 7.

selected because it had been given to the Samaritans by none other than the patriarch Jacob: "our father Jacob," as the woman called him, "who gave us this well, and drank from it himself, and his sons, and his cattle" (4:12). (A site at the foot of Mount Gerizim, the sacred mountain of the Samaritans, is identified to this day as Jacob's well.) The more immediate ancestor of the Samaritans (as the father of Ephraim and Manasseh) was Jacob's son Joseph, whom he called "a fruitful bough by a spring" in his final blessing (Gen. 49:22). So the well was ideally situated for a conciliatory conversation between a Samaritan woman and a man she explicitly designated as a Jew (4:9), belonging to the great tribe of Judah (all of whom were descended from Judah, another of Jacob's sons), the long-standing enemy of the Samaritans.

In reading this chapter we should bear in mind the exceptional importance of the figure of Moses in Samaritan traditions. As Wayne Meeks says, Moses "dominates Samaritan religious literature to an extent scarcely equaled in any circle of Jewish tradition, with the possible exception of Philo."[6] Deuteronomy 18:18, the key text in any explanation of the discovery of Jesus in John 1:45, lies behind the expectation of the Taheb no less than it does behind the Jewish expectation of a future prophet. Commentators are agreed that the woman's use of the Jewish term *Messiah* when speaking of her own expectation (4:25) must be interpreted as a reference to the Samaritan Taheb,[7] not a Davidic Messiah but a Moses-like prophet. Moses, although not actually named in this passage, was considered to be the author of the Samaritan Torah, guaranteeing that their future expectations would be fulfilled.[8] Neither of these two missionary documents would have been welcomed or accepted if it did not accord somehow with the hopes of those for whom it was composed. A successful outcome of the mission is explicitly recorded among the Samaritans (4:39-42) and, in the case of the Jews, must be inferred from the subsequent presence in the synagogue of followers of Jesus. So two documents testifying to a calmly positive attitude to Moses have been taken over and included in the Gospel.

JOHN 3:14

There is a further instance in the Gospel of Moses in his role as antitype or precursor, perhaps the most intriguing of all: "And as Moses lifted up the serpent

---

6. Wayne A. Meeks, *The Prophet-King. Moses Traditions and the Johannine Christology,* Supplements to Novum Testamentum 14 (Leiden: Brill, 1967), 216.

7. In a helpful note (*Prophet-King,* 250 n. 1), Meeks points out that the word תהב, active participle of the verb תוב (= Hebrew שוב) can be understood either transitively ("the Restorer") or intransitively ("the Returning One"). Scholars disagree about which of these is more likely to be correct.

8. See further Martyn's discussion of Samaritan expectations in *History and Theology,* 106–7.

in the wilderness, so must the Son of man be lifted up" (3:14). The reference is clear and undisputed: "And the Lord said to Moses, 'Make a fiery serpent, and set it on a pole; and every one who is bitten, when he sees it, shall live.' So Moses made a bronze serpent, and set it on a pole; and if a serpent bit any man, he would look at the bronze serpent and live" (Num. 21:8-9). But how did the elevation of the bronze serpent by Moses in the desert come to be associated with the elevation of Jesus on the cross? To put the question in this way may seem to imply that the association was suggested by the use of the word *elevation*; but in fact where John uses ὑψοῦν ("exalt") the Greek version of Numbers uses the simple verb ἱστάναι ("set up").[9] Commentators have had a field day in their search for a verbal connection between the two passages, and many different ambiguous Aramaic words have been proposed as a solution of the puzzle—though as Rudolf Bultmann remarks drily with regard to one such suggestion concerning 12:34 (where the word ὑψοῦν also occurs): "this verse was composed by the evangelist, who wrote Greek."[10] It must be relevant that gazing at the bronze serpent was a guarantee of survival, since John saw the purpose of the lifting up of the Son of Man to be "that whoever believes in him may have eternal life" (3:15). Bultmann thinks that "the Evangelist was probably acquainted with the typological interpretation which the Christian tradition had given to Num. 21.8f, for it also occurs in Barn 12.5-7; Just. *Apol.* I 60; *Dial.* 91, 94, 112."[11] But Barnabas and Justin were second-century writers; and if someone had to be the first to associate the setting-up of a bronze effigy for the purpose of preserving life with the life-giving elevation of Jesus on the cross, why should it not have been the evangelist John? I began this paragraph by referring to Moses as an antetype or precursor, but this is not quite right.[12] For the (literally) crucial connection is the actual act of elevation, the lifting up of the pole in one case and of the cross in the other. If we were to push the comparison further we would have to conclude that what Moses actually prefigured was the action of the Roman soldiers in hoisting up the cross, and that Jesus, bizarrely, was being compared with a snake. (And indeed Barnabas and Justin, and, later, Tertullian, do treat the serpent as a type of Christ.) The real link is to be found in the notion of life, but the evangelist is very far from associating life with Moses.

9. For a fuller discussion, see my *Understanding the Fourth Gospel,* 2nd ed. (Oxford: Clarendon, 2007), 268-70.

10. Rudolf Bultmann, *The Gospel of John: A Commentary* (Oxford: Basil Blackwell, 1971), 354 n. 6.

11. Bultmann, *Gospel,* 152 n. 1.

12. See Howard M. Teeple, *The Mosaic Eschatological Prophet,* Journal of Biblical Literature Monograph Series 10 (Philadelphia: Society of Biblical Literature, 1957), 96; Meeks, *Prophet-King,* 292.

JOHN 5:31-47

We now turn to the conclusion of chapter 5, the chapter in which for the first time in the Gospel Jesus is accused by the Jews of claiming equality with God. From this it may be inferred that this chapter must have been composed after the breakup with the synagogue, and so may be expected to exhibit some hostility to the principles of its leaders.

We might conclude from a cursory reading of the first part of this passage (5:31-40), where the key word is *witness* (μαρτυρία), that Jesus is appealing here to a variety of witnesses. He starts by discounting his own witness,[13] but then, in rapid succession, he speaks of God (the one who sent him), of John the Baptist, of his own works, of Moses, and finally the Scriptures. A more attentive reading, however, reveals that John's testimony is rapidly set aside (v. 34: "I do not receive testimony from man"), and that the three witnesses that Jesus does allow, his works (v. 36), the Father (v. 37), and the Scriptures (v. 39), can be reduced to the single witness of the Father, inasmuch as Jesus' works are performed only in obedience to the one who sent him, and the authority of the Scriptures comes from the God who inspired them.

At this point Jesus speaks to the Jews of the Scriptures as a whole: "You search the scriptures because you think that in them you have eternal life; and it is they that bear witness to me; yet you refuse to come to me that you may have life" (5:39-40). That Jews looked to find life in the Scriptures is almost a truism.[14] Yet Jesus does not enter into an argument here. Instead, almost as an afterthought, he closes his discourse in this chapter by talking of Moses—not, though, to attack him, for at this point he is relying on the authority of Moses to provide him with an argument his adversaries would be forced to accept. So the evangelist takes the opportunity of bringing Moses into the discussion in a sort of *argumentum ad hominem* that conceals a real opposition he is not yet prepared to disclose.

---

13. The usual translation of 5:31, "If I bear witness to myself, my testimony is not true," makes no sense. The word ἀληθής should be translated here as "valid." The same rendering is required in 8:14: "Even if I do bear witness to myself, my testimony is valid." Although these two verses appear to contradict each other, the contradiction is only apparent, for in both passages the underlying appeal is to the testimony of God. For a full discussion, see my *Understanding the Fourth Gospel*, 118–22.

14. Raymond E. Brown (*The Gospel according to John: Introduction, Translation, and Notes*, 2 vols., Anchor Bible 29, 29A [New York: Doubleday, 1966, 1970], 1:225) has two citations—strong ones—from *Pirqe Aboth*: "He who has acquired the works of the Law has acquired for himself the life of the world to come" (2:8), and, "Great is the Law, for it gives to those who practice it life in this world and in the world to come" (6:7). See too Bultmann, *Gospel*, 268 n. 2, and the literature cited there.

Yet there is no prevarication in his acknowledgment of the *witness* of the Scriptures, in particular of the Torah. Along with all the other writers of the New Testament, the fourth evangelist was fully conscious that the Christian message was not properly intelligible without support from Jewish tradition. So neither here nor at any other point in the long discourse in chapter 5, built out of the controversy surrounding the healing of the cripple, does he target Moses directly. Like all Jews at the time, John had no doubt that Moses was the author of the book of the law. Here, at the end of the chapter, he hits upon the idea of appropriating Moses' work, or rather of extracting from it the testimony he needed. He knew that he had somehow to separate the man and the book, but to do so openly would have weakened his own position. Hence the remarkable conclusion of this chapter, in which Jesus attempts to drive a wedge between *Moses* and *the Jews*: "it is Moses who accuses you, on whom you set your hope. If you believed Moses you would believe me, for he wrote of me. But if you do not believe his writings, how will you believe my words" (5:45-47). It is an astonishing accusation: the Jews, asserts Jesus, did not truly believe what Moses had written, even though they pretended to put their trust in him. The book of the law on which they relied actually supported his own claim: "Moses wrote of me" (5:46).

We may recall that this was precisely what Philip said to Nathanael after Jesus had summoned him to follow him just after his baptism: "We have found him of whom Moses in the law and also the prophets wrote, Jesus of Nazareth" (1:45). But that was in a context where there was not yet so much as a whisper of controversy. The situation is now one in which Jesus is directly confronting people who have accused him of making himself equal with God. And he introduces the name of Moses simply to score a point. As I have observed, it is an *argumentum ad hominem*.

The Jews might have been expected to respond to the claim that Moses had really written of Jesus by asking, "Where? Can you point to a single passage where he wrote of you?" And they would certainly not have been satisfied with a simple citation of Deut. 18:18. (As we shall see in relation to chapter 9, this was another contentious issue.) One would like to have been able to listen in to a debate between representatives of the two groups on this point, in the manner of Justin's *Dialogue against Tryphon*. But here, as elsewhere in the Gospel, the Jews speak the words dictated to them by the evangelist, and the chapter ends with a rhetorical question to which Jesus expects no reply: "If you do not believe his writings, how will you believe my words?"

JOHN 7:15-24

From a structural point of view John 7 is among the most complex in the Gospel.[15] The main reason for its complexity is that, although it includes what was originally the direct continuation of chapter 5 (for 7:15 follows on from 5:47),[16] the subsequent insertion of chapter 6 compelled the evangelist to make certain alterations.

In the first place, the opening of chapter 7, the story of Jesus' reluctant decision to go up to the feast (once the commencement of a miracle story) has been adapted and extended to serve as a preface to the controversy material beginning in 7:11. This material, however, is quickly interrupted, as we have just seen, by the Jews' puzzlement at Jesus' learning (7:15), expressed in a question that originally furthered the argument that now concludes chapter 5. This question enables both the reintroduction of the motif of personal glory (7:18; see 5:44) and the reversal back to the main theme of chapter 5, Jesus' claim to be speaking with the authority of God (7:16-17; see 5:19, 30). Then comes Jesus' sudden question, "Did not Moses give you the law?" (7:19), which takes a different tack by once again introducing the name of Moses in an *argumentum ad hominem* adding to that of the conclusion of chapter 5, which it continues.

In the second place, the other question (in the same verse) that looks so abrupt and out of place in its present context—"Why do you seek to kill me?" (7:19c)—is readily intelligible if we see it as a reference back to the long opening paragraph of chapter 5 that climaxes in the first attempt upon Jesus' life (5:18). The reference is confirmed by Jesus' response: "I did one work [ἓν ἔργον], and you all marvel at it" (7:21). Jesus' one work, the healing of the cripple that caused all the trouble in the first place, is thus contrasted, in a typical rabbinic *qal waḥomer* argument, with the behavior of the Jews in continually infringing on the Sabbath by practicing circumcision on that day.

Bultmann's concluding comment on this argument is masterly:

---

15. See my *Understanding the Fourth Gospel*, 233-39 (Excursus V: The Composition of John 7).

16. Bultmann, relying partly on the fact that the relatively rare word γράμματα occurs both in 5:47 and in 7:15, argues plausibly that this passage (7:15-24) is the response of the Jews to Jesus' appeal to Moses at the end of chapter 5: "How is it that this man knows his letters, when he has never studied?" Rightly understanding the word ἐθαύμαζον in 7:15 to express surprise rather than admiration, Bultmann picks up the inference: "He does not belong to the guild of the Scribes." C. K. Barrett (*The Gospel according to St. John: An Introduction with Commentary and Notes on the Greek Text*, 2nd ed. [London: SPCK, 1978] 317), supported by Barnabas Lindars (*The Gospel of John* [London: Marshall, Morgan & Scott, 1972], 288), rejects this argument on the grounds that the reference is to specific writings in the first instance, to intellectual training in the second. But his knowledge of the law is what gives Jesus his authority to teach. See Bultmann, *Gospel*, 273 n. 3.

There is only one way in which we can attach any meaning to this confused speech, in which the Jews are accused on the one hand of breaking the Mosaic law (v. 19) and on the other of breaking the Sabbath in compliance with the Mosaic law (v. 23). It must mean that the Jews break the Mosaic law, because even though they act in compliance with the law of circumcision they fail to ask what Moses' real intention was.[17]

We should not infer from this passage that the evangelist himself continues to respect the actual legislation found in the Torah;[18] for Jesus clearly dissociates himself from Jewish practice—"Moses gave *you* circumcision," and "*you* circumcise"—just as elsewhere he refers to "*your* law" (8:17; 10:34; cf. 15:25). Similarly, when Pilate invited the Jews to assume responsibility for Jesus' fate, what he said was, "Take him yourselves and judge him by *your* law" (18:31). All that was left by way of a law for John and his community was the "new commandment" of mutual love enjoined upon them on the eve of Jesus' departure (13:34-35). Here in chapter 7, Jesus is simply using arguments that his opponents will find difficult to refute: Lindars comments on the clever use of the issue of circumcision, which "provides a double-edged argument: on the one hand, it gives a precedent for Jesus' action, which justifies him on the Jews' own ground; on the other, it adduces an example of the way in which the Jews themselves break the Law, which is Jesus' accusation in verse 19."[19] Moses is no longer the unchallenged spokesman of God, but simply a name to be conjured with when arguing with traditionally minded Jews.

JOHN 9:27-28

Passing over John 3:13 (which should arguably have been included here because although Moses is not named in this verse he must have been among those Jewish seers of whom it was denied that they had ascended into heaven),[20] we come to the most important passage of all—the angry response to the sarcastic question of the recently healed blind beggar: "Do you too want to become his disciples?" To which the immediate response is: "You are that fellow's disciple, but we are the disciples of Moses" (9:27-28). I will comment in chapter 7 on the momentous implications of this reply. Here it is enough to say that the man's

---

17. Bultmann, *Gospel*, 278 (punctuation altered).

18. Meeks (*Prophet-King*, 287-99) gives a very good analysis of the passage, but I think he is wrong to infer from 7:19 that "the Torah is not rejected."

19. Lindars, *Gospel*, 291.

20. This verse will receive a lengthy discussion later.

immediate expulsion was a signal instance of a more general excommunication that had already been determined. Jesus was now thought of as usurping the place of Moses.

CHAPTER 14

Moses is nowhere named in the second half of the Gospel, but his shadow is perceptibly present throughout the Farewell Discourse, for Jesus' parting words to his disciples, cast in the form of a testimony, are clearly modeled on Moses' final address to the whole people of Israel in the book of Deuteronomy. Paradoxically, although Moses is nowhere named in Jesus' discourse, Jesus is named in that of Moses (at any rate in the Greek version of this, for the Hebrew Joshua is rendered Ἰησοῦς in Greek). Joshua is Moses' successor, commissioned to lead the people into the promised land after his death. Taking on an analogous role in John's account is the Paraclete, who, as the Spirit of Truth, is thereby the spirit of Jesus (who has just declared himself to be the truth). In John 16 (which belongs to the second edition of the Gospel) the analogy is extended, for here the promise is made that the Paraclete will lead the disciples "into the truth" (16:12), a richer realm than the promised land.[21]

JOHN 6:30-33

"We would dearly love," remarks Barnabas Lindars in his comment on John 5:46, "to have a specimen of the way in which John understood the OT witness to Christ; fortunately, for the second edition of his work, he has provided precisely such an example in his great interpolation of chapter 6, in which the whole issue is treated at length. We generally think of chapter 6 as the discourse on the Bread of Life, but it is a much more a discourse on the interpretation of Scripture"[22]—an observation repeated on the next page of his book, where he says of chapter 6 that

> its present position is peculiarly suitable because of the way in which it serves as an illustration of Jesus' claim in 5.39, 46f. For this is the most biblical section of the whole Gospel. The discourse is not merely a development of the implications of the miracle of feeding with which the chapter opens; on the contrary, that is really a brilliant use of traditional material as an opening gambit for a

---

21. These ideas are fully developed in the chapter of *Understanding the Fourth Gospel* entitled "Departure and Return."

22. Lindars, *Gospel*, 233.

discourse which is fundamentally an exposition of an OT text—the story of the manna in the Wilderness in Exod. 16.

Subsequent commentators have not taken up this suggestion of Lindars; but it provides an astute and satisfying solution to the puzzle of the present position of John 6: "an independent composition, inserted by John into the second edition of his work."[23] Apart from the Prologue, to be considered shortly, this is the only additional occurrence of the name of Moses in what may be thought of as the second edition of the Gospel, and deserves our attention for that very reason.

Early on in their debate with Jesus in John 6, the people who found him on the other side of the lake (not yet called Jews in this chapter) asked him for a sign: "What work do you perform? Our fathers ate the manna in the wilderness; as it is written, 'He gave them bread from heaven to eat' " (6:30-31). Although this is probably a (slightly adapted) quotation from Psalm 78, the underlying text is undoubtedly the manna story in Exodus. And Jesus has the answer: "Truly, truly, I say to you, it was not Moses who gave you the bread from heaven: my Father gives you the true bread from heaven' (6:32). Peder Borgen has argued that this is a rabbinic-type exegesis of the pattern, "Do not read *that*, but rather read *this*." That is to say, "Do not read the 'he' as Moses, but as the Father, and do not read 'gave' but 'gives,'"[24] But this reading gives more prominence to Moses than he is allowed in the text. Jesus might have said (but did not), "Moses gave you manna, but my Father gives the true bread." What he says instead is a simple denial: "Moses *did not* give you bread from heaven," or rather, "not [οὐ] Moses gave . . . but [ἀλλά] my Father gives." As J. Louis Martyn points out, "the emphatic negative by means of which [Jesus] introduces his reply stands immediately before the word 'Moses.' And the subject of the second line is changed. The 'correction' therefore is, 'not Moses gave, but my Father gives.' John is strongly contrasting Moses with God!"[25]—and in doing so taking Moses out of the story altogether. Although there is what looks like a form of midrash at this point, the evangelist is effectively denying Jesus' interlocutors the right to make any typological comparison between Moses and Jesus. Jesus is about to say, "I am the bread of life" (6:39), and that bread is what God is giving now. Wayne Meeks says of this passage that "the polemical intent is evident: Moses is reduced to a mere

---

23. Lindars, *Gospel,* 234. See Excursus II below on the problem of the position of chapter 6.

24. Peder Borgen, "Observations on the Midrashic Character of John 6," *Zeitschrift für die neutestamentliche Wissenschaft* 54 (1963): 232-40.

25. Martyn, *History and Theology,* 122. "Only in the final analysis," Martyn says, "do I think Borgen's suggestions are misleading" (121 n. 187).

mediator of the gift, and the gift itself is derogated in comparison with its Christian counterpart."[26] But the gift of the bread from heaven in the original quotation (6:31) is rapidly interpreted to refer to the true bread of life, a gift stated in such a way that even the name of Moses is deliberately excluded.

Earlier in the chapter, having seen the miracle of the loaves, the people had declared of Jesus: "This is indeed the prophet who is to come into the world" (6:14)—the clearest acknowledgment in the whole Gospel that Jesus had now taken over the role of Moses as *the* prophet of God. So in a story that, among other things, justified Jesus' claim in the preceding chapter that Moses did indeed write of him, the evangelist pursues his own agenda: to refute the Jewish belief that Moses had the key role in the story of God's revelation to his people, and to reassign that role to Jesus.[27]

It might be observed that if those responsible for the theological program behind the decoration of the walls of the Sistine Chapel had remembered the story of John 6 they might well have chosen the scene of the distribution of the manna as a parallel to the Last Supper instead of the end of Moses' life, where in one part of the picture he is shown handing over his staff to Joshua and in another (the center of this fresco) reading out the law to the people. If the manna scene had been preferred Moses would have figured, as he does in the other pictures on the south wall, as the precursor or antitype of Jesus. But that is not how John read the story.

THE PROLOGUE

The first mention of Moses in the Gospel as it has come down to us occurs in the Prologue. After the astounding statement in verse 14 that "the Word became flesh and dwelt among us, full of grace and truth; and we have beheld his glory, glory as of the only Son from the Father," we read (in the RSV): "And from his fullness have we all received, grace upon grace. For the law was given through Moses; grace and truth came through Jesus Christ" (John 1:16-17). The word χάρις ("grace") comes four times in these two verses. There must be an allusion to the Hebrew coupling חֶסֶד וֶאֱמֶת (*ḥesed wĕ'emet*) as found, for instance in Exod. 34:6—"a God abounding in steadfast love and faithfulness," even though the term חֶסֶד is generally translated ἔλεος ("pity, compassion") in the Septuagint. Raymond Brown renders it as "love": "And

---

26. Meeks, *Prophet-King*, 291.

27. In the same context Martyn also cites the following verse (6:15) concerning the determination of the crowd to make Jesus king. This verse, he says, may indicate that certain persons in the synagogue had gone beyond identifying Jesus as the Mosaic prophet "to the opinion that he is the Prophet-Messiah" (*History and Theology*, 110). But Jesus evades the attempt to make him king.

of his fullness we have all had a share—love in place of love. For while the law was a gift though Moses, this enduring love came through Jesus Christ." Here is a positive view of the role of Moses, much the same as that of Pope Sixtus and of his theological advisers responsible for the design on the walls of his great chapel. But was this how the author of the Prologue saw things? Surely not. "For John," as C.K. Barrett rightly concludes, "Jesus is certainly not a new Moses."[28] Brown's translation is skewed by his insertion of the noun "gift" (from the Greek verb "was given") to define and describe the law. Judaism, unquestionably, saw the law as a gift and a grace bestowed by God on his people.[29] But this sentence from the Prologue, with its stark opposition between Moses and Christ, is a denial that the gift was a grace.[30] As I pointed out in the introduction, it is the clearest statement in the whole of the New Testament of the stark opposition between Christianity and Judaism. It is my task in the remainder of this book to try to explain it.

THE RABBINIC VIEW

The article on Moses in the *Encyclopaedia Judaica*, after a pages-long analysis of all the biblical texts concerning Moses, concludes with a short section headed "Rabbinic View." This is how it opens:

A marked ambivalence is to be observed in the Jewish tradition with regard to the personality of Moses. On the one hand, Moses is the greatest of all the Jewish teachers, a powerfully numinous figure, the man with whom God speaks "face to face," the intermediary between God and man, the master of the prophets, and the recipient of God's law for mankind. On the other hand, the utmost care is taken to avoid the ascription of divine or semi-divine powers to Moses. Moses

---

28. Barrett, *Gospel according to St. John*, 169.

29. Lindars (*Gospel*, 97) observes that according to rabbinic exegesis the grace and the truth of God are revealed in the law: he refers to a midrash on Ps. 25:10, which includes the phrase *ḥesed wĕʾemet*.

30. *Contra* Brown, who argues against "the theory that vs. 17 contrasts the absence of enduring love in the Law with the presence of enduring love in Christ: on the grounds that it 'does not seem to do justice to John's honorific reference to Moses (i 45, iii 14, v 46)'" (*Gospel*, 1:16). Brown seems to have momentarily forgotten his own theory that the Prologue was an independent composition (see chapter 8 below); but in any case the verses he cites, as I have argued, do not really support the suggestion of "honorific reference." It may be questioned, in fact, whether the concluding verses of the Prologue (1:17-18) were part of the original hymn or whether one or both of these verses were added by the evangelist. We cannot exclude the possibility that the evangelist inserted the verse we have been considering as a deliberate statement of the view he was now taking about Moses and the law. But even if it formed part of the hymn in the first place, he was unquestionably adding his authority to it.

is a man, with human faults and failings. Strenuous attempts are made to reject any "personality cult," even when the personality in question is so towering as Moses. Judaism is not "Mosaism" but the religion of the Jewish people. God, not Moses, gives His torah to his people Israel.[31]

Yet the "utmost care" and the "strenuous attempts" would hardly have been necessary if the rabbis were not aware of tendencies in Judaism to place Moses too high. I will be looking at some of those tendencies later.

I will argue in Excursus III that if we want to use the Gospel as a historical source, with the aim of reconstructing as far as possible the birth and development of the Johannine community, we have to read it diachronically: we cannot take for granted that the Gospel was composed in the order in which it is printed. Of every passage in the Gospel the historian is entitled to ask what it can tell us about the author and his community—what stage of the history of the community it reflects. If we take this approach (excluded a priori, of course, by the self-styled literary or narrative critics), the Prologue confronts us with an immediate challenge. For we are compelled to recognize that the statement in 1:17 we have just been looking at could not possibly have been written by a believing Jew. In attributing grace and truth to Christ rather than to Moses, the author of this sentence knew—cannot but have known—that he was dissociating himself from Judaism in any of its forms.

Conclusion

What have we learned from this inquiry about the status of Moses in the eyes of the fourth evangelist?

1. In his prophetic role, Moses was the precursor of Jesus, who fulfilled the prediction that Moses would be followed by a prophet like himself.
2. Moses wrote of Jesus. In the Pentateuch, the Torah, there were stories that foreshadowed events in the life of Jesus.
3. It was through Moses that Israel received the law; but the legal prescriptions of the law, such as the Sabbath and circumcision, no longer had any relevance.
4. God's revelation to Moses, the core and foundation of the Jewish tradition, has been superseded by the revelation of Jesus, and Jesus himself has taken the place of Moses.

---

31. *Encyclopaedia Judaica* (Jerusalem: Keter Publishing House, 1972), 12:394.

Excursus I: The Gospel Genre

What are the Gospels? This is the title of a book by Richard Burridge in which he sets out "to establish the case positively and finally for the biographical genre of the gospels to become the new scholarly consensus and orthodoxy."[1] Consensus? Orthodoxy? Should the torrent of critical applause that greeted this work, liberally quoted in the second edition,[2] be allowed to drown out any misgivings one might have about these grandiloquent claims?

Let us begin by tackling the question of genre: "Genre is at the heart of all attempts to communicate," declares Burridge.[3] Even if we limit ourselves to *literary* genres this is patent nonsense, though *genre* is a category tossed around comfortably and casually by literary critics of all persuasions. Sometimes it may be useful. *Tragedy*, for instance, is a term applied particularly to three groups of writings, the first composed in fifth-century Athens, the second in Elizabethan and Jacobean England, and the third at or around the court of Louis XIV of France. We have a sufficient number of well-preserved examples of all three of these groups to make comparison straightforward and illuminating. The audience of each of the three groups is well known and well documented, and in spite of some dispute about the origins of the first two groups it is easy to trace probable influences. So here is an example in which the term *genre* performs a useful function.

Compare this happy situation with Greek *bioi* and Latin *vitae*, generally classed together as Greco-Roman biographies, written in two different languages over some nine centuries in a wide variety of styles, and with a number of different aims in view. Burridge has selected ten illustrative examples. Five of these predate the Gospels. Isocrates' *Evagoras* is a funeral eulogy of Evagoras, king of Cyprus c. 411–374 BCE. Xenophon's *Agesilaus* gives an account of its subject's life (king of Sparta 398–360 BCE), followed by a systematic review of his virtues. Satyrus's *Euripides*, extant only in fragments, recounted various episodes of the life of the Greek tragedian and concluded with his death. Nepos's *Atticus* tells the story of the political career of Cicero's

---

1. Richard A. Burridge, *What Are the Gospels? A Comparison with Graeco-Roman Biography* (Cambridge: Cambridge University Press, 1992), 99.

2. Richard A. Burridge, *What Are the Gospels? A Comparison with Graeco-Roman Biography*, 2nd ed. (Grand Rapids: Eerdmans, 2004), 253-55.

3. Burridge, *What Are the Gospels?* 2nd ed., 48.

famous friend and correspondent; while Philo's *Moses*—exceptional among his works, which are otherwise mostly pure allegories—is an apologetic account of the career of Moses, written with a Gentile readership in mind. Three of Burridge's other examples (Tacitus's *Agricola*, Plutarch's *Cato Minor*, Suetonius's *De vita Caesarum*) were composed soon after the Gospels, the final two (Lucian's *Demonax* and Philostratus's *Apollonius*) considerably later. (The last named, frequently cited in discussion of the Gospels, will receive further discussion.)

Suppose that we put the Greco-Roman *bioi* completely out of our mind: suppose they never existed. Would we then have to conclude that the Gospels could never have existed either, because then there would have been no preexisting genre for them to be slotted into? The form critics brought to light the great variety of forms, or *Gattungen*, that make up the bulk of the Synoptic Gospels. Add the necessary connective links, plus a passion narrative, and you have a Gospel. Anyone who then wished to speak of a Gospel genre would have to say, as Bultmann did, that the Gospels are *sui generis*. Burridge objects: "It is hard to imagine how anyone could invent something which is a literary novelty or unique kind of writing,"[4] and elsewhere that "the gospels cannot be *sui generis*, but must be set within the web of literary relationships of their own day"[5]—comments that appear to suggest that the first person to write a Gospel must have had some already existing model in mind. Yet nowhere does he actually claim (how could he?) that the Christian evangelists were influenced by any of the *bioi* prior to their own, or that they knew even a single one of them.

Bultmann also saw that the Gospels cannot be classed as biographies in the modern sense of the word, because they show no interest in the *character* of Jesus. It is largely because the Greco-Roman *bioi* are equally uninterested in the character development of their subjects that the Gospels can plausibly be ranged among them. Burridge concluded of his survey that it "has provided a clear picture of the βίος genre: there is a family resemblance, yet the overall impression is of a diverse and flexible genre, able to cope with variations in any one work."[6] Yet it is worth asking just how much these vastly different works have in common. Two things: they were all written either in Greek or in Latin sometime between 500 BCE and 400 CE, and they were all concerned with the life and career of a particular individual.

4. Burridge, *What Are the Gospels?*, 2nd ed., 12.
5. Burridge, *What Are the Gospels?*, 2nd ed., 101.
6. Burridge, *What Are the Gospels?*, 2nd ed., 84.

Admitting that the Gospels match these very broad criteria used for detecting Greco-Roman *bioi*, we can hardly object to giving them the name; but we may still wish to ask whether this is all that can or should be said in reply to the question, What are the Gospels? I think not. I suggest that to call the Gospels *Lives of Christ* without further ado is inadequate and misleading, simply because we have not yet taken account of the primary aim of the evangelists, which was to promote faith in Jesus as Messiah and Son of God.

In 1987, five years before the publication of Burridge's book, David Aune defended the thesis that the Gospels are indeed Lives of Christ. In the first two chapters of his book *The New Testament in Its Literary Environment*,[7] he gives a perfectly adequate defense of this thesis. Burridge was to criticize Aune for defining biography as the portrayal of "a whole life" (thus ruling out both the Gospels and many ancient biographies), for paying insufficient attention to what he calls *genre theory*, and for failing to "establish the case positively and finally for the biographical genre of the gospels to become the new scholarly consensus and orthodoxy."[8] Many readers like myself, however, content with Aune's more concise exposition, will not have needed Burridge's rather more labored treatment of the same subject to persuade them that, while the Gospels are not biographies in the modern sense of the word, it is reasonable to put them in the same category as Greek and Roman *bioi*, not because they have borrowed from any individual Greek *bios* or Roman *vita*, but because they meet the not very stringent criteria—they were written at the right time, in the right language, and with the right focus on a single individual. Reasonable, but still misleading, because the kerygmatic purpose of the Gospels is so different from that of the bulk of the writings with which they are thus aligned.

Aune objects to the concentration of many New Testament scholars on the proclamatory aims of the evangelists because this is often theologically motivated, resting on the false supposition that kerygma (proclamation) and history are mutually exclusive. Hellenistic biographers, he argues, "often wrote with rhetorical purposes and techniques," because they were interested in providing incentives to virtue:[9]

History and biography focused on the past as a source of lessons for the future. Hellenistic history and biography, no less than the Gospels, tended to merge the past with the present. If the Gospels and Acts deserve the (exaggerated) designation "theology in

---

7. David E. Aune, *The New Testament in Its Literary Environment* (Philadelphia: Westminster, 1987).

8. Burridge, *What Are the Gospels?*, 2nd ed., 98–99 (emphasis added).

9. Aune, *New Testament*, 64.

narrative form," then Greco-Roman history and biography fully merit the label "ideology in narrative form." Functionally the differences are minimal.[10]

It is here that, with respect, I part company with Aune, for two reasons. He provides no example of lives "written with rhetorical purposes and techniques"; and as far as I can see the only Hellenistic biographer to fit this description, and to have written, sometimes, "to provide incentives for virtue," was Plutarch—nobody else.[11] More importantly, in urging their readers to believe that Jesus is Messiah and Son of God the evangelists had in mind something quite different from "ideology in narrative form." This is not the right way to describe the Gospels, which were certainly not written "to provide incentives to virtue." Rather, as I put it in *Understanding the Fourth Gospel*, "a Gospel is a narrative of the public career of Jesus, his passion and death, told in order to affirm or confirm the faith of Christian believers in the Risen Lord."[12]

Three late *bioi* (dating from the third and fourth centuries CE) have a closer resemblance to the Gospels than all the others, because they deal with the lives of men who were regarded as gods or sons of gods—Philostratus's *Vita Apollonii* (one of Burridge's chosen examples), Porphyry's *Vita Pythagorae*, and Iamblichus's *Vita Pythagorica*. Patricia Cox says of these that "they exhibit the idealizing and propagandist features of Graeco-Roman biography but with a crucial addition. They were involved in religious controversy and so *attempted to sway not mere opinion but belief*."[13] She goes on to point out that, although

---

10. Aune, *New Testament*, 62.

11. Nepos, Suetonius, and Tacitus were historians. But they can hardly be said to provide "a source of lessons for the future." Some of Suetonius's *Lives of the Caesars*, in fact, were quite derogatory—the lives of of Divus Julius and Divus Augustus are followed by the lives of Tiberius, Gaius Caligula, Divus Claudius and the truly villainous Nero; and against Plutarch's lives of the virtuous Cato and his Greek counterpart Phokion one might set the lives of Pyrrhos and Marius, object lessons in the dangers of overreaching oneself, or, more simply, of discontent. Lucian, another writer placed by Burridge among his writers of *bioi*, was not primarily a biographer or historian but a humorist, writing to amuse, and a satirist, writing to disabuse, as in *Alexander or the Pseudo-Seer*, a savage exposure of the charlatan Alexander of Abonuteichos. Lucian's sole purpose was to undermine Alexander's credibility, along with that of Glycon, whose cult he had founded. This work, like *Timon the Misanthrope* (an early though indirect source of Shakespeare's famous play) is arguably a much more characteristic example of Lucian's writing than the laudatory life of his friend Demonax.

12. John Ashton, *Understanding the Fourth Gospel*, 2nd ed. (Oxford: Clarendon, 2007), 332; also, for a fuller discussion, 24–27.

13. Patricia Cox, *Biography in Late Antiquity: A Quest for the Holy Men*, Transformation of the Classical Heritage 5 (Berkeley: University of California Press, 1983), 16 (emphasis added).

the philosopher sage was a time-honored and traditional paradigm, "in later biographies by such authors as Philostratus, Porphyry . . . and Iamblichus the great wisdom and noble character of the philosopher are augmented, and sometimes overshadowed, by specific qualities and talents linking him to divinity."[14] As characteristic traits of the divine philosopher she names wisdom, insight into human nature, a real sympathy and concern for his fellow human beings, and finally a desire to communicate his wisdom. Moreover, the lives of the "sons of god" are marked first by birth stories that credit them with divine parentage, and, second, by the working of miracles, for they have the power to dominate nature by curing diseases, both mental and physical, and by manipulating natural phenomena.

Other striking resemblances between the Christian Gospels and the *Lives* of Philostratus and Iamblichus had already been noticed by the eminent historian of religion Jonathan Z. Smith, in an essay entitled "Good News Is No News: Aretology and Gospel."[15] Of those figures for whom the claim is made that they are sons of god, he argues, their biographies "serve as apologies against outsiders' charges that they were merely magicians and against their admirers' sincere misunderstanding that they were merely wonder-workers, divine men or philosophers." All of these biographies are characterized by a double defense against the charge of magic—"against the calumny of outsiders and the sincere misunderstanding of admirers."[16]

"The solution of each group or individual so charged," he continues, "was the same: to insist on an inward meaning of the suspect activities. The allegedly magical action, properly understood, is a sign. There is both a transparent and a hidden meaning, a literal and a deeper understanding required. At the surface level the biography appears to be an explicit story of a magician or a *Wundermensch*: at the depth level it is the enigmatic self-disclosure of a son of god." The various literary devices employed in all these stories (including riddle, aporia, joke, and parable) "depend upon a multivalent expression which is interpreted by admirers and detractors as having univocal meaning and thus invites misunderstanding. The function of the narrative is to play between various levels of understanding and misunderstanding, inviting the reader to assume that both he and the author truly do understand and then cutting the ground out from under this confidence."[17]

14. Cox, *Biography in Late Antiquity*, 34.

15. Jonathan Z. Smith, *Map Is not Territory: Studies in the History of Religions* (1978; repr., Chicago: University of Chicago Press, 1993), 190–207.

16. J. Z. Smith, *Map Is Not Territory*, 193. Smith includes the Gospel of Mark among the biographies so designated.

"What an Apollonius, a Pythagoras, a Jesus," concludes Smith, "reveals in the narratives concerning them, is their own enigmatic nature, their *sui generis* character. What was said by one of these sons of god might have been said by the others: 'You will seek me and you will not find me, where I am you cannot come' (Jn 7:34)—a saying which was misunderstood by opponent and disciple alike."[18]

Many of the points made in this rich and suggestive essay are, I suspect, intentionally provocative. By and large, New Testament scholars have either deliberately ignored it or simply failed to notice it.[19] If they were to pay it the attention it deserves, they would no doubt cavil at not a few of Smith's comparisons. But he and Cox discuss in some depth the very few Roman *vitae* that have a real resemblance to the Gospels, and in doing so show how dim a light the simple classification of the Gospels as ancient *bioi* sheds on their real nature.

In an appendix to the second edition of his work (2004), Burridge shifts his attention to the christological aspect of the Gospels, something to which he had already drawn attention in an article written for a collection edited by Richard Bauckham: "The historical, literary, and biographical methods [of Gospel scholarship] combine to show us," he states, "that the Gospels are nothing less than Christology in narrative form, the story of Jesus." But if "Christology in narrative form" (only a hair's breadth away from Aune's "theology in narrative form") is an essential element in the definition of the Gospel genre, would not this imply that the Gospels are indeed *sui generis*? Burridge goes on immediately (in the very next sentence, opening a new paragraph): "The implication of this biographical hypothesis is that the Gospels are about a person, not about theological ideas."[20] But what is Christology if not a branch of theology—a reasoned organization of theological ideas? The purpose of the evangelists, as their name suggests, is not to do theology but to proclaim the good news. (And who thinks of theology as good news?) The Gospels are not theology (Aune, with some hesitation) nor are they Christology (Burridge). And to call them Greco-Roman *bioi* without further qualification is, as I have argued, if not wrong, insufficient and misleading.

17. J. Z. Smith, *Map Is Not Territory*, 194.

18. J. Z. Smith, *Map Is Not Territory*, 203–4.

19. Neither Aune nor Burridge refers to Smith's essay, close though it is to their concerns. Burridge does not mention Cox either, although her book does figure in his bibliography.

20. Richard A. Burridge, "About People, by People, for People: Gospel Genre and Audiences," in *The Gospels for All Christians: Rethinking the Gospel Audiences*, ed. Richard Bauckham (Grand Rapids: Eerdmans, 1998), 113-45.

I find some support for this argument in an unexpected quarter. Martin Hengel begins a lecture called "The Four Gospels and the One Gospel of Jesus Christ" (summarizing a book of the same title) with a zealous defense of the view that the Gospels are biographies. Aware, however, that this is not enough, he adds, with reference to Mark, that it is a "*kerygmatic* biography." "Because 'biography' and 'proclamation' are fused in his work," he continues, "Mark can call his narrative about Jesus '[a] saving message,' that is an account of Jesus' activity which brings about faith and thus salvation."[21] Leaving aside the tendentious translation of εὐαγγήλιον as "saving message," I might point out that the addition of the word *kerygmatic* effectively guards against the misleading implications of the simple term *life* or *biography* if this is used without qualification. For *kerygma* is the traditional term for the early promulgation of the Christian message that was subsequently expanded in the Gospels. It should no doubt be said that all the Gospels have much more in them than kerygma—the moral teaching in the Synoptics, for instance, and the bitter controversies in John. Yet the stated purpose of John, writing "that you may believe that Jesus is the Messiah, the Son of God" (20:31), indicates that none of this extra material affects the main thrust of his work.

It seems that some of the most ardent champions of the hypothesis that the Gospels are Greco-Roman *bioi* feel compelled to add a word such as *theology* (Aune), *Christology* (Burridge), or *kerygma* (Hengel) to specify them further. It is my contention, therefore, that to call the Gospels biographies without more ado is radically mistaken: we should think of them primarily in terms of the stated purpose of John, and of the implicit purpose of Mark (since his word, εὐαγγέλιον, gospel—good news, is equivalent to a statement of intent).

21. Martin Hengel, "The Four Gospels and the One Gospel of Jesus Christ," in *The Earliest Gospels: The Origins and Transmission of the Earliest Christian Gospels. The Contribution of the Chester Beatty P45*, ed. Barbara Aland and Charles Horton, Journal for the Study of the New Testament: Supplement Series 258, (London: T&T Clark, 2004), 22.

2

Consciousness of Genre

Such was the impact of the life and teaching of Jesus of Nazareth, and of the stories told about him after his death, that soon afterwards, in the religiously combustible regions of Palestine and the Jewish Diaspora, a new religion was kindled into flame. Bright little fires of faith in Jesus began to burn, and within a hundred years or so these had coalesced into the single blaze of Christianity. We associate these little fires with the leading writers of the New Testament, Matthew, Mark, Luke, and John—and of course Paul, the first Christian writer. At least three of these, Paul, Matthew, and John, were Jewish, and they all confront us, in different ways, with the puzzle of how Christianity emerged from Judaism. This book is concerned with one of these figures, John, with the Gospel he wrote, and with the community to which he belonged.

We continue our own inquiry by reflecting on the gospel genre, best conceived, as I have just argued in Excursus I, not as a biography or life, but as a proclamatory narrative.

Like other works of literature, the Gospels may be approached either from the inside or from the outside. The approach from the inside, the attempt to understand the meaning of the text, is what we call interpretation, or, particularly where the Bible is concerned, exegesis. (Literary criticism is too broad a category.) The approach from the outside, the attempt to find out how any particular text came to be written, is the one taken by historians. In practice the two approaches are often combined; but from a formal point of view they are different and must be held apart. In the bulk of this book I shall be asking historical questions about the origins of the Gospel of John; but in the present chapter, starting from the text of the Gospel itself, I want to ask how it presents itself. I will be arguing that its author, who had a very clear idea of what he was doing, has found ways of informing his readers about the nature of the gospel genre and of how he himself conceived it. The title of this chapter, however, "Consciousness of Genre," requires some explanation.

All four Christian Gospels tell the story of the brief public career of Jesus of Nazareth, of his arrest, trial, and execution at the hands of the Roman authorities, and of his resurrection from the dead. Yet these stories, designed to show that he is really the long-awaited Jewish Messiah and also the Son of God in a special sense that renders him unique, have an inbuilt contradiction that has to be recognized and acknowledged if we are to have any real understanding of what makes the gospel genre so different from the many biographies of great Greeks or Romans—emperors, generals, politicians, writers—who lived around the turn of the era. For the earliest Christian writers saw, right from the start, that Jesus could not be recognized for who he truly was until after he had risen from the dead.

"Let all the house of Israel know assuredly that God has made him both Lord and Messiah, this Jesus whom you crucified." So says Peter in his Pentecost speech in Acts (2:34), just after his extraordinary proclamation that Jesus had been raised up from the dead and exalted at God's right hand; and Paul, quoting an even older statement of Christian belief, asserts in Rom. 1:4 that it was at his resurrection that Jesus was *designated* Son of God. In both of these passages there is a clear affirmation of a change in status. Not until he had risen from the dead could Jesus properly be called Messiah, Lord, or Son of God. Viewed retrospectively, numerous recollections—oral traditions—of his life and teaching could be seen to support the claims that came to be made on his behalf—what is sometimes called the *kerygma*. The evangelists' central purpose, one might say, was to piece together these fragmentary traditions in a story designed to corroborate their claim that he was truly the Messiah, the Son of God, and thus prove that Christian believers were right to worship him as their risen Lord. But they had a problem. On the one hand, they knew that the key element in the story they had to tell was the resurrection; on the other hand, this story was all about the Jesus' life *before* the resurrection.

The great German scholar William Wrede was the first to highlight this problem, in a book called *Das Messiasgeheimnis* (*The Messianic Secret*), which is how the problem has been referred to ever since this book was published, in 1901. Wrede cited the passages from Acts and Romans mentioned in the preceding paragraph, but for him the key to Mark's own understanding of his Gospel is the Jesus' injunction to Peter, James, and John on their descent from the mountain of the Transfiguration "to tell no one what they had seen until the Son of man should have risen from the dead. So they kept the matter to themselves," the passage continues, "questioning what the rising from the dead meant" (9:9–10; cf. 8: 30).[1] Mark frequently exhibits his awareness that, except for this brief glimpse of Jesus' future glory (which the three disciples did not comprehend at the time), his real identity remained hidden during his lifetime. Only when Jesus had risen did it dawn on them who he really was—when, as Wrede put it, "the scales fall from their eyes."[2]

Matthew and Luke skate over this difficulty by including early in their Gospels stories designed to show that Jesus was truly divine from his very conception. (And Wrede, writing about their work in a chapter entitled, "The Later Gospels: Matthew and Luke," shows that although they retain some traces of Mark's secrecy motif it has lost most of its significance for them.) But the other two evangelists, Mark and John, have no infancy narrative in their Gospels, and they both fully recognize the difficulty caused by Jesus' change of status at his resurrection.

In the Gospel of John, Jesus' glory, already announced in the Prologue (1:14), was manifested to his disciples at the wedding-feast of Cana, right at the start of his public career (2:11). This was not just a fleeting glimpse, as it was for Peter, James, and John at the Transfiguration (an episode not recorded by John); so the problem presents itself differently. John too has a double purpose, first to tell the story of Jesus and, second, to persuade his readers that he is Messiah and Son of God. But he is fully aware that there could be no full understanding of who Jesus was, or indeed of any of his words and actions, until after the resurrection. (The similarity between Mark and John in this respect was clearly seen by Wrede, who devoted a whole chapter to the Fourth Gospel in his book on the Messianic Secret.) [3]

THE TEMPLE EPISODE

We may start our examination with the story of Jesus' very first confrontation with "the Jews" in the second half of chapter 2, where the evangelist seizes the chance to suggest that the whole of Jesus' public career will be lived out under

1. William Wrede, *The Messianic Secret* (Cambridge: James Clarke, 1971), 67. Literally, when the blindfold is removed from from their eyes: "bis die Zeit kommt, wo die Binde von ihren Augen genommen wird" (*Das Messiasgeheimnis in den Evangelien* [Göttingen: Vandenhoeck & Ruprecht, 1901], 113).

2. Wrede, *Messianic Secret*, 112.

3. Wrede, *Messianic Secret*, 181–207. In the course of this chapter, Wrede makes the important admission that Mark, unlike John, does not at any point single out the resurrection as the moment at which the disciples recognized Jesus for who he really was. "Nevertheless," he says, "I have interpreted him in the light of this idea" (p. 186).

the shadow of the cross.[4] The Jews have just demanded an explanation (a sign) of his action in ejecting the sellers from the Temple:

> Jesus answered them, "Destroy this temple [τὸν ναὸν τοῦτον], and in three days I will raise it up [ἐγερῶ αὐτόν]." The Jews said, "It has taken forty-six years to build this temple, and will you raise it up in three days?" But he spoke of the temple of his body. When therefore he was raised from the dead, his disciples remembered [ἐμνήσθησαν] that he had said this; and they believed the scripture and the word which Jesus had spoken. (2:19–22)

Wrede cites the concluding verse of this passage (it is in fact the first of several quotations from the Gospel in his chapter on John) but does not comment on it at any length. Yet there is a lot here that requires discussion.

It should first be pointed out that when Jesus makes his prediction it is hardly surprising that neither the Jews nor the disciples understand him. Just after he has expelled first the sellers of sheep and oxen and then the money-changers from the temple precincts, he goes on to speak of "this temple," saying that after its destruction he would raise it up again. But how could any of his listeners, watching and hearing him speak within the temple precincts, be expected to know that he was really speaking of the temple of his body? The word for "raise," ἐγείρειν, was commonly used to refer to the erection of a building, and this would have added to their confusion. No doubt any Christian reader with some knowledge of Greek would think immediately of resurrection; but that is part of the evangelist's purpose, underlining the difference in perception between his own readers and the characters in the story. The evangelist would not have expected *Jesus' listeners* to realize that he was talking about himself; but he would certainly have expected *his own readers* to understand. Precisely this point was made by Xavier Léon-Dufour

---

4. In the Fourth Gospel as it has come down to us, this episode is placed toward the beginning of Jesus' public career rather than toward the end. But it is very likely that in the first edition it occupied much the same position as it does in the Synoptics (cf. also Acts 6:14), where it provides the immediate cause of the authorities' decision to plot Jesus' death. In the second edition, the Lazarus episode gives the chief priests and Pharisees a different motive for wanting Jesus dead, and so an alternative place had to be found for the temple episode. (See my *Understanding the Fourth Gospel,* 2nd ed. [Oxford: Clarendon, 2007], 201.) Although some have attempted to argue that John's positioning of the episode is historically correct, most scholars, I think rightly, take the opposite view. For a careful and detailed argument, see Ernst Bammel, "Die Tempelreinigung bei den Synoptikern und im Johannesevangelium," in *John and the Synoptics,* ed. Adelbert Denaux, Bibliotheca ephemeridum theologicarum lovaniensium 101 (Leuven: University Press, 1992), 507–13.

in an article entitled "Le signe du Temple selon saint Jean," summing up his insight in the phrase "deux temps de l'intelligence."[5] This is unquestionably a correct observation, for a distinction certainly has to be drawn between the time in which the story of Jesus took place and the time in which the Gospel was composed and first read. (We shall be considering some of the implications of this difference of time in the next chapter.) But it has to be said that it is not the point that the evangelist himself is making. He is concerned here with the difference between what was understood (or rather misunderstood) in Jesus' lifetime, and what was understood after his resurrection. The distinction he is drawing is not between Jesus' listeners and the Gospel's readers, but between *two different stages of the experience of the disciples within the story*. Right up to the resurrection they are in the dark. Afterwards, like Thomas, who believes as soon as he sees the risen Jesus, they are finally in a position to understand.[6]

Also in this story we have the very first of the riddling sayings that crop up frequently in the first half of the Gospel. The term ναός ("temple"), it should be emphasized, is not a metaphor but a riddle, and its ambiguity is not removed but reinforced when it is made the object of the verb ἐγείρειν ("raise, erect"), a perfectly ordinary word, as we have seen, to use of the erection of a building.

In fact, the riddle is one of the literary devices employed by the evangelist to underline the habitual misunderstanding of Jesus' words by the other characters in the story. The incomprehension both of the disciples and of the Jews, friends and foes, is *predetermined*, proceeding as it does not from any information at the disposal of the evangelist that Jesus' hearers did not grasp what was said to them at the time, but from an authorial decision on his part to portray them in this way. The underlying logic, however, is very different in the two cases. The Jews are regarded as constitutionally incapable of accepting the message of Jesus, and indeed this incapacity is their essential characteristic: it is what makes them what they are. This is made all too plain in a later question addressed to the Jews:

5. Xavier Léon-Dufour, "Le signe du Temple selon saint Jean," *Recherches de science religieuse* 39 (1951–52), 159.

6. Nevertheless, the distinction between Jesus' hearers in the narrative and the Gospel's readers is worth making, for it helps us to see that in this respect the Gospel is no different from other works of literature written long after the events with which they are concerned. The authors of certain nineteenth-century novels constantly interject comments of their own to explain to their readers the significance of the action. Moreover, the literary technique involved is not far from the dramatic irony common in stage plays. In Sophocles' *Oedipus*, for example, and in Shakespeare's *Othello*, the audience knows immediately what is going on, but the eponymous heroes of these plays are kept in the dark right up to the final denouement. (Though one should add that Jesus, the central character of the Gospel, unlike Oedipus and Othello, is always fully aware of the situation, and in a certain sense actually controls the action.)

Why do you not understand what I say? It is because you cannot bear to hear my word. You are of your father the devil. . . . When he lies, he speaks according to his own nature, for he is a liar, and the father of lies. But because I tell the truth, you do not believe me . . . He who is of God hears the words of God; the reason why you do not hear them is that you are not of God. (8:43-47)

This is far from being the case with the disciples. In the present instance, on hearing Jesus' rebuke to those he had thrown out of the temple, "You shall not make my Father's house a house of trade," they had been reminded of a verse in Psalm 69: "Zeal for thy house will consume me." So some of Jesus' sayings did make sense to them. Yet they too failed to grasp the significance of the prophecy that the temple, once destroyed, would be rebuilt in three days. In their case, however, this failure was only temporary; for "*when he was raised from the dead* they remembered that he had said this; and they believed the scripture and the word which Jesus had spoken" (2:22).[7]

REMEMBERED INCIDENTS

In two incidents in the Gospel, both of them discussed by Wrede, we see that the disciples were baffled by Jesus' actions just as much as by his words. One of these incidents is the washing of the feet, where Jesus tells Peter: "What I am doing now you do not know now [οὐκ οἶδας ἄρτι] but afterwards you will come to know [γνώσῃ]" (13:7).[8] Wrede suggests that the secret meaning veiled from Peter at the time is the purificatory function of water in the rite of baptism, a function indicated by the words of Jesus: "He who has bathed does not need to wash, but is clean all over" (13:10).[9] But this verse, which continues, "you are clean, but not every one of you," is picked up further on, in 15:3: "You are already made clean by the word which I have spoken to you," where the word

---

7. So the new insight into the real meaning of Jesus' words partly depends on a recollection of "the scripture." The importance that the Scriptures hold for the evangelist is confirmed by an aside embedded in the resurrection narrative, where a knowledge of "the scripture that he must rise from the dead" is seen to be conditional on the experience of the resurrection: "for as yet they did not know the scripture, that he must rise from the dead" (20: 9).

8. Raymond Brown translates γινώσκειν here as "understand." Recognition and understanding go hand in hand.

9. Wrede thinks that the words εἰ μὴ τοὺς πόδας ("except for his feet"), omitted by Sinaiticus, should be deleted. C. K. Barrett, in a long and illuminating note, argues that although these words were inserted into the text very soon, they were nevertheless a later addition (*The Gospel according to St. John: An Introduction with Commentary and Notes on the Greek Text*, 2nd ed. (London: SPCK, 1978), 441–42.

καθαρός involves a punning allusion to the preceding καθαίρειν (normally "cleanse," but here "prune"). So if 15:3 is a comment on 13:10 the evangelist is reading the washing of the feet as a symbolic anticipation of the full founding of the community outlined in the allegory of the vine.

The other incident, which took place a few days earlier, is the occasion of Jesus' final entry into Jerusalem. "Jesus found a young ass and sat upon it; as it is written, 'Fear not, daughter of Zion; behold thy king is coming, sitting on an ass's colt.' His disciples did not understand [οὐκ ἔγνωσαν] this at first; but when Jesus was glorified, then they remembered that this had been written of him and had been done to him" (12:14-16). As Wrede points out, the solemn entry of Jesus and the homage of the crowd that accompanies it "stand in a relationship to the glorification or resurrection of Jesus that is *no more special* than any other significant event in his life or any important pronouncement. Here manifestly there lies behind the material *the general idea* that certain facts of his history remained obscure to begin with, even to the disciples, but after his victory over death became clear and transparent."[10]

THE ROLE OF THE SPIRIT

The Farewell Discourse (chapters 14–16) serves many purposes, but, most importantly, it offers an explanation of the new situation that the disciples (that is, the Johannine community) are about to find themselves in after Jesus' departure. Far from being utterly bereft once Jesus has left them, they are in some respects better off, because, with the assistance of the Paraclete, they are now at last in a position to understand fully all that he said while he was still on earth. So the sayings concerning the Paraclete or the Spirit of Truth embedded in these chapters are of vital importance in helping us to understand the evangelist's own understanding of the gospel genre.

Before turning to these, however, we may usefully consider three other passages that speak of the Spirit, the most remarkable of which (whose significance is generally lost in translation) comes in chapter 7, where the action takes place in the temple, on the feast of Tents or Tabernacles (a water feast):

> On the last day of the feast, the great day, Jesus stood up and proclaimed, "If any one thirst, let him come to me, and let him who believes in me drink. As the scripture has said, 'Out of his belly shall flow rivers of living water.'" Now he said this about the Spirit, which those who believed in him were to receive; for *as yet there was no*

---

10. Wrede, *Messianic Secret*, 185 (trans. modified; emphasis added).

Spirit [οὔπω γὰρ ἦν πνεῦμα] because Jesus was not yet glorified (7:37-39).

Although we should retain the literal translation of the words οὔπω γὰρ ἦν πνεῦμα ("for as yet there was no Spirit"), they should be taken in conjunction with two later comments of the evangelist, the first concerning Jesus' death, the second concerning one of the very last of his actions on earth, after his resurrection. John says first that in dying Jesus "gave up the ghost" (παρέδωκεν τὸ πνεῦμα; 19:30) and, second, that before taking his final leave of his disciples he breathed upon them (ἐνεφυσήσεν), and said, "Receive the Holy Spirit" (Λάβετε ἅγιον πνεῦμα; 20:22). In giving up the ghost he was at the same time *handing over* the Spirit (the literal meaning of the verb παραδιδόναι), and in breathing upon the disciples he was at the same time *infusing them* with the Spirit.

THE FAREWELL DISCOURSE

Taken together, these passages show that for this evangelist there was no role for the Spirit until after Jesus' death and resurrection; and this conclusion is confirmed when we turn to the sayings concerning the Paraclete in the Farewell Discourse. There are five of these, two in chapter 14 (vv. 16-17, 26), one in chapter 15 (v. 26), and two in chapter 16 (vv. 7-11, 12-15). Four of these are relevant to our present purpose. (I omit 16:7-11 from consideration here.)

1. "And I will pray the Father, and he will give you another Paraclete, to be with you for ever—the Spirit of truth, whom the world cannot receive, because it neither sees him nor knows him; you know him, for he dwells with you, and will be in you [ἐν ὑμῖν ἔσται] (14:16-17). This other Paraclete (taking over from Jesus himself, who preceded him in his various functions)[11] is thought of as the Spirit of *Truth*, with all that this implies; moreover, he will remain forever with the community, not just present *to* them but also, in some sense, present *in* them. Later on in the same chapter Jesus promises anyone who loves him and keeps his word that he and his Father "will come to him and make our home with him [καὶ μονὴν παρ' αὐτῷ ποιησόμεθα]" (14:23). (The word μονή is the substantival equivalent of the verb μένειν, which in these passages we translate

---

11. See Raymond E. Brown, *The Gospel according to John: Introduction, Translation, and Notes,* 2 vols., Anchor Bible 29, 29A) (New York: Doubleday, 1966, 1970), 2:1141–42. Brown shows how the Paraclete is seen to have copied Jesus in teaching, reminding, bearing witness, and so on.

as "dwell" or "abide.") The presence of Father and Son in the soul of the believer is made possible by, or rather is equivalent to, the presence of the Paraclete.

2. "But the Paraclete, the Holy Spirit, whom the Father will send in my name, will teach you all things [διδάξει πάντα], and bring to your remembrance [ὑπομνήσει] all that I have said to you" (14:26). Part of the Paraclete's role will be to remind (ὑπομιμνήσκειν) the disciples of all that Jesus has told them up to this point. This is to be taken along with what is said concerning Jesus' prophecy in the temple in chapter 2, that the disciples would remember it after he was raised from the dead. Only then, reminded by the Paraclete, would they fully understand; only then would they fully believe. Less clear is what is meant by saying that the Paraclete would teach them *everything* (πάντα). Not, surely, everything that there is to know, but rather everything that they needed to know in the one area that concerned them, summed up a little further on as "the truth." And once again, not the truth about everything, but the truth about Jesus, who had just identified himself as *the* truth (14:6). Moreover, since the Paraclete would remain with them forever, this promise also holds good for those to whom the evangelist is addressing his Gospel, the Johannine community.

John 14 comes in the first edition of the Gospel. The fact that it contains such clear indications of the role of the Paraclete shows that by the time the evangelist had composed a first version of his work that could be regarded as complete he had a full grasp of the essential nature of the gospel form. And the fact that further reflections are found in the two subsequent chapters, which belong to the second edition, demonstrates the importance he attached to this aspect of his work.

3. "But when the Paraclete comes, whom I shall send to you from the Father, the Spirit of truth, who proceeds from the Father, he will bear witness concerning me [μαρτυρήσει περὶ ἐμοῦ]; and you also are witnesses [καὶ ὑμεῖς δὲ μαρτυρεῖτε], because you have been with me from the beginning" (15:26). Bultmann has an insightful comment on this passage:

> The word μαρτυρήσει [*he will bear witness*] indicates that the Spirit is the power of proclamation in the community, and this is made fully clear by the juxtaposition of the disciples' witness and that of the spirit; καὶ ὑμεῖς δὲ μαρτυρεῖτε [*and you also are witnesses*] (v. 27). For the witness of the disciples is not something secondary, running alongside the witness of the Spirit. . . . The community's preaching

is to be none other than witness to Jesus; for the word μαρτυρεῖτε is of course to be supplemented by the περὶ ἐμοῦ [*to me*] of the μαρτυρήσει. . . . Their witness is not a historical account of that which was, but—however much it is based on that which was—it is "repetition," a "calling to mind" [14:26] in the light of their present relationship with him.[12]

At the end of chapter 21, rightly regarded by most scholars as an appendix to the Gospel, it is said of the evangelist that "he bears witness to these things," and that "his testimony is true" (21:24). His Gospel contains nothing apart from his witness or testimony to Jesus (μαρτυρία) in the sense that this word has in the verse under discussion.

4. "I have yet many things to say to you, but you cannot bear them now. When the Spirit [πνεῦμα, *neuter*] of truth comes, he [ἐκεῖνος, *masculine*] will guide you into the whole truth [ἐν τῇ ἀληθείᾳ πάσῃ];[13] for he will not speak on his own authority, but whatever he hears he will speak, and he will expound to you [ἀναγγελεῖ ὑμῖν] the things that are to come. He will glorify me, for he will take from what is mine and expound it to you. All that the Father has is mine; therefore I said that he will take what is mine and expound it to you" (16:12-15).[14]

---

12. Rudolf Bultmann, *The Gospel of John: A Commentary* (Oxford: Basil Blackwell, 1971), 553–54.

13. The words ἐν τῇ ἀληθείᾳ πάσῃ, by far the best-attested reading, might be translated, "within the sphere of the whole truth." Two important manuscripts, however, Vaticanus and Alexandrinus, read εἰς instead of ἐν at this point, probably because their scribes (rightly in my view) interpreted the ἐν to mean "into." As Brown points out (*Gospel*, 2:715), the two prepositions were used quite loosely around this time.

14. The word ἀναγγέλλειν, which occurs three times in this short passage, I have translated as "expound" (instead of the usual "declare"), because this is what it means in several contexts involving the explanation of a riddle or mystery. It is the verb used by Theodotion in his translation of Daniel 2 (which the evangelist may have known) to translate the Aramaic word החוי [the haphel of חוה], which means "to expound or interpret" and is used in conjunction with with פשרא, the Aramaic equivalent of the Hebrew פשר ("pesher"). It is used with the same meaning in a passage in *4 Ezra* that recounts how the angel Uriel poses three riddles (*similitudines* = παραβολαί) to the seer: "Three paths I have been sent to show you and three riddles to set you: if you can explain one of these to me [*si mihi renunciaveris unam ex his*] I in turn will show you the way you long to see." (4:3-4). Here the Latin *renunciare* is certainly a rendering of ἀναγγέλλειν, the verb used in Adolf Hilgenfeld's Greek retroversion, *Messias Judaeorum* (Leipzig, 1869). Finally, it is used in 1 Peter of the explanation given to Christians of the new revelation by preachers of the gospel: "the things which have been explained to you" (ἀνηγγέλη ὑμῖν) (1 Pet. 1:1-10). Ignace de La Potterie also points to *2 Baruch* and *Hermas, Vis.* ii.1.3; iii.3.1 as standing in the

Giving his last instructions to his disciples on the eve of his death, Jesus appears to be saying at this point that he has yet more to tell them. But how are we to understand this? There is now no time left for him to speak plainly in his own person of all that he has left to say. Even if he continued to speak, they could not take it in: so why continue? As the readers of the Gospel should know by now, the disciples *cannot* understand until Jesus had risen from the dead. He has already told them that it will be the work of the Paraclete to remind and instruct them. Now he puts it another way: he is to lead them into the truth.

Relevant here is the distinction made elsewhere between enigmatic and open discourse. In 7:26 "some of the people of Jerusalem" reflect admiringly that even though Jesus has been speaking quite openly (παρρησίᾳ), he has not been challenged; and asked later by the Jews to tell them plainly (παρρησίᾳ) if he is the Messiah, Jesus replies, "I *have* told you, and you do not believe" (10:24). Later still, in response to questions about his teaching addressed to him by the high priest at his trial, he declares, "I have spoken openly [παρρησίᾳ] to the world: I have always taught in the synagogues and in the temple, where all Jews come together; I have said nothing in secret [ἐν κρυπτῷ]" (18:20). Yet toward the end of the Farewell Discourse he admits to his disciples that up to that point he had been speaking to them enigmatically (ἐν παροιμίαις), and he continues: "the hour is coming when I will no longer speak to you enigmatically [ἐν παροιμίαις] but tell you plainly [παρρησίᾳ] of the Father" (16:25). Yet—to add to the reader's confusion—when he has concluded this discourse, the disciples thank him for at last speaking plainly (παρρησίᾳ) and no longer enigmatically (παροιμίαν οὐδεμίαν λέγεις), adding, "now we know that you know all things and do not need to be asked" (16:29).

What are we to make of these apparent contradictions? The answer is that in spite of an occasional wobble the evangelist makes an absolute principle of his distinction between all that transpired in Jesus' lifetime—both words and actions—and the quite different situation after his death and resurrection. *Before* the resurrection the disciples hear and see but cannot understand. *After* the resurrection they can no longer see and no longer hear (because Jesus is no longer with them), but with the assistance of the Paraclete, they can now (at last) understand. Wrede is quite right to say that "so far as the evangelist is concerned, Jesus would speak ἐν παροίμιαις even if nothing of the sort existed."[15]

---

same tradition (*La vérité dans saint Jean*, 2 vols., Analecta biblica 73, 74 [Rome: Biblical Institute Press, 1977], 1:445–49).

15. Wrede, *Messianic Secret*, 206.

Wrede also saw very clearly that "the prophecy of teaching through the Spirit of Truth and all the related sayings refer to the teaching of the Gospel itself";[16] and he did not shrink from pointing out the implications:

> I am thereby ascribing to the Gospel of John a manifest contradiction. Jesus refers to the future revelation and to the importing of information on a higher level than the disciples have meanwhile experienced, and yet during his life he said everything that was to be said. And this contradiction could not in any circumstances be evaded by the evangelist if he was going to postpone the unveiling of the truth to the disciples till the time of the glorification.[17]

Rudolf Bultmann comments approvingly on these remarks, agreeing that the contradiction is intentional on the part of the evangelist and underlining the point that the statements "Jesus has already said everything that he is still concealing" and "he has as yet said nothing in such a way that it could be understood" belong together.[18] But in ascribing to the disciples a failure to understand Jesus' words at the time they were uttered, the evangelist was not contradicting himself; rather, he was accepting that Jesus' resurrection enabled and involved a new understanding. Also perhaps, as we shall see later, he was deliberately adopting the apocalyptic convention of two stages of revelation.

The idea of being guided or led into the truth, I suggest, is borrowed from the farewell discourse of Moses in the book of Deuteronomy. On the eve of his own death, Moses told the Israelites that his successor, Joshua, would lead them into the promised land, thus investing Joshua with his own authority. So too Jesus here tells his disciples that *his* successor, the Paraclete, the Spirit of Truth, will "lead them into all truth." Moses, knowing that he is about to die, entrusts to Joshua the task of leading his people into the promised land; similarly Jesus promises to send the Paraclete to lead his disciples into the truth—the full revelation of all that he has told them. The Paraclete is the successor of Jesus as Joshua was the successor of Moses.[19]

---

16. Wrede, *Messianic Secret*, 192.

17. Wrede, *Messianic Secret*, 193.

18. Bultmann, *Gospel,* 573 n. 2.

19. The foregoing paragraph is a summary of a fuller argument in *Understanding the Fourth Gospel,* 445–53.

CONCLUSION

I have been arguing in this chapter that John the evangelist, fully aware of the contradiction intrinsic to and inseparable from the gospel genre, has exploited it for his own purposes so as to underline the essential difference between the reception of Jesus' words and actions during his lifetime and the enhanced understanding of these words and actions that was available to him and his community. Inherent in the full acceptance of all that the gospel genre implies is the awareness that all the works and words of Jesus are operative in the evangelist's own present: he includes himself and his community as among the people Jesus was talking of when he uttered the words, "we must work the works of him who sent me, while it is still day" (9:4). He knows that the risen Jesus is an abiding presence and the source of life for himself and his community. He knows that the new understanding is a revelation from above, but that the *content* of this new revelation is nothing more (and nothing less) than the story he has just told. I reserve until the last chapter of this book any comment on the full significance of this perception. Meanwhile it is of some importance to recognize that John was not just "writing theology in a book that was to be a possession for ever," as Barrett has maintained,[20] but a book with immediate relevance to his own situation and that of his readers about an individual Jew called Jesus of Nazareth who had lived a half-century earlier.

20. C. K. Barrett, *The Prologue of John's Gospel* (London: Athlone, 1971), 8.

3

Chief Priests and Pharisees

With reference to Julius Wellhausen's commentaries on the Synoptic Gospels, published just over a century ago between 1905 and 1911, Rudolf Bultmann wrote (in English):

> Wellhausen brought clearly to light a principle which must govern research. We must recognize that a literary work or a fragment of tradition is a primary source for the historical situation out of which it arose, and is only a secondary source for the historical details for which it gives information.[1]

Written in 1926, these words are as true today as they were then and are no less appropriate as a defense of historical criticism against what its advocates call *the third quest* than they were as Bultmann used them, that is to say, as a defense of form criticism against attempts being made at the time to use the Synoptic Gospels as sources for the life of Christ.

So let us consider the significance of the simple fact that the Gospels were written many years after the events that they record. Though narrating events that took place in the first half of the first century CE, the evangelists were addressing themselves to their own contemporaries in the second half of the same century. So we have to bear in mind the differences between the social and political conditions prevailing during Jesus' lifetime and those of the time of the composition of the Gospels.[2] That these differences were so great is almost entirely consequent upon the catastrophic failure of the Jewish uprising

---

1. Rudolf Bultmann, "The New Approach to the Synoptic Problem," *Journal of Religion* 6 (1926): 337–62. These words were also cited by Willi Marxsen in support of what he was the first to call Redaction Criticism, at that time still a fledgling method of Gospel research (*Der Evangelist Markus: Studien zur Redaktionsgeschichte des Evangeliums,* Forschungen zur Religion und Literatur des Alten und Neuen Testaments 67 [Göttingen: Vandenhoeck & Ruprecht, 1956], 13 n. 1). It was Marxsen who coined the term *Sitz-im-Leben-des-Evangeliums.*

against Rome in 66 CE. In the remainder of this chapter I will illustrate these differences by reflecting on the significance of one expression ("chief priests and Pharisees"), which occurs five times in the Gospel of John (7:32, 45; 11:47, 57; 18:3), and twice in Matthew (21:45; 27:62), always in a context of these two groups' murderous opposition to Jesus. I want to ask first how far this conjunction was plausible during Jesus' lifetime (for the two groups arguably had at best an uneasy relationship), and, second, what it will have meant to John's readers, living as they did in a period when the priests had lost their power and authority had reverted to the Pharisees.

If we are primarily concerned with the period of Jesus' public career, the problem arises from the presence of the Pharisees; for in the passages in the Fourth Gospel where they are seen to be actively cooperating with the priests, they appear to be credited with much more than the moral authority they had throughout their history. We have already seen that John is not the only evangelist to implicate the Pharisees in this conspiracy. Matthew, who makes his animosity toward the Pharisees all too plain, uses the conjunction "chief priests and Pharisees" at one point, like John, in telling of an attempt to arrest Jesus (21:45-46; cf. 27:62). Mark, surprisingly early in his Gospel, concludes a series of controversy stories by declaring that "the Pharisees went out, and immediately held counsel with the Herodians against him, how to destroy him" (Mark 3:6).

2. Just how important the confusion between the two can be, and how pervasive, is illustrated by the following quotation from a recent book by Daniel Boyarin: "I submit that it is possible to understand the Gospel only if both Jesus and the Jews around him held to a high Christology whereby the claim to Messiah was also a claim to being a divine man. Were it not the case, we would be very hard-pressed to understand the extremely hostile reaction to Jesus on the part of Jewish leaders who did not accept his claim" (*The Jewish Gospels: The Story of the Jewish Christ* [New York: New Press, 2012], 55).

THE CHIEF PRIESTS

First, though, let us reflect on the authority of the chief priests,[3] which is best understood from a consideration of the historical context. At least from the time of Ezra, in the second half of the fifth century BCE, the high priest was not just a priest but a prince, the political leader of the nation. The authority of the high priest was at its height during the reign of the Hasmonean priest-kings, a period of some eighty years (142–63 BCE), the only time in the Second Temple era that Israel could claim to be truly independent of any foreign power. This period of independence came to an end in 63 BCE, when the reigning king Aristobulus was defeated by the Roman general Pompey. Aged forty-three at the time, Pompey was then the most powerful man in the western world. Two years later, celebrating a magnificent triumph in Rome, he forced Aristobulus to walk in front of his chariot. The last of the Hasmonean priest-kings was Aristobulus's son, Antigonus, who reigned (with the consent and approval of Rome) for a brief three years, between 40 and 37 BCE, when Herod the Great finally succeeded in gaining control of Jerusalem and getting him killed. The Roman authorities, who had already taken charge of the appointment of the high priest (which meant that tenure of this office was no longer for life), passed on their power of appointment to Herod. Having no intention of restoring power to the priests, Herod withdrew their hereditary rights permanently; moreover, his own choice did not always fall upon a member of one of the traditional priestly families. The power of appointment rested with Herod and his son Archelaus

---

3. The nomenclature can be confusing. The simple form ἱερεύς ("priest") occurs only once in John's Gospel (1:19) and is not very frequent in the other Gospels either. The confusion comes from the much more common ἀρχιερεύς, because when this term occurs in the singular it is translated as "high priest," whereas the plural form, ἀρχιερεῖς, is always translated as "chief priests." How are we to explain this? The word is found only four times in those parts of the Septuagint that translate the Hebrew Bible, and in three of these instances other manuscripts have the simple form ἱερεύς instead. There is one occurrence in Leviticus (4:3), a book largely concerned with the sacrificial responsibilities of the high priest, where once or twice the qualification 'the anointed' (המשיח) is added to the simple form כהן (kohēn). Elsewhere (e.g. Haggai) he is sometimes called the great priest (הגדול). On the other hand, the word occurs frequently in 1 and 2 Maccabees (books composed in Greek and not found in the Hebrew Bible), but always in the singular, referring, in 1 Maccabees, to the high priests Jonathan, Simon, or Simon's son John, and in 2 Maccabees to Onias or Alcimus. To the best of my knowledge the first use of the plural form is in the Gospels, but the historian Josephus too uses it to refer to members of the priestly aristocracy, whereas the singular form, in his writings as elsewhere, is always used of the high priest. In John 18:19 the title is erroneously given to Annas (Ananos), who was high priest between 4 and 15 CE, even though, as the evangelist knew perfectly well, the high priest at the time of Jesus' arrest was Caiaphas. The anomaly is discussed by Raymond Brown in a long note on John 18:13, *The Gospel according to John: Introduction, Translation, and Notes,* 2 vols., Anchor Bible 29, 29A (New York: Doubleday, 1966, 1970), 2:820–21.

until 6 CE, when Archelaus (never given the title of king) was dismissed and exiled by the emperor Augustus. Rome then took back the right to appoint the high priest and exercised it, through the governors of the province of Syria, until the fall of the temple in 70 CE.

Since some of the governors used this power of appointment quite frequently, besides the incumbent high priest there were often several ex–high priests around. All of them had at one point held the actual title, so the historian Josephus refers to them by the plural form of the word. The translation "chief priests" (never "high priests" in the plural) reflects the fact that only one of them could be high priest at a time. Josephus also occasionally used the term of members of the four leading families who had not in fact officiated as high priest. (In any case they were a privileged lot, aristocrats.) "Different races," he comments, at the beginning of his *Life*, "base their claim to nobility on various grounds; with us a connection with the priesthood is the hallmark of an illustrious line" (1.1). In what he says next he emphasizes that this is really true only of a relatively small number of families, of which his own was the most eminent. And he goes on to list his own pedigree, a series of high priests, starting from his own great-grandfather's grandfather.

So how much power was the high priest left with under Roman dominion? The answer is, quite a lot. Not only did he perform all the major sacrifices in the temple, but he presided over the Sanhedrin, and hence over the civil affairs of the nation, and was still usually chosen from among a few privileged families. So under the sovereignty of the Romans and Herodians the families from which the high priest was mostly drawn were still an influential aristocracy (Josephus, *Ant.* 2. 227-28), and the Sanhedrin, the supreme legislative council, retained its original character, which was that of a representation of the nobility, not a council of scholars, even though it will have included some Pharisees in its ranks. At the same time one consequence of the subordination of the high priest (and of the Sanhedrin) to the Roman authorities must have been a loss of some of their prestige in the eyes of the people.

THE PHARISEES

So much, then, for the chief priests. What about the Pharisees? In the first couple of centuries of the postexilic period (539–333 BCE) the two leading influences on Israel's internal development were the priests and the scribes, reflecting the double focus of the life of the nation: the temple and the Torah—the law. In this early period there was no reported dissension between the two groups; but during the first two centuries of the so-called Greek era that followed (333–63) they grew farther and farther apart, until by the end of the Maccabean wars (175–135) they were in sharp opposition. The Sadducees, who were primarily aristocrats, keen on maintaining both political power and social standing, emerged from priestly circles.[4] The Pharisees, whose first concern was always with the strict observance of the law, came from among the scribes, or Torah scholars, and were distinguished from the outset by their legal orientation.

It is not easy to give a clear picture of the Pharisees, largely because the society of ancient Israel was so different from our own. Of all countries it is perhaps present-day Iran that offers the closest analogue. We call these societies theocracies, a term that seems to suggest that they are governed by God. But their real rulers are the religious leaders. Think of the literal sense of the word hierarchy, formed from the same two words as ἀρχιερεύς, one meaning priest, the other chief or leader. Like modern Iran, whose supreme leader, the Ayatollah Ali Khamenei, is first and foremost a prominent cleric, ancient Israel, once it had recovered from the traumatic experience of exile in Babylon, and once the temple had been rebuilt, was a hierarchy in this, the etymological sense of the word, with the high priest as the supreme authority in the land. In the second place, just as present-day Iran, like other Muslim countries, claims that its people should live their lives according to the precepts of the Qur'an, so the lives of the people of ancient Israel were largely controlled by the Torah (as of course is true of Orthodox Jews today).

Accordingly we may think of Second Temple Judaism as an era when the lives of the people had a double focus: first there was the temple, which automatically ensured that the high priest in particular, but also more generally the priestly aristocracy to which he belonged, enjoyed great powers and privileges; second, there was the law or Torah. Like any other corpus of legal precepts, the Torah requires interpretation, and it was in this area that the Pharisees came to acquire a moral authority different from that of the priests. For most of what we know about the Pharisees we are indebted to the Jewish historian Josephus, who writes of them first as one of three different forms of philosophy: εἴδη φιλοσοφεῖται (War 2.119) or Jewish sects (αἱρέσεις; War 2.162), asserting that they are considered the most accurate interpreters of the νόμιμα, that is, the precepts of the Torah (Life 191), and hold the position of the leading sect. Himself a member of the priestly aristocracy by birth, Josephus

---

4. The Fourth Gospel says nothing at all directly about the Sadducees, who retained a dominant political position right up to the fall of the temple in 70 CE The word *Sadducees* never occurs in the Gospel (an omission partly to be explained by the fact that, as we shall see, the fall of the temple meant the loss of their authority), and the Johannine community never had any involvement with them.

says that he began his political career by following the sect of the Pharisees (*Life* 12), a remark that illustrates one crucial difference between the two groups: you are *born* a priest, you *choose* to be a Pharisee. (It should be added that it is quite wrong to think of the Pharisees as a sect in the sense of a religious group that has seceded from the main body.)

The history of the Pharisees is far too long and complicated to be discussed in detail here, but two events recounted by Josephus illustrate the nature of their authority. The first of the Hasmonean priest-kings, John Hyrcanus I (134–104 BCE) regarded them with some favor early in his reign, but when they subsequently urged him to give up the high priesthood, he responded angrily by abrogating previous legislation that had favored Pharisaic teaching (Josephus, *Ant.* 13.288-98). Some time later (76–69), under the reign of Queen Alexandra, the widow of Hyrcanus's son, the violent and irascible Alexander Jannaeus, they came into favor again: Alexandra put them in charge of the internal affairs of the nation, with the result that for a short period of six or seven years they came to dominate Jewish public life.

These episodes show, first, that by the closing decades of the second century BCE at the latest, the Pharisees had become a political interest group, eager to attain as much authority as they could over the Jewish people, but also, second, that they could not manage this without the consent of the government in power at the time.[5]

The fortunes of the Pharisees during the long reign of Herod the Great (37–4 BCE) confirm these conclusions, since once again they enjoyed Herod's support early in his reign but lost it when they allied themselves with a faction that opposed him. In this respect things were the same under the Roman governors (6–66 CE): the Pharisees won political clout by ranging themselves

---

5. The opposition of the Pharisees to the Sadducees is often portrayed as religiously slanted, but the religious element can be overstated. The Pharisees were mainline Jews, not a religious sect, and what set them against the Sadducees was largely the natural resentment of ordinary folk toward bossy aristocrats. Anthony J. Saldarini, whose study *Pharisees, Scribes and Sadducees in Palestinian Society* has the subtitle *A Sociological Approach* (Wilmington, Del.: Michael Glazier, 1988) is careful not to portray the Pharisees either as a political party or as a religious sect, and he thinks of them rather as the kind of grouping which, following Gerhard E. Lenski (*Power and Privilege: A Theory of Social Stratification* [New York: McGraw-Hill, 1966]), he entitles a *retainer class*, that is to say, a diverse group of people that serves the needs of the ruler or governing class and in so doing acquires some authority of its own. But although, as we have seen, the Pharisees were always eager to exercise some authority within the community, this was not out of concern for the needs of the rulers. We should recognize that, although most of their members were not aristocrats, some probably were. We have seen that Josephus, himself the scion of an aristocratic priestly family, chose to be a Pharisee, and it is widely acknowledged that the Sanhedrin will have had some Pharisees within its ranks.

alongside the imperial power. In an attempt to avert Roman wrath, Josephus tells us, the most powerful people of Judea, shortly before the outbreak of the Jewish war, faced with what seemed to be certain disaster, assembled with the chief priests and the most notable Pharisees (*War* 2.411). So during Jesus' lifetime, when both priests and Pharisees were collaborating with the Roman authorities, we should not be surprised when John tells us repeatedly that they joined forces in a matter of common concern. Nevertheless, a word of caution is in order. For reading the Gospels today and focusing on the story of Jesus, we can all too easily attach as much importance to the Pharisees as to the priests and, furthermore, associate the whole Pharisaic movement with the handful of men who may have joined with the senior members of the Sanhedrin in persecuting Jesus. When the term *Pharisees* is used in the Gospels to refer to people cooperating with the chief priests, we should probably understand it to refer, as it does in the passage from Josephus I have just quoted, to the most notable among them. With this proviso, the conjunction "chief priests and Pharisees," used as it is in John's Gospel exclusively in contexts where they join forces to arrest Jesus and cause him to be condemned by the Roman authorities, makes perfect sense.

Should we conclude, therefore, that these passages are historically reliable? By no means. The decision to seek Jesus' death is ascribed by Mark (14:1) and, following him, Luke (22:2) to "the chief priests and the scribes," while Matthew, in the same context, writes of "the chief priests and the elders" (27:1). John's only mention of the scribes and the elders is in the spurious account of the woman taken in adultery (8:2, 9). When he implicates the Pharisees, along with the chief priests, in the two attempts on Jesus' life—first in the earlier episode in the temple (7:32, 45) and then in the final, successful, effort (11:47, 57; 18:3)—he is probably retrojecting his current enmity with the Pharisees back into the story. It could be said that for him the coupling "chief priests and Pharisees" is equivalent to "the Jews" in the typically hostile sense in which he uses this appellation. But in the two contexts in which a decision is taken to have Jesus arrested and killed, the fourth evangelist needs a more specific designation—though whether he was aware that the Pharisees (or some of them) did on occasion cooperate with the chief priests is open to doubt. We should never forget Wellhausen's salutary warning concerning sources and Bultmann's reminder of it, quoted at the beginning of the present chapter. Of course John wanted to tell the story of Jesus, but only because, as newly remembered, it had an immediate bearing on the life of his community. In certain respects the Fourth Gospel resembles Shakespeare's history plays, insofar as Shakespeare too was prepared to play fast and loose with the historical facts if by doing so he could shed his own light upon what he found in his sources. Shakespeare was not a historian; nor was John. They were much less concerned with historical accuracy than with putting their own particular slant on the story they were telling.

The earliest of the British monarchs chosen by Shakespeare as subjects for his history plays is King John, who came to the throne in 1199, the latest Henry VIII, who died in 1547. The time gap between the end of Henry's reign and Shakespeare's play is roughly the same as the gap between the death of Jesus and the composition of the Fourth Gospel. But the social and political situation of the Jewish people had changed no less dramatically within a span of roughly sixty years than had that in the three centuries between the reign of King John and that of Queen Elizabeth, which was when Shakespeare wrote his history plays.

To understand why, we must consider the enormity of the change undergone by the Jewish people as a consequence of their disastrous revolt against Rome. The war that followed lasted from 66 to 73 CE. Seven bloody years of war—just think of it! Longer than either of the two world wars of the twentieth century, longer than the American Civil War, just a year shorter than the American War of Independence. And as far as the city of Jerusalem was concerned, an agonizing five-month siege was followed by complete and absolute defeat. Though repulsed time and time again, the Romans, having already destroyed the temple, eventually broke through the last ineffective ramparts erected by the defenders, and swarmed through the city, murdering, burning, and looting, leaving nothing behind that could be called a city at all. Jerusalem was an area of utter devastation, and was, for the time being, deserted. Josephus tells us that those who visited it at this time could not believe that it had ever been inhabited (*War* 7.3). All the survivors fled, many of them to the coastal town of Yavneh, about forty miles west of Jerusalem, a few miles south of Tel Aviv, sometimes known by its Greek name of Jamnia. This rapidly became a special center of scholarly activity. It was the home first of Yohanan ben Zakkai and later of Gamaliel II, the two best known of a large circle of early rabbinical scholars. But of course their influence was not restricted to this one small town. It extended beyond Palestine into the Jewish Diaspora.

Let me quote Emil Schürer on the consequences of the war:

> The destruction of Jerusalem resulted in a violent upheaval in the inner life of the Jewish people. The disappearance of the Sanhedrin and the suspension of the sacrificial cult were the two great factors which profoundly affected Jewish life. . . . The Sanhedrin embodied

the last vestige of Jewish political independence, and with it the last remains of the power of the Sadducean nobility. The latter's influence had already been reduced since the time of Alexandra by the growing power of Pharisaism.[6] Nevertheless, as long as the Sanhedrin existed, it still had a role to play. For the competence of this aristocratic senate of Judaea was, during the time of the procurators, quite far-reaching; and at its head were the Sadducean High Priests. . . . The Pharisees and the rabbis entered into the heritage of the Sadducees and the priests. They were excellently prepared for this role, for they had been pressing for leadership during the last two centuries. Now, at one stroke, they acquired sole supremacy, as the factors which had stood in their way sank into insignificance.[7]

The priests did not lose all their authority immediately: taxes continued to be paid to them as before.[8] They had suffered more than most from the defeat by Rome and had retained, at least for a time, the respect of the people. And the amount of legislation in the Mishnah relating to temple worship suggests that those responsible for its redaction (including the Pharisees) still had hopes that the temple would eventually be rebuilt. But in those parts of the Gospel of John that can be shown to relate to the period of the composition of the Gospel, the priests play no part.

The Pharisees, on the other hand, play a significant part, but it is largely obscured by John's general preference for the term *Jews* ('Ιουδαῖοι) when referring to Jesus' adversaries. Most scholars think that he uses the two terms synonymously, but there are reasons for thinking that, in its most common, adversarial use in the Gospel, the term οἱ 'Ιουδαῖοι had come down from the self-appellation of the closely knit band of exiles who returned to Israel from Babylon when they were at last permitted to do so by the Persian king Cyrus in 538 BCE.[9] From that time on the name *Jews* denoted primarily an inner group within Israel characterized by particularly strong monotheistic

6. As we have seen, in the course of her ten-year reign Alexandra, who succeeded her husband Alexander to the throne of Judea in 76 BCE, gave such strong support and encouragement to the Pharisees that from then on they were a force to be reckoned with in Judean politics (see Josephus, *Ant.* 13.405-8).

7. Emil Schürer, *The History of the Jewish People in the Age of Jesus Christ (175 B.C.–A.D. 135)*, rev. and ed. Geza Vermes, Fergus Millar, and Martin Goodman, 3 vols. in 4 (Edinburgh: T&T Clark, 1973–87), 1:521–24.

8. See Schürer, *History of the Jewish People*, 1:524.

9. See John Ashton, *Understanding the Fourth Gospel*, 2nd ed. (Oxford: Clarendon, 2007), 69–78.

beliefs—beliefs associated with the exilic prophet Second Isaiah—what Morton Smith called "the Yahweh-alone party." [10] The returning exiles who held these beliefs distinguished themselves from those who had remained behind, who came to be given the derogatory appellation *the people of the land*.[11] Centuries later, taking advantage of the disarray that followed the fall of Jerusalem in 70 CE, this powerful party gradually assumed authority over the people of Israel as a whole and determined the nature of what we now call Judaism, which was pretty well settled by the time of the publication of the Mishnah, around 200 CE. The Pharisees, numbered by Josephus at roughly six thousand, must have had great influence within this inner group, but they are rarely mentioned after the end of the Jewish war. (There are only three occurrences of the name in the whole of the Mishnah.) Perhaps it was at this time that they managed to rid themselves of the separatist implications of their name by identifying themselves simply with the Ἰουδαῖοι.[12] If so, then this would explain why the evangelist uses the term Ἰουδαῖοι in passages of the Gospel relating directly to the conflict between the Jesus group in the synagogue and those who rejected the message of Jesus.

In some passages of the Gospel, however, the discussion is not with the Ἰουδαῖοι but with the Pharisees. These passages, as the Cambridge scholar Ernst Bammel pointed out in a little-known essay, reflect some very early disputes. "The Jews (Ἰουδαῖοι)-level," he says, "is later," whereas "the Pharisees-passages represent old valuable tradition,"[13] dating from a time when the two groups in the synagogue were still talking to one another. (I will have much more to say on this topic later.)

The quarter century that followed the defeat of the Jewish rebels saw the birth of two religions, not just one. Both of these emerged from the ruins of the temple to contend for dominance, a contention that went on for centuries, often accompanied by bitterness, misunderstanding, and mistrust. Both rabbinic

10. Morton Smith, *Palestinian Parties and Politics That Shaped the Old Testament*, 2nd ed. (London: SCM, 1987), 71 and passim.

11. See Shemaryahu Talmon, "The Emergence of Jewish Sectarianism in the Early Second Temple Period," in *Ancient Israelite Religion: Essays in Honor of Frank Moore Cross*, ed. Patrick D. Miller et al. (Philadelphia: Fortress Press, 1987), 587–616; Daniel Boyarin, "The Ioudaioi in John and the Prehistory of 'Judaism'," *Pauline Conversations in Context: Essays in Honor of Calvin J. Roetzel*, ed. Janice Capel Anderson, Philip Sellew, and Claudia Setzer, Journal for the Study of the New Testament: Supplement Series 221 (Sheffield: Sheffield Academic Press, 2002), 216–39.

12. See John Ashton, "The Jews in John," in idem, *Studying John: Approaches to the Fourth Gospel* (Oxford: Clarendon), 71–89.

13. Ernst Bammel, "'John did no miracle': John 10:41," in *Miracles: Cambridge Studies in Their Philosophy and History*, ed. C. F. D. Moule (London: Mowbray, 1965), 175–202, here 199.

Judaism and primitive Christianity can be traced back to the period following what we now call Second Temple Judaism (which, as the name suggests, lasted no longer than the Second Temple itself). But Second Temple Judaism already had its differences. That rabbinic Judaism sprang out of Pharisaism is beyond dispute. But what, precisely, were the origins of Christianity? That is a question to which there is no single answer. It would be wrong to think of the differing understandings of Jesus represented by, say, the writings of Paul, of Matthew, and of Mark, as if they had but a single provenance. In the remainder of this book I will continue to discuss one writing only, the most singular of all—the Gospel of John.

4

The Essenes

INTRODUCTION

I ended the last chapter with a discussion of the fate of the Jews after the debacle
of their uprising in 66–73 CE, and the flight to Yavneh, a bustling coastal town
not far from present-day Tel Aviv. In this chapter we take a huge fifty-mile
leap eastward away from the coast to what is (or at any rate used to be) one
of the most desolate places on earth, the western shore of the Dead Sea, about
eight miles from Jericho, where we find ourselves standing in the middle of
a pile of ruins called Khirbet Qumran. In 68 CE, two years after the start of
the revolt against Rome, when a small religious community that had settled
there a century or more earlier was forcibly disbanded, some of its members
gathered together a large number of manuscripts that had constituted their
precious library, scrambled up the nearby cliffs, and placed them in eleven
separate caves—hiding them so successfully that they remained undiscovered for
the best part of nineteen centuries.

The first find, by a Bedouin shepherd boy searching for a lost goat, was
in the spring of 1947. Soon afterward a hunt took off for more caves and
more manuscripts. The eleventh and last of the caves, which were numbered
in the order that they came to light, was discovered in 1956, but it was not
until 1997, a half-century after the first fortuitous find, that all the manuscripts
became available to anyone wanting to inspect them. The tangled story of their
agonizingly slow publication is well told by the Jewish scholar Geza Vermes,
who declared in 1977 that the protracted delay was becoming "the academic
scandal *par excellence* of the twentieth century."[1] The first edition of his own
Dead Sea Scrolls in English was published in 1962, and eventually, after three

---

1. Geza Vermes, *The Complete Dead Sea Scrolls in English* (London: Penguin, 1997), 7. In a later book,
The Story of the Scrolls: The Miraculous Discovery and True Significance of the Dead Sea Scrolls (London:
Penguin, 2010), after remarking that "the miserable handling by de Vaux [a Dominican priest who was
the first person to be given general charge of the publication of the scrolls] and his successors of the

revised and enlarged editions, there came at last, in 1997, *The Complete Dead Sea Scrolls in English*. Not only does Vermes offer "a bird's-eye view of fifty years of Dead Sea Scrolls research,"[2] but he also gives us a summary account of the Qumran community, its history and its religious life. A useful and easily accessible introduction.

For three very good reasons historians rapidly became convinced that the people who lived at Qumran must have belonged to a Jewish sect called the Essenes, mentioned by the Roman geographer Pliny the Elder and described, though with some disagreements, by the Jewish Alexandrian philosopher Philo and the historian Josephus.[3] The first reason is that the location given by Pliny for the Essene settlement, on the western shore of the Dead Sea, tallies remarkably well with the actual site of the Qumran community. The second reason is the close correspondence between the account given by Josephus of the admission procedures of the sect (*War* 2.137-42) and the very precise delineation of the rules for admission in a section of one of the very first documents to be discovered at Qumran, now generally known as the *Community Rule* (1QS 6:14-23). And the third reason is the fact that various social practices outlined in the Greek sources—the sharing of property, the habit of communal living, and the observation of a strict state of ritual purity—are also outlined in the *Community Rule*.

archaeological finds has stretched the scandal well into the third millennium" (p. 172), he goes on to defend the Essene hypothesis outlined below against various alternative theories.

2. Vermes, *Complete Dead Sea Scrolls*, 1.

3. Since the secondary sources, Pliny, Philo, and Josephus, are all clearly wrong about some things, how can we be sure when they are right? Pliny, for instance, says that the Essenes do not use money: the plentiful supply of coins discovered at Qumran proves him to be mistaken. And he is equally wrong to maintain that they survived for thousands of centuries (though he does remark at the same time how difficult this is to believe, since no children are ever born to them!) (*Natural History* 5.15.73). Josephus, who distinguishes between two orders of Essenes, the first celibate, the second not, is more interested in the first group, which he numbers at rather more than four thousand (*Ant.* 18.20-21). The *Community Rule* at Qumran makes no provision for women, and the great majority of skeletons found in the cemetery were male; so if the community also included members of the second (married) order of Essenes, they will have been much in the minority. Philo's account is distorted by his philosophical preoccupations, and whereas Josephus says that Essenes were to be found in every city of Judea, Philo says that they avoided cities, which they regarded as dens of vice. Yet although, given these discrepancies, it is scarcely surprising that historians come to different conclusions, especially with regard to place and numbers, much of what Philo and Josephus say about the nature of Essene communities has in fact been confirmed by archaeological and, more especially, by the extensive manuscript discoveries at Qumran and elsewhere. (The classical sources—Philo, Pliny, Josephus—are conveniently gathered together, with translations, in *The Essenes according to the Classical Sources*, ed. Geza Vermes and Martin Goodman, Oxford Centre Textbooks 1 (Sheffield: JSOT Press, 1989).

To the best of my knowledge no other book on the Gospel of John discusses the Dead Sea Scrolls as thoroughly as I am attempting to do here. Most such studies (including my own) contain cursory references to lines or passages in the scrolls that appear to shed light on particular themes that are also of importance in the Gospel, themes such as truth and life. Yet without some fuller discussion such as I am giving here, the light that is shed can only be flickering and fitful. I am convinced that a broader comparison will lead to a fuller understanding—not because there is necessarily a direct indebtedness on the part of the evangelist, but because the scrolls gives us a greater insight into certain characteristics of Second Temple Judaism that throw John's Gospel into sharp relief. I do not discount the possibility of a direct debt (which I have argued for in the past); but I now believe that an overall comparison is more instructive.[4]

We must begin by observing that modern scholarship offers two very different pictures of this sect. Since the discoveries at Qumran, which have brought to light an abundance of genuinely firsthand material, most scholars have focused their attention on the Qumran community itself, and I myself will be taking this path here. If we except the elder Pliny's remark about money, the rapid sketch that he gives in his *Natural History* seems to have been fairly accurate: "sine ulla femina, omni venere abdicata, sine pecunia, socia palmarum" (5.15.73): no women, no sex, no money, with only palm trees for company—that is to say a reclusive, strictly celibate, monkish community of maybe a couple hundred men, hiding themselves away in the desert on the edge of the Dead Sea. (Pliny adds that with no children ever born to them they were fortunate to have a plentiful supply of new recruits among men who were tired of life!)

A few scholars, however, have shown more interest in what Josephus says about the rest, some four thousand celibate men, holding all that they possess in common, scattered around in most if not all of the towns and villages of Judea (see *War* 2.124 and *Ant.* 18.20-21). An especially daring suggestion comes from Brian Capper:

---

4. Introducing a collection of essays published in 2013 based on my suggestion (in *Understanding the Fourth Gospel*) that the Gospel of John was "an apocalypse in reverse," I argued that John (as an Essene) had carefully read the Book of Daniel and that he had also studied the parts of *1 Enoch* available at Qumran ("Intimations of Apocalyptic: Looking Back and Looking Forward," in *John's Gospel and Intimations of Apocalyptic*, ed. Christopher Rowland and Catrin H. Williams [London: T & T Clark, 2013]: 1–33). Since 2010, when this essay was written, I have radically revised my opinion: I now think that it is only a mere rather than a near possibility that the evangelist was an Essene before he came to follow Jesus.

This powerful, firmly united core of more than four thousand skilled, educated, and highly disciplined male celibates was supported by at least several thousand families of the second Essene order [those that do not choose celibacy]. . . . The long-standing, honored presence of the celibate male Essene order throughout Judea . . . may indeed mean that virtually all the families of Judea's villages, and many laborers and artisans in Jerusalem, had been absorbed into the second order by the time of Jesus.[5]

In rejecting the theory that Essenism was a sect in the proper sense, and calling it instead a "virtuoso religion," even a religious order, Capper ignores the evidence, first, of what is known as the *Damascus Document*, which, as I shall show, cannot be regarded as anything other than the manifesto of a new sect, and, second, of the so-called *Halakhic Letter* (4QMMT), which states that "we have separated ourselves from the majority of the people . . . from intermingling and participating with them in these matters."[6] Nonetheless, the bold suggestion that one form of Essenism was omnipresent in first-century Judea opens up the possibility that if the evangelist was acquainted with that sect he did not necessarily acquire his knowledge at Qumran.

The Essenes are never mentioned in the New Testament, but it was not long before scholars began to look to the Dead Sea Scrolls found at Qumran and in a few other places for evidence relating to early Christianity. Some of the wilder speculations are sketched out by Vermes, who mentions in particular an early thesis of the Cambridge scholar Jacob Teicher that two of the most prominent personages mentioned in the scrolls, the Teacher of Righteousness and the Wicked Priest, could be identified, respectively, as Jesus and Saint Paul. Weirdest of all is the theory of the Australian Barbara Thiering that the Wicked Priest was Jesus, a married man with four children.[7] Certain features of the scrolls, such as their interest in messianism and their eschatological expectations, are clearly comparable with similar concerns on the part of the New Testament writers. There is no immediately obvious link between the Dead Sea Scrolls and the Gospel of John, but in fact there is at least one very important feature shared by the teachers of the community and the fourth evangelist (along, of

5. Brian J. Capper, "John. Qumran, and Virtuoso Religion," in *John, Qumran, and the Dead Sea Scrolls: Sixty Years of Discovery and Debate*, ed. Mary L. Coloe and Tom Thatcher, Society of Biblical Literature Early Judaism and Its Literature 32 (Atlanta: Society of Biblical Literature, 2011), 107–8.

6. See John J. Collins, *The Scepter and the Star: The Messiahs of the Dead Sea Scrolls and Other Ancient Literature*, Anchor Bible Reference Library (New York: Doubleday, 1995), 6.

7. See Vermes, *Complete Dead Sea Scrolls*, 21.

course, with all other Christian believers), namely, *a readiness to accept further divine revelations*. I will start, however, with a rough description of the Qumran library and a brief history of the Essenes. I have to say something about the library because I shall be drawing very extensively in the remainder of this book upon a number of different documents found in it. About the history of the sect I can afford to say less, because it does not directly affect my argument.

THE QUMRAN LIBRARY

The library is made up of around nine hundred documents, representing several different genres of writing, all of which, in one way or another, are religiously inspired. Some of these were books of the Bible; others were works composed by members of the community. These include rules for living, hymns, halakhic compositions (that is to say, particular legal rulings), and commentaries on Scripture. Still others (such as the book of *Jubilees*), though not composed at Qumran, were clearly highly prized there. If the whole collection (which contains thousands of fragments, some large, but most quite tiny) had been discovered much earlier, not by an Arab but by an orthodox Jew, it would have been either ignored or destroyed. Although we have quite a lot of writings from the Second Temple period besides the Bible, almost all of them have come down to us through Christian channels. Virtually the only exceptions are the books that came to be reckoned as canonical by the scribes. Even thoroughly Jewish works listed under the heading Apocrypha—writings such as the books of Maccabees and the Wisdom of Solomon—would have been lost to us had they not received Christian recognition. The same is true of the works of great Jewish writers like Philo of Alexandria and the historian Flavius Josephus, and also—for the purposes of this book most significant of all—large-scale apocalypses such as *1* and *2 Enoch, Syriac Baruch,* and *4 Ezra.* All but one of these apocalypses were composed after the Qumran community had ceased to exist. I will be reflecting later on the significance of the single exception, *1 Enoch.*

THE *DAMASCUS DOCUMENT*

None of the writings found at Qumran is historical in the strict sense of the word. Yet there is one text, known as the *Damascus Document,* that provides us with some important information about the sect's essential nature. It was known to scholars well before the discoveries at Qumran, because significant sections of it had been found decades earlier in Cairo and published by Solomon Schechter in 1910 as *Fragments of a Zadokite Work.* The subsequent discovery at

Qumran of fragments of the same document established a direct link between the Qumran community and a sectarian group known to have been already in existence. The Qumran community represents *one branch* of the sect of the Essenes, which according to Josephus, as we have seen, had members in every town in the region. The *Damascus Document* shows that the rules and regulations at Qumran were much the same as those of the Essenes as a whole, with the important exception that the *Document* assumes the presence of women throughout.

Before offering an exegesis of part of this document, I want to say a little about Second Temple Judaism. It has been suggested that the diverse cultural phenomena of Second Temple Judaism may be treated "as a protracted discussion of the question, 'What is it that really constitutes Israel?' "[8] The first task of the Jews on returning from their long exile in Babylon was to rebuild the temple, which immediately became the center of the life of the nation and gave an immediate boost to the social significance both of the priests and of the Torah for which they were responsible. The Torah (the Pentateuch, the first five books of the Hebrew Bible) directly concerns Israel's origins and juridical organization, and so had acquired a uniquely authoritative status by providing a necessary ideological basis for the survival of Israel as a people both during the exile and later, under the Persian Empire. In an important essay entitled, significantly, "Interpretation and the Tendency to Sectarianism," Joseph Blenkinsopp explains how "the interpretation or reinterpretation of tradition expressed in texts determined the self-understanding and self-definition of Judaism in Palestine"; or, put in another way, "how interpretation served as a factor in shaping alternative versions of an ideal envisioned in or presupposed by the texts [that were being interpreted]."[9] Starting with the Second Temple, his essay does not go beyond the Hasmonean monarchy toward the end of the second century BCE (by which time both Pharisees and Essenes had already emerged as recognizable groups); but Blenkinsopp makes clear that he thinks the same is true for the later period that saw the emergence of the early Christians. In what follows, focusing on the Essenes, I want to argue for a modified version of Blenkinsopp's thesis: namely, that one crucial factor in the self-understanding of this sect was not just an alternative interpretation of the law but an alternative theory of the very principles of interpretation.

8. Carol A. Newsom, *The Self as Symbolic Space: Constructing Identity and Community at Qumran,* Studies on the Texts of the Desert of Judah 52 (Leiden: Brill, 2004), 4.

9. Joseph Blenkinsopp, "Interpretation and the Tendency to Sectarianism: An Aspect of Second Temple History," in *Jewish and Christian Self-Definition: Aspects of Judaism in the Greco-Roman Period,* ed. E. P. Sanders et al., 3 vols. (London: SCM, 1981), 1:1–26.

No one has yet given a totally convincing literary analysis of the extraordinary work that we call the *Damascus Document*.[10] Although it is now almost universally acknowledged to have been the foundation document of the sect of the Essenes, I doubt if its author (or authors, for there may have been more than one) thought of it in this way: it was clearly intended as a manifesto, a written declaration of the beliefs and principles of a breakaway sect or party. (In this respect it resembles the Christian Gospels, which, though less obviously so, are also manifestos.) The *Damascus Document* is directed both to believers and to unbelievers, to those already convinced and to those not yet convinced of the truth it proclaims, *which is a new revelation.*

The *Document* opens (1:1) with a formula ("And now listen, all who know righteousness, and understand the actions of God") that recurs twice, with slight variations, in the first two columns: "And now listen, all who enter the covenant, and I will open your ears to the paths of the wicked" (2:1); "And now, O sons, listen to me and I will open your eyes so that you can see and understand the actions of God" (2:14). His addressees, envisaged as listening to what they are in fact reading, are first invited to "understand the actions of God"; then, in the second paragraph, the writer promises to open their ears, and finally, in the third paragraph, their eyes. Without his assistance, we are entitled to infer, the people he is addressing would be both blind and deaf.

In the course of the opening admonition (1:1—2:1) we learn of the misdeeds of the Scoffer, or man of mockery, who "sprinkled upon Israel waters of falsehood and led them astray in a chaos without a way" (1:14-15), with the result that "they sought smooth things [*ḥălāqôt*] and chose delusions and sought out loopholes" (1:18-19). The accusation of looking for easy interpretations and loopholes in the law, substituting overly simple readings for what the writer knows to be the truth, is encapsulated in the phrase "the Seekers of Smooth Things," which appears more than once in the Qumran manuscripts and is generally taken to refer to the Pharisees.[11] Those whose knowledge of

10. Perhaps the most impressive attempt, drawing upon the work of Jerome Murphy-O'Connor, Hartmut Stegemann, and others, is that of Philip R. Davies, *The Damascus Covenant: An Interpretation of the Damascus Document,* Journal for the Study of the Old Testament: Supplement Series 25 (Sheffield: JSOT Press, 1982). Davies criticizes both Murphy-O'Connor and Stegemann for their excessive reliance on the scriptural interpretations found at Qumran known as *pesharim* (on which I have more to say later). But it may be that he makes the opposite mistake of failing to give them sufficient attention.

11. Two examples from the Scrolls: (1) The phrase "the city of blood" in Nah. 3:1 is interpreted as "the city of Ephraim, *those who seek smooth things* during the last days, who walk in lies and falsehood" (4QpNah 3-4 ii 2); (2) In two of the hymns called the *Hodayot,* the leader of the community sees himself an object of attack by "the interpreters of error" and "those who seek *smooth things*" (1QH 10:14-15) and

the Pharisees has been hitherto restricted either to the works of the historian Josephus or to the Christian Gospels (or both), and who therefore think of the Pharisees as rigorous sticklers for the law, are likely to be surprised to learn that they are scornfully referred to by the Essenes as "the Seekers of Smooth Things."

The *Damascus Document* proposes a startlingly new model of interpretation. "Of those who held fast to God's ordinances," the writer declares, "God established his covenant with Israel forever, revealing to them hidden things [*nistārôt*] in which all Israel had strayed. . . . (These) he opened before them and they dug a well of abundant water" (3:12-16). We learn from this text (1) that the people with whom God has established his new covenant lay claim to the same proud name, Israel, that belonged to those who had strayed, one of the characteristics of any breakaway sect being an assured conviction that it is the only true representative of what the parent body formerly claimed to be. In the second place (2) we learn that Israel's grievous offenses, far from being obvious, are the object of a special revelation, so that even those who committed them could not have been aware of this at the time. Their faults, where they had strayed, are called "hidden things": knowledge of their own wrongdoing was unavailable to them because the special revelation required to recognize these misdeeds for what they were was reserved for others. (3) This revelation is somehow connected with the digging of "a well of abundant water." The explanation of this well is given somewhat later:

And God recalled the covenant with the first ones, and he raised up from Aaron men of discernment and from Israel wise men; and he allowed them to hear. And they dug the well (of which it is written) "the well was dug by the princes and excavated by the nobles of the people, with a staff." The "well" is the Torah and those who "dig" it are the penitents of Israel [the choice of *penitents* rather than the alternative translation, *returnees*, is significant] and those who depart from the land of Judah and dwell in the land of Damascus. God called them all *princes*, for they sought him, and their honor was not rejected by anyone's mouth. And the "staff" is the Interpreter of the Law, of whom Isaiah said, "He takes out a tool for his work" (Isa. 54:16). . . . And "the nobles of the people" are those who come to excavate the well with the staves [statutes] that the staff decreed . . .

again by "lying interpreters and deceitful seers," who "have concocted base schemes against me, to exchange your law, which you impressed upon my heart for *smooth things* for your people" (1QH 12:10-11).

and without which they will not obtain it until there arises one who will teach righteousness in the end of days. (6:2-11)

The men of knowledge and the wise men, of course, are the leaders of the community. The first biblical passage quoted here, from the book of Numbers, alludes to an episode during Israel's forty-year sojourn in the wilderness:

And from there they [the people of Israel] continued to Beer [b'r, Hebrew for well], that is the well of which the Lord said to Moses, "Gather the people together, and I will give them water." Then Israel sang this song: "Spring up, O well!—Sing to it!—the well which the princes dug, which the nobles of the people delved, with the scepter and with their staves." (Num. 21:16-18)[12]

This well, which, with an exercise of a brilliantly imaginative midrashic exegesis, they interpreted as referring to the law, was at the center of the life of the community, and it had to be dug by people qualified to do so. In the interpretation of the biblical passage the word *staff* is employed first in the singular (*scepter*) to indicate the Interpreter of the Law and, second, in the plural, to refer to the nobles, who are told how to dig by the Interpreter. The proper interpretation of the law demanded not only competence but effort. The choice of metaphor is interesting and significant. Understanding the Scriptures is not simply a matter of seeing a light or hearing a voice (and indeed, as we have observed, it had already been made plain to them the outset that they could not even open their eyes or their ears without help). Correct interpretation involves hard digging. Seeing it in this way, the writer expresses his contempt for people who failed to realize the need for effort, his own predecessors, who "sought out smooth things, chose delusion and sought out loopholes" (1:18-19).

To sum up, then, what I want to emphasize most particularly is that all the deviations of the author's adversaries, which justified him and his new sect in splitting away from the parent body, are attributed ultimately to a single cause—their failure to read Scripture correctly. And the reason for this failure is that they were not favored with the new revelation that was granted to the Interpreter of the Law and the members of his community. These two reasons,

---

12. An elaborate pun makes it impossible to translate this passage effectively. The verb *ḥāqaq* means "to cut or inscribe (on a tablet)" and hence "to decree," and the participial form of the verb, *ḥōqēq*, can mean either a commander's staff (which explains the translation "scepter" in the RSV) or else something decreed—a statute. The document exploits this ambiguity: במחוקקות אשד חקק חמחוקק—*bimmĕḥóqĕqót 'ăšer ḥāqaq hammĕḥóqēq*, "with the statutes (staves) that were decreed by the ruler (staff)" (CD 6:9).

on the face of it, are contradictory. How could the "Seekers of Smooth Things" be blamed for wrong interpretations when, with the key withheld from them, it was impossible for them to find the correct ones? A good question, but this is simply one example of a deep conceptual faultline that runs throughout the teaching of the Essenes, and indeed throughout the teaching of any religion (Calvinism is the best known example) that proclaims at the same time both divine predestination and human guilt.

The History of the Essenes

Most of our information concerning the history of the Essenes comes from the document we have just been considering, the *Damascus Document*. Besides a program of the sect's principles and intentions, the text also includes some account of the group's history and the nature of its organization. The document opens with an account of the origins of a sect that seems to have broken away much earlier from what is loosely called mainstream Judaism, stating that 390 years after delivering Israel into the hands of Nebuchadnezzar, king of Babylon, God "left a remnant of Israel and did not deliver them up to destruction,"[13] but "caused to grow out of Israel and Aaron a root of planting, to inherit his land and grow fat in the goodness of his soil." But this was not the end of Israel's disobedience, and the document now switches to speak of people who "discerned their iniquity." For twenty years these people blindly groped for a way. Nevertheless, the writer asserts, they sought God wholeheartedly, and so he "raised up for them a Teacher of Righteousness to guide them in the way of his heart" (CD 1:5-12).[14] So the members of the sect were convinced from the outset of their own sinfulness and of the need to repent, and yet at the same

---

13. Most scholars think that the 390 years should be calculated from the destruction of the First Temple in 586 BCE By adding twenty (the number given for the years of searching), we arrive at the date of 176 BCE. for the beginning of the sect and the appearance of the Teacher of Righteousness. Three hundred and ninety years looks like a precise figure, but it may well have been borrowed from a prophecy of the prophet Ezekiel relating to Israel's punitively long exile. In the relevant passage, after commanding the prophet to lie on his left side, God declares: "I will lay the punishment of the house of Israel upon you; for the number of days that you lie upon it, you shall bear their punishment. For I assign to you a number of days, three hundred and ninety days, equal to the number of years of their punishment" (Ezek. 4:4-5). In a note on this number, one editor of the document (Daniel Schwartz) comments that although it is canonical (insofar as is taken from Ezekiel), "it may, nevertheless, be approximately correct." Clearly he might just as well have said, "being canonical, this number is unreliable." But the author evidently believed that the sect to which he belonged was no more than a few decades old.

14. "Teacher of Righteousness" is the literal translation of a Hebrew expression, *mōrēh haṣṣedeq*, which could be rendered in more idiomatic English as "Righteous Teacher." But I will continue to employ the more literal rendering, the one generally used by commentators.

time they were convinced that in the Teacher of Righteousness they had found a leader who could direct them in the right path, enabling them to remain true to God by faithful adherence to the law of Moses. Then there was yet another breakaway, or at least a temporary lapse, led by a villainous personage called "the Scoffer" (or a man of mockery), who "sprinkled upon Israel waters of falsehood and led them astray in a chaos without a way," with the result that they "sought smooth things and chose delusions and sought out loopholes . . . and caused the covenant to be broken." This provoked the wrath of God, who set "the angels of destruction" upon "those who willfully depart from the way and despise the statute," so as to leave not a single survivor (2:6-7). Nevertheless, "out of those who held fast to God's ordinances, with those who remained of them, God established his covenant with Israel forever, revealing to them hidden things in which all Israel had gone astray" (3:12-14). So the document represents the views of those who remained faithful. Confident that their strict interpretation of the law was the correct one, they all took a solemn oath to adhere, or rather "return" to it (CD 15:5—16:2).[15] In the last sentence of this passage the name *Israel* refers both to the sinful people and also to the new covenanters, who now see themselves as the true Israel.

THE HABAKKUK PESHER

I now turn to a very different document. Under the heading "Bible Interpretation" Vermes lists a number of commentaries on biblical prophets.[16]

---

15. Somewhat further on the document speaks of "the penitents of Israel and those who depart from the land of Judah and dwell in Damascus" (CD 6:5) and of "those who entered the new covenant in the land of Damascus" (6:19). Hence its name: the *Damascus Document*. The C in the abbreviation CD is for Cairo—where it was found—and the D for Damascus. The location of Damascus is disputed.

16. The word generally used to refer to these commentaries is *pēšer*, a Hebrew word (borrowed from the Aramaic *pišrah*) designating a continuous commentary on a biblical text: the corresponding verb *pāšar* was used of the act of interpretation. Several pesharim, as they are now called, have been found at Qumran—and nowhere else! The word is found only once in the Hebrew Bible (Qoh. 8:1), in the sense of explanation, but the cognate noun *pōtēr* and the corresponding verb *pātar* occur in Genesis in the context of Joseph's interpretation of the dreams of "the butler and the baker of the king of Egypt," and of Pharaoh himself (Genesis 40–41). This being so, it seems likely that the author of Daniel, who uses the Aramaic word *pišrah* repeatedly of Daniel's interpretation of Nebuchadnezzar's dreams (Daniel 2), was borrowing the word, and with it the idea of dream interpretation, from the story of Joseph. It is equally likely, I believe, that the author of the Qumran pesharim was similarly borrowing from the story of Daniel, for just as Daniel could not interpret dreams without divine assistance, the *pesharim* show that the words of Scripture, like Nebuchadnezzar's dreams, are mysteries (*rāzîm*), and consequently cannot be properly understood except by an interpreter inspired by God. (The word *rāz*, "mystery," rare in the Hebrew Bible, is quite common in the scrolls in the sense of a deep secret that human beings are unable

The commentary on the first two chapters of the prophet Habakkuk, the best preserved of these, was an early find. In a reflection on Hab. 1:5, we are told of "a priest" in whose heart God set understanding (the word *bînâh* is conjecturally restored at this point) "that he might interpret the words of his servants the prophets, through whom he foretold all that would happen to his people and [his land]" (1QpHab 2:8-9). So we know already of the writer's conviction that what Habakkuk foretold relates to a distant generation, the generation of the writer himself and the community; and indeed the same conviction underlies all the other pesharim as well. Each verse is assumed to have a direct bearing on the situation of the writer, the Teacher of Righteousness ("to whom God made known all the mysteries of the words of his servants the prophets" [1QpHab 7:4-5]). The Teacher of Righteousness, *mōrēh haṣṣedeq*, is, as we have noticed, the name given to the leader of the sect in the *Damascus Document*, where it is said of him that God raised him up to guide his people in the way of his heart (CD 1:11); and we have seen that he was also a priest (1QpHab 2:8; cf. 4Q171 2:18, 3:15—a pesher on Psalm 37). Other characters too are named in these commentaries, especially enemies of the community, the Wicked Priest, the Spouter of Lies, the Scoffer in Jerusalem, also people called the Kittim (a term now generally agreed to refer to the Romans) whose future destruction is assured. We have already remarked that the name of one of Joseph's sons, Ephraim, is associated with the Seekers or Searchers of Smooth Things (the Pharisees). The descendants of Ephraim and of Manasseh, another of Joseph's sons, founded the northern, breakaway kingdom, and most scholars, Vermes among them, now agree that Manasseh refers to the Sadducees. If this is correct, the Qumran community was asserting that both the Pharisees and the Sadducees, the two main branches of Judaism at the time, were actually illegitimate, and that the members of the Qumran community alone were the true Israel.

Let us take a closer look at this pesher:

> ... and God told Habakkuk to write down that which would happen to the final generation, but he did not make known to him when time would come to an end. And as for that which he said, *That he who reads may read it speedily* [Hab. 2:2]: interpreted this concerns the Teacher of Righteousness, to whom God made known all the mysteries of the words of his servants the prophets.

to penetrate without God's special aid.) So here, though in a very different context, we come across once more the now familiar theme of the essential element in the interpretation of Scripture.

For there shall be yet another vision of the appointed time. It shall tell of the end and shall not lie (Hab. 2:3a).

Interpreted, this means that the final age shall be prolonged, and shall exceed all that the prophets have said, for the mysteries of God are astounding.

If it tarries, wait for it, for it shall come, and shall not be late (Hab. 2:3b).

Interpreted, this concerns the men of truth who keep the law, whose hands shall not slacken in the service of truth when the final age is prolonged. For all the ages of God reach their appointed end as he determines for them in the mysteries of his prudence. (1QpHab 7:1-14)

This passage concerns the community's perception of Scripture. We have already seen from the *Damascus Document* that they regarded the law as their own special preserve: a well requiring excavation. Now we see that they think the same about the prophets,[17] whose utterances have come to be thought of as mysteries that cannot be understood without a special revelation, a conviction that entails the surprising belief that the prophets themselves did not really understand what they were saying. Moreover, we now learn that this divinely inspired insight into the meaning of Scripture is the prerogative of the Teacher of Righteousness.

THE COMMUNITY RULE

The passage from the *Damascus Document* that we have already discussed sheds light on another document, perhaps the most important of all the manuscripts found at Qumran. This document, which soon came to be called the *Community Rule*, was one of the first to be found, and was published as early as 1951 under the title of *The Manual of Discipline*. (Subsequently a number of smaller fragments of ten other manuscripts of the Rule were found in Caves 4 and 5.) This is how Vermes describes its contents: it "contains extracts from liturgical ceremonies, an outline of a tractate on the spirits of truth and falsehood, statutes concerned with initiation into the sect and with its common life, organization and discipline, a penal code, and finally a poetic dissertation on the fundamental religious duties of the Master and his disciples, and on the

---

17. With a single exception, a pesher on one of the Psalms, all the pesharim are interpretations of prophetic texts—Isaiah and some of the minor prophets. No doubt the community thought of David, to whom they ascribed the authorship of the Psalms, as yet another prophet.

sacred seasons proper to the community."[18] Here is part of a section that deals with the formal acceptance of aspirants into the community:

> Whoever approaches the Council of the Community shall enter the Covenant of God in the presence of those who have freely pledged themselves. He shall undertake by a binding oath to return to every commandment of the Law of Moses *in accordance with all that has been revealed of it to the sons of Zadok, the Priests, Keepers of the Covenant and Seekers of his will, and to the multitude of the men of their Covenant* who together have freely pledged themselves to his truth and to walking the way of his delight. (1QS 5.9-10, trans. Vermes)

The clear implication here is that the law cannot be properly understood without some additional revelation reserved for the priests, the sons of Zadok, who are those who keep the covenant. A little further on, still in the context of the solemn admission into the community, the Interpreter is enjoined not to conceal from those "set apart as holy . . . any of those things hidden from Israel which have been discovered by him" (8:11), secrets, that is to say, disclosed to the Interpreter but hidden from Israel as a whole. At this point the new members are urged to "separate from the habitation of the unjust and go into the wilderness to prepare there the way of him," that is to say, the path spoken of by Isaiah, which the writer understands to mean "the study of Law which he commanded by the hand of Moses" (1QS 8:16-17; 4Q259 frag. 3, lines 4-5).

It all fits together. We know from the *Damascus Document* that among the secrets hidden from Israel was the proper understanding of the law. In that document the metaphor for the law, drawn from the book of Numbers, was a well of abundant water. Here, as he pictures the members of his community studying the law in the wilderness of the shore of the Dead Sea, the writer thinks of them as fulfilling the injunction of Isaiah to prepare for the coming of God.

THE PROVIDENCE OF GOD

I will conclude this chapter with some consideration of a particularly important motif that runs through many of the manuscripts salvaged from Qumran. This is the motif of the providence of God, which we may sum up as the divine plan for humankind. Faith in the providence of God, of course, far from being confined to Qumran, pervades the entire Jewish tradition. At Qumran,

---

18. Vermes, *Complete Dead Sea Scrolls*, 97.

however, what is particularly underlined is their belief that God has planned out the whole of human history from the outset, including the course that would be taken by individual human lives, and that insight into this plan comes through a special revelation.

I start with some reflections on an important corpus of manuscripts known as the *Hodayot*—songs of praise with a peculiar twist not found anywhere else in Jewish writings.[19] Many of these hymns oscillate between exultation and despairing self-loathing, except that what looks like despair turns out to be grounds for hope, since total self-abandonment results in an unquestioning faith in the providence of God, which is what I want to focus on. Here are a few typical passages:

I know that the inclination of every spirit is in your hand [and all] its [activity] you established before you created it. . . . You alone created the righteous, and from the womb you prepared him for the time of favor, to be protected in your covenant and to walk in all [your ways]. . . . But the wicked you created for the [time of] your wrath; and from the womb you dedicated them for the day of slaughter. (1QH 7:16-20)

And these are the ones whom [you] pre[pared from ages] of old to judge through them all your creatures before you created them—together with the host of your spirits and the congregation of [the heavenly beings wi]th your holy firmament and [al]l its hosts, together with the earth and all that springs from it in the sea and in the depths—[according to]all that was planned for them for all the everlasting epochs and the eternal visitation.

For you yourself prepared them from ages of old and the work of [. . .] among them so that they might make known your glory in all your dominion. . . .

And in the mysteries of your knowledge you apportioned all these things, in order to make known your glory. (1QH 5:13-19)

In your wisdom [you] es[tablished the generations of] eternity, and before you created them, you knew their deeds for everlasting ages. For without you nothing] is done, and nothing is known without your will . . .

. . . and in the wisdom of your knowledge you established their destiny before they existed. According to your will everything

19. In what follows and for the translation I am indebted to a long chapter of Carol Newsom entitled "What Do Hodayot Do?" in eadem, *Self as Symbolic Space*, 204–86.

[comes] into being: and without you nothing is done. . . . These things I know because of the insight that comes from you, for you have opened my ears to wondrous mysteries. (1QH 9:19-21)

Underlying all the hymns from which these passages are drawn is a firm belief in the Creator God. But in addition to this belief is the conviction that everything was planned out by God beforehand. In a certain sense the providence of God *precedes* creation. This is even clearer in the famous Two Spirits section of the *Community Rule*, 1QS 3:15—4:26: Commenting on this text, Carol Newsom points to its peculiar relationship to the opening chapter of the book of Genesis, a relationship especially evident from the number of words common to both (kinds, signs, hosts, create, rule, fill, darkness, light, generations): "what 1QS 3–4 manages to do is to open up a space behind Genesis 1 and to insert itself into that space. It establishes itself as the pre-text for Genesis 1. Where Genesis 1 is concerned with creation, 1QS 3–4 is concerned with the מחשבה [i.e. the plan, literally *thought*, of God] that grounds creation." ("From the God of knowledge comes everything that is and will be. Before they existed he fixed all their plans [מחשבתם] and when they come into existence they complete their work according to their instructions in accordance with his glorious plan [מחשבת כבודו] and without changing anything" [1QS 3:15-16].) "It is not just that 1QS 3–4 is to be read in the light of Genesis 1 but that henceforth Genesis 1 must be read in the light of 1QS 3–4."[20]

The great hymn that concludes the *Community Rule* (it takes up nearly two whole columns of this eleven-column manuscript) states the message of God's plan for humankind with particular clarity: "all things come to pass [כול הווה] by his knowledge; he establishes all things by his design [במחשבתו] and without him nothing is done" (1QS 11:11). This hymn follows the same pattern as many of the other *Hodayot*, with their combination of exaltation and self-loathing. (Certain of these we have just looked at.) But it is alone in summing up the nature of God's providence in two words, רז נהיה, *raz nihyeh*, "the mystery of what is coming to pass."[21] Here is the relevant passage:

---

20. Newsom, *Self as Symbolic Space*, 86.

21. At first this term was translated as a future—"the future mystery." I have argued, however, that a present tense is more appropriate—"the mystery that is coming to pass." See John Ashton, "'Mystery' in the Dead Sea Scrolls and the Fourth Gospel," in Coloe and Thatcher, *John, Qumran, and the Dead Sea Scrolls*, 53-58. See also *Qumran Cave 4.XV: Sapiential Texts, Part 1*, ed. T. Elgvin et al., in consultation with J. A. Fitzmyer, Discoveries in the Judaean Desert 20 (Oxford: Clarendon, 1997), 105, where the editors say of the term רז נהיה: "This refers to the secret of that which is coming into being," and they point to Sir. 43:19 and 48:25, "where נהיות is parallel to נסתרות, secrets."

For my light has sprung from the source of his knowledge; my eyes have beheld his marvelous deeds, and the light of my heart, the mystery that is coming to pass [*raz nihyeh*]. He that is everlasting is the support of my right hand; the way of my steps is over stout rock which nothing shall shake; for the rock of my steps is the truth of God, and his might is the support of my right hand. From the source of his righteousness is my justification, and from his marvelous mysteries is the light in my heart. My eyes have gazed on what is eternal, and wisdom concealed [*nistārâh*] from men, on knowledge and wise design (hidden) from the sons of man; on a fountain of righteousness and a storehouse of strength, on a spring of glory (hidden) from the assembly of flesh. (1QS 11:3-7)

The writer emphasizes repeatedly in this passage how extraordinarily privileged he feels to have been granted access to truths hitherto concealed from all humankind, a design of God stretching back into eternity which he sums up in the phrase *raz nihyeh*, the mystery of what is coming to pass. This is the source of his assurance that in the path he has chosen he is walking on solid rock: "the rock of my steps is the truth of God." For the vast majority of humankind this truth is unavailable; "marvelous mysteries"—for the term also occurs in the plural—involve "a wisdom concealed [*nistārâh*] from men." This hidden wisdom extends further and deeper than the mysteries regarding the law, which themselves require a special revelation if they are to be properly understood: it is probably an allusion to the great hymn of Job 28, which also speaks of a wisdom that is in principle inaccessible to humankind, "hidden from the eyes of every living thing and concealed [*nistārâh*] from the birds of the sky" (28:21).

The term *raz niyeh* occurs frequently in a manuscript known as 4QInstruction, not properly published until 1999.[22] There *raz nihyeh* appears, like the Johannine Logos ("we have gazed on his glory"), as *an object of contemplation*: "By day and night meditate upon the mystery that is coming to pass and study it always. . . . For the God of knowledge is the foundation of truth, and by the mystery that is coming to pass he has laid out its foundation, and its deeds he has prepared with . . . wisdom. . . . Gaze on the mystery that is coming to pass, and know the paths of everything that lives and the manner of

---

22. See *Qumran Cave 4.XXIV: 4QInstruction (Musar leMevin): 4Q415 ff.*, ed. J. Strugnell, D. J. Harrington, and T. Elgvin, in consultation with J. A. Fitzmyer, Discoveries in the Judaean Desert 34 (Oxford: Clarendon, 1999).

his walking that is appointed over his deeds" (4Q417 frag. 2, lines 6–19; cf. 1 i 9, where it is stated that God "has laid out the foundation of truth [i.e., creation] and its works [i.e., history]").[23]

CONCLUSION

In reflecting on the similarities between certain of the Dead Sea Scrolls and some early Christian texts, one must be careful not to exaggerate them. Both the *Damascus Document* and a number of other texts from Qumran (*hodayot* and *pesharim*) emphasize the need for a special revelation from God when interpreting Scripture and exhibit an awareness that for this reason the leaders of the sect are especially privileged to know the real meaning of the law and the prophets: they are the men of truth. What is more, there is evidence that they particularly prized another revelatory source, the *raz nihyeh*, also reserved to the members of the sect. The new sect is clearly veering away from the insistence on the definitive nature of the revelation to Moses that already characterized the dominant party in Israel (which, I have suggested, was later identified by the fourth evangelist as the ʼΙουδαῖοι). Yet they remained fervent adherents of the law, and criticized their opponents for being less so.

23. In chapter 8 I will give further reasons for stressing the similarity between the Logos and the *raz nihyeh*.

Excursus II. The Johannine Community

In this excursus I want to confront a strong challenge to the concept of the Johannine community as this is found in the work of Raymond E. Brown, J. Louis Martyn, and myself.[1] The subject of *The Sheep of the Fold*, by Edward W. Klink III, is apparent from its subtitle, *The Audience and Origin of the Gospel of John*.[2] Following the lead of his doctoral supervisor, Richard Bauckham,[3] Klink altogether rejects the idea of a Johannine community and proposes instead that the Gospel of John, like the other Gospels, was written for a much more general audience.

He begins his discussion with some wide-ranging reflections on the meaning of community; but here I will restrict my comments to his treatment of the Gospel of John, which starts in his third chapter, entitled "Early Christian Gospel: Gospel Genre and a Critique of the Two-Level Reading of the Gospel of John."

First comes the affirmation that "recent discussions in the Gospel community debate have shown the importance that genre plays in the interpretation of a text's audience."[4] As I made clear in Excursus I, my own view is that it has no importance whatsoever. Even if the Gospels are correctly classified as Greco-Roman *bioi* they owe nothing to previous examples of the genre and are so different from these that nothing at all can be inferred from this "fact" about their intended readership. Klink thinks it "important to define the exact role the literary genre plays in determining the size of their intended readership"[5]—to which the answer should be, without further specification, none at all. Harping on, he continues, "If the role of genre is, by definition, to inform the reader of a narrative's content, and to instruct the reader how to read it, then the *bios* genre does just that."[6] But this remark about "the role of

---

1. See Raymond E. Brown, both his commentary and *The Community of the Beloved Disciple: The Life, Loves, and Hates of an Individual Church in New Testament Times* (New York: Paulist, 1979); J. Louis Martyn, *History and Theology in the Fourth Gospel*, 3rd ed. (Louisville: Westminster John Knox), 2003; John Ashton, *Understanding the Fourth Gospel* (Oxford: Clarendon, 1991).

2. Edward W. Klink III, *The Sheep of the Fold: The Audience and Origin of the Gospel of John*, Society for New Testament Studies Monograph Series 141 (Cambridge: Cambridge University Press, 2007).

3. See especially Richard Bauckham, "For Whom Were the Gospels Written?" in *The Gospels for All Christians: Rethinking the Gospel Audiences*, ed. Richard Bauckham (Grand Rapids: Eerdmans, 1998).

4. Klink, *Sheep of the Fold*, 108.5.

5. Klink, Sheep of the Fold, 109.

genre" is odd to the point of unintelligibility. Surely it is the other way around? One has to know the contents of a narrative first before deciding on its genre. And if we know the genre already—perhaps from a publisher's list—this will tell us nothing about its contents. Equally unintelligible is the assertion that the genre *instructs* us how to read a narrative.

The next section of the chapter, headed "John's two-level drama: a critique," begins with the question, "how would a first-century audience have appropriated a Gospel text?" There soon follows a long digression—revolving around a theoretical construct named *the first-century reader* (fabricated with the help of Hans Frei and Frances Young),[7] whose chief characteristic is that he/she is "pre-critical." Martyn is then rebuked for imposing "a modern (or critical) grid of understanding on the first-century readers of the Fourth Gospel."[8] According to this logic, first-century readers of Virgil's *Aeneid*, a story of a mythical hero composed in the preceding century, cannot possibly have understood its many subtle references to contemporary issues, simply because they lived in a pre-critical era and therefore had the misfortune of being pre-critical readers. And what of Pindar (fifth century BCE), what of Callimachus (third century BCE) or, for that matter, what of the book of Wisdom, written probably in the first century CE? In the light of the subtlety and sophistication of all these writers (and one could name more) the terms *pre-critical era* and *first-century readers* can be seen to be no more than vapid and thoroughly misleading generalizations.

Klink begins his direct criticism of Martyn's work by quoting him: "Someone created a literary genre quite without counterpart in the body of the Gospels. We may indeed call it a drama," and he concludes "that Martyn is claiming that the Fourth Gospel's genre is different from the genre of the Synoptics."[9] But Martyn is writing here about the construction of a sequence of scenes based on the miracle story of chapter 9, not about the genre of the Gospel as a whole. Such a blatant misreading is not an encouraging start. Nor do things improve when he turns to discuss 9:22, the entry point into the two-level reading, though he is right to regard Martyn's exegesis of this passage as crucial to his whole enterprise. He also correctly singles out Martyn's most important

---

6. Klink, Sheep of the Fold, 115.

7. Hans Frei, *The Eclipse of Biblical Narrative: A Study in Eighteenth and Nineteenth Century Hermeneutics* (New Haven: Yale University Press, 1974); Frances M. Young, *Biblical Exegesis and the Formation of Christian Culture* (Cambridge: Cambridge University Press, 1997).

8. Klink, *Sheep of the Fold*, 125.

9. Klink, *Sheep of the Fold*, 116 n. 39.

observation, which is a comment on 9:28: "You are that man's disciple [μαθητὴς ἐκείνου], but we are disciples of Moses."

> This statement is scarcely conceivable in Jesus' lifetime, since it recognizes discipleship to Jesus not only as antithetical, but also as somehow comparable, to discipleship to Moses. It is, on the other hand, easily understood under circumstances in which the synagogue has begun to view the Christian movement as an essential and more or less clearly distinguishable rival.[10]

Klink makes two critical comments on this observation. "We cannot assume," he says, "that the Jewish-Christian tension being described is anything more than a general reference to Jewish-Christian conflict. . . . Would not any messianic confession be found in almost any 'Christian' literature in early Christianity, and would not that be found disagreeable to any non-Christian Jew?"[11] But he appears to have forgotten that the conflict portrayed in John 9 is recorded in a Gospel narrative that, on the face of it, is a story about events that occurred in Jesus' lifetime. There is *one* messianic confession recorded in the Synoptic Gospels, namely, the confession of Peter; but there is not the slightest indication that there was any controversy over this title between Jesus and the Pharisees, or between Jesus and any other Jewish group. Indeed, it is safe to say that such a controversy is highly unlikely to have occurred in Jesus' lifetime.

Second, argues Klink,

> the use of the adverb "already" (ἤδη) ["the Jews had *already* agreed"] implies . . . that whatever the "expulsion" is implying, it was already in process during Jesus' lifetime. That is, the conflict with the "Jews" that occurred in the earthly life of Jesus is no different in kind than what is being experienced by the Johannine readers, in fact, in retrospect, what "the readers" are experiencing was "already" in process in Jesus' day.[12]

But to read the *already* as reaching back to Jesus' lifetime is to beg the question. Once again, there is not the slightest likelihood that the expulsion of Jesus' disciples from the synagogue began during his lifetime.

---

10. Martyn, *History and Theology*, 47.
11. Klink, *Sheep of the Fold*, 140.
12. Klink, *Sheep of the Fold*, 140.

Scratching at Martyn's case in just two paragraphs without even denting it, Klink only succeeds in revealing its strength. But feeble as these two arguments are, they do at least attempt to address the question. We are still left, however, with what is surely Martyn's most important observation. This concerns the recognition of a rivalry or comparability between the disciples of Jesus and the disciples of Moses. As Martyn says, such a rivalry, implying as it does that the two groups can properly be compared together because they have a similar prestige and importance, is scarcely conceivable in Jesus' lifetime. How could a few dozen followers of Jesus, all good Jews, ever have been thought to present a challenge to the religious beliefs of the whole Jewish nation? On this point Klink has not a word to say. Halfway through his thesis on the Gospel of John, once he has temporarily abandoned theoretical generalities to deal with the text itself, the weakness of his case becomes all too apparent.

It is appropriate at this point to quote Dwight Moody Smith's admirable summary of Martyn's argument:

> His entire proposal is based upon two fundamental assumptions or insights. First, the prominence of the Jews and their hostility to Jesus and his disciples likely represents a genuine historical setting (that is, it is not an exercise in theological symbolism). Secondly, this historical setting can scarcely be that of Jesus and his actual, original disciples and opponents. Therefore, one is not only justified, but also impelled to look for a historical setting and state of affairs corresponding to the nature and direction or thrust of the Gospel's tensions and conflict. Martyn is actually invoking the modern, form-critical principal that the Gospels bear testimony primarily to the life-setting in which they were produced, and only secondarily to their subject matter.[13]

I turn now to Richard Bauckham's article "The Audience of the Fourth Gospel."[14] This is divided into a number of different sections. In the first of these Bauckham summarizes the case he had already made that the Gospels were intended to be read by all Christians, already dispersed throughout the

13. Dwight Moody Smith, "The Contribution of J. Louis Martyn to the Understanding of John," in Martyn, *History and Theology*, 3rd ed., 6.

14. Richard Bauckham, "The Audience of the Fourth Gospel," in *Jesus in Johannine Tradition*, ed. Robert T. Fortna and Tom Thatcher (Louisville: Westminster John Knox, 2001), 101–11, reproduced, with slight changes, in Bauckham, *The Testimony of the Beloved Disciple: Narrative, History, and Theology in the Gospel of John* (Grand Rapids: Baker Academic, 2007), 113–36.

Mediterranean.[15] After that he embarks on an argument restricted to the Gospel of John, opening with a very fair outline of Martyn's general position, and then turning to the problems raised by the decision recorded in John 9 to expel professing Christians from the synagogue. He is right to say that "the historical issue of the status of Jewish Christians in the late first century has been much debated, and it is not all clear that what happened to Diaspora-Jewish Christians resembles what happens to the blind man in John 9."[16] Bauckham shrewdly concentrates on the weakest section of Martyn's book, where he discusses the *Birkat ha-Minim*, the curse against heretics (which I will consider later in another context). It must be confessed that there is considerable uncertainty surrounding this. But why does he completely ignore Martyn's strongest argument, that is to say, the virtual impossibility that Jesus' disciples could have been recognized during his lifetime as rivals of the disciples of Moses? Is it because he failed to recognize its strength, or simply because he had no answer?

Bauckham continues: "More generally, the most damaging criticism of Martyn's two-level reading strategy is the fact that it has no basis in the literary genre of the Fourth Gospel. The genre of a particular text generally guides readers to the appropriate strategy of interpretation. . . . Recent discussion of the gospel genre strongly favors the view that first-century readers would have recognized all four canonical gospels as a special form of Graeco-Roman biography."[17] I have dealt with this issue in Excursus I. Most first-century readers of the Gospels are unlikely ever to have come across any example of Greco-Roman biography; even so their ignorance of this genre will scarcely have worried them. The *bios* genre of the Gospels, if this is indeed a proper designation, is of no value whatever in determining the nature of their audience or in indicating how the works should be read.

In the next section of his article ("A Two-Level Text?") Bauckham deals with two further issues. First he questions the viability of a (diachronic) reading of the text based on discontinuities or contextual aporias:

15. Bauckham, "For Whom Were the Gospels Written?" I dealt with this essay briefly in *Understanding the Fourth Gospel*, 2nd ed., 28–29, and will not now repeat what I wrote there. But it is worth noting that five years earlier, criticizing Martin Hengel for suggesting "that the Gospel was intended to circulate far beyond the circle in which the beloved disciple was well known," Bauckham wrote that the plausibility of this suggestion "depends upon two gratuitous assumptions," the first being "that the Gospel was primarily intended for churches beyond the circle of the Johannine churches" ("The Beloved Disciple as Ideal Author," *Journal for the Study of the New Testament* 49 [1993]: 30). This comment was quietly dropped from a modified version of the article included in *Testimony of the Beloved Disciple*, 73–91.

16. Bauckham, "Audience," 104.

17. Bauckham, "Audience," 104.

In light of literary criticism's sensitivity to the strategies of the text, many of the apparent aporias on which source criticism depends are seen to be much less problematic. A passage that seems awkward to the source critic, whose judgment often amounts merely to observing that he or she "would not have written like that," can appear quite reasonable to a critic who is attentive to the literary dynamics of the text.[18]

It is impossible to deal directly with this airy dismissal of genuine difficulties in the text, some of them first recognized by Julius Wellhausen over a century ago[19] and the object of intense debate ever since, because there is nothing specific to aim at. (I will, however, tackle this problem in some depth in Excursus III.)

Next Bauckham questions the significance of apparent tensions that arise because of discontinuities in the text:

We need to be much more open to the possibility that these tensions belong to the character and method of the Fourth Evangelist's theology. . . . It is no more difficult to view these tensions as the deliberate theological strategies of a single author. . . . Perhaps we are dealing with the work of a creative theologian who . . . developed his own distinctive interpretation of the history of Jesus.[20]

Although I am inclined to agree that almost the whole Gospel was the work of a single individual, this is another objection whose vague generality makes it impossible to counter. As I will make clear in the body of this book, I think that the unspecified tensions Bauckham is probably thinking of are caused by additions and alterations the author made to his own text.

The next section of the article ("In-group Language?") commences strongly: "With this topic we reach the point where it will be possible to turn the tables on those who argue that an isolated Johannine Community was the intended audience of the Fourth Gospel."[21] Bauckham is convinced that the evangelist designed the (so-called) in-group language precisely to introduce it to readers not already familiar with it. Before turning to argue from specific passages, however, Bauckham makes what is, to me, a quite

18. Bauckham, "Audience," 105–6.

19. Julius Wellhausen, *Erweiterungen und Änderungen im vierten Evangelium* (Berlin: Georg Reimer, 1907).

20. Bauckham, "Audience," 106.

21. Bauckham, "Audience," 106.

astonishing declaration: "In the modern church's experience, the Fourth Gospel has been seen as the most accessible of the New Testament books both to Christians with little education in the faith and to complete outsiders who have minimal knowledge of the Christian tradition."[22] I can understand that it may be accessible to Christians (though scarcely those with little education in their faith), because it has been an integral element in Christian teaching for centuries. But where is the evidence "in the modern church's experience" that this difficult and complex work is readily accessible even to complete outsiders?

When Bauckham at long last turns to the text of the Gospel, he takes his first example from the temple episode in John 2: "Destroy this temple, and in three days I will raise it up" (2:19). At the time neither the Jews nor the disciples understood this saying, although the evangelist explains that "he was speaking of the temple of his body" (2:21). The evangelist, suggests Bauckham, "surely intends this to be an illustrative example: he will not always help his readers on later occasions but he has shown them how to figure out what Jesus means."[23] The truth is that help is always at hand, because the evangelist (like most authors) wants his intended readership to understand what he writes. (It would be odd if he did not.) But the most important lesson of this episode concerns not the readers of the Gospel but the disciples, and specifically their delayed understanding: "When therefore he was raised from the dead, his disciples remembered that he had said this; and they believed the scripture and the word which Jesus had spoken" (2:22). When they first heard him talk of the temple of his body, however, speaking in the real temple while he was still on earth, they did not—indeed could not—understand this enigmatic saying, but they would fully understand later, once Jesus had risen, *at which point they became indistinguishable from the members of the community*, who are reminded of what Jesus said by the Paraclete and are then continually instructed by him. In the Farewell Discourse, where the Paraclete is spoken of for the first time, Jesus is ostensibly addressing his own disciples. But the emphasis on the enduring presence of the Paraclete, who is to be with them forever, shows that the evangelist is also thinking of those to whom he is addressing his Gospel. While it cannot be proved that he has not also a wider audience in mind, the most natural inference is that he is thinking of the people he knows best and among whom he lives. Read properly, therefore, the temple episode is a good indication of the two-level reading that Bauckham rejects.[24]

---

22. Bauckham, "Audience," 107.
23. Bauckham, "Audience," 107–8.
24. I have already discussed this passage in chapter 2.

In his next paragraph Bauckham discusses the riddling sayings that so confuse Nicodemus (John 3) and the Samaritan woman (John 4) as if these were no different from the "temple of his body" image in John 2. But Nicodemus, who never arrives at a full understanding, and the Samaritan woman, never seen again after her appearance at the well, are not disciples in the full sense, and they play different roles in the scheme of the Gospel. The "lifted up sayings" used to prophesy the passion are different again, as might be inferred from the varied contexts in which they occur.

On the last page of his article, under the heading, "Universal References," Bauckham points to the evangelist's use of the word *world* as evidence of a strong universal perspective "quite irreconcilable with the outlook of a community that deliberately set itself apart from the worldwide [*sic*] Christian movement."[25] But I doubt if Martyn ever envisaged the Johannine community as deliberately distancing itself from other Christian groups[26]—I myself have never done so. The purpose of the insider language cultivated by the community was to strengthen their conviction of their privileged status in having been given a special revelation (*the truth*) that others did not share and that justified their secession from the larger Jewish community. So it has to be read not, as Bauckham supposes, with reference to other Christians but in the context of their recent controversy with more traditional Jewish believers.

There is evidence that at some point the community began to think of "other sheep that are not of this fold" (10:16), an expression that, I think, affords a glimpse of the larger Christian community, the church outside, to which the Johannine group had not yet become affiliated, but which they would now like to see enter into "the one true fold."[27] Martyn makes a strong case for thinking that the people that the Johannine community now wants to gather into its own fold are not Gentiles but other Jewish Christians.[28]

Lastly Bauckham turns to John 21, where, as all agree, the flock that Jesus commissions Peter to tend is the larger church outside. For those scholars (the

---

25. Bauckham, "Audience," 111.

26. Though he does go so far as to say that "the community stood at some remove not only from the parent synagogue—from which it had been excommunicated—but also from the emerging Great Church" (J. Louis Martyn, "A Gentile Mission That Replaced an Earlier Jewish Mission?" in *Exploring the Gospel of John: In Honor of D. Moody Smith*, ed. R. Alan Culpepper and C. Clifton Black (Louisville: Westminster John Knox, 1996), 124.

27. See my article, "The Shepherd," in Ashton, *Studying John: Approaches to the Fourth Gospel* (Oxford: Clarendon, 1994), 114–40, esp. 129–30; J. Louis Martyn, "Glimpses into the History of the Johannine Community," in idem, *History and Theology*, 3rd ed., 163–66.

28. Martyn, "Gentile Mission?" Martyn answers the question of his title in the negative.

great majority) who see this chapter as a later addition to the Gospel the chapter is perfectly reconcilable with the thesis that up to that point the Johannine community had been more narrowly confined. This extra chapter suggests that it eventually came to look further afield, to a different Christian community, which, though equally committed to Jesus, owed immediate allegiance not to John but to Peter—hoping that both groups might acknowledge the desirability of mutual recognition and respect. Bauckham ends his article by admitting that "the alternate view, that chapter 21 is an epilogue and an integral feature of the design of the Fourth Gospel, cannot be argued here." [29]

All in all, Bauckham's conviction that he has turned the tables on those who argue that a relatively isolated Johannine community was the intended audience of the Fourth Gospel is not warranted by the evidence he offers. On the contrary, as I hope to have shown, the theory stands up well to close examination; and I shall not hesitate to rely upon it in the remainder of this book.

---

29. Bauckham, "Audience," 111. To be fair, I should add that Bauckham had briefly defended this view in his article, "Beloved Disciple," 27–28. In *Understanding the Fourth Gospel*, 42–44 and 49–52 I argue that John 21 is a later addition to the finished Gospel, and I deal with the problems arising from the conclusion of John 20.

5

The Situation of the Gospel

The Gospels, as I argued in Excursus I, are not simply Lives of Christ. A Gospel (and by that I mean one of the four Gospels recognized by the Christian church) is a proclamation in narrative form of faith in Jesus as Messiah and Son of God. Ostensibly historical documents, entirely concerned with events that had occurred in the past, they are actually addressed to the evangelists' own communities and speak to their hopes and fears. Such, at least, is the hypothesis that underlies what is known as redaction criticism, a method of Gospel research characterized by its interest in the particular concerns (sometimes referred to as the *theology*) of the four evangelists.[1] It was widely practiced round about the 1950s and 60s. One might have expected that the redaction critics would show an equal interest in the situation of the communities to which the Gospels were addressed, but this has not always been the case. The exegetical inquiry into the meaning of the Gospels (except occasionally in the case of Matthew) is seldom accompanied by historical research into the circumstances in which they were composed.

Such research is never straightforward, largely because the history of Palestine in the last few decades of the first century CE (after the end of the Jewish war) is so poorly documented. Josephus, by far our most important source for the long history of the Second Temple, says virtually nothing about the period that followed; and the many valuable nuggets of early rabbinic sayings are difficult to extract from the complex writings, published long afterward, in which they are embedded. In any case, most students of the Gospels are, quite understandably, more interested in what they say about

---

1. This hypothesis was strongly challenged by Richard Bauckham in the collection he edited, *The Gospels for All Christians: Rethinking the Gospel Audiences* (Grand Rapids: Eerdmans, 1998), but his challenge left many scholars unconvinced. See my *Understanding the Fourth Gospel*, 2nd ed. (Oxford: Clarendon, 2001), 28–31; and Excursus II above for a refutation of Bauckham's arguments against the theory of a Johannine community.

Jesus than in what they tell us about the time of their composition. Such historical questions as they do put—questions about the historical Jesus—are mostly directed to the stories themselves. Inquiry into the immediate circumstances of the evangelists and their communities, however fundamental this must seem to anyone preoccupied with the puzzle of the rise of Christianity, is less common. Historical research into the Gospel of John in particular has been patchy and episodic. That, however, is our present concern.

The earliest (dating from 1820) and one of the most interesting reflections on the immediate purpose of the Fourth Gospel came from the pen of a German scholar, Karl Gottlieb Bretschneider, who compared it with the writings of the second-century apologist Justin Martyr:

> The Fourth Gospel appears to have been composed in the same historical context: its apologetic and polemical purpose is plain to see. . . . It is more an apologia than a work of history, and its author assumed the role of a polemicist rather than of a historian. Hence (1) the frequent clashes between Jesus and the Jewish Scribes, whom he calls Jews (οἱ 'Ιουδαῖοι) to distinguish them from the people (λαός) or the crowd (ὄχλος); (2) all those debates; (3) the foolishness of the Jews, who never understood Jesus' words, a foolishness the author was really using to depict the stubborn objections of Jewish adversaries *of his own day*; (4) the debates and doctrinal sections (*dogmata*), which concerned controversies not between Jesus and the Pharisees but between Christians and Jews of the second century.[2]

The aspect of Bretschneider's work that caused most offense was his denial of apostolic authorship.[3] Written in Latin, and therefore inaccessible to the general public, it aroused such a storm of controversy among his fellow scholars (the *eruditi* whom he was addressing) that he felt compelled, some four years later, to publish a retraction in which he declared that he had written his book in the first place in order to provoke the response it received.[4]

---

2. Karl Gottlieb Bretschneider, *Probabilia . . .* (Leipzig: Jo. Ambros. Barth, 1820), 118–19.

3. The title page of his little book reads as follows: *Probabilia de evangelii et epistularum Joannis, apostoli, indole et origine eruditorum judiciis modeste subjecit Carolus Theophilus Bretschneider.* To which he added the Greek epigraph, παντα δοκιμαζετε. το καλον κατεχετε. ("Peruse everything carefully: hold on to the good bits."). In supplying a title that appeared to uphold the apostolic authorship of the writings under discussion he was about to deny, and even in "modestly submitting his findings to the judgment of the learned," Bretschneider not surprisingly infuriated his critics.

4. *Tschirners Magazin für Chr. Prediger* 2 (1824): 153, quoted by Maurice Goguel, *Introduction au nouveau Testament*, 4 vols., Bibliothèque historique des religions (Paris: Leroux, 1922–26), 2:23.

Bretschneider did not get it all right. His dating (late second century) is too late, and he overstresses the polemical aspect of the Gospel. But his observation that the evangelist uses the term Jews (οἱ Ἰουδαῖοι) of Jesus' adversaries, is spot on and raises difficulties that we noticed in chapter 3. Some time later (1861) another scholar, Moriz von Aberle, wrote a long and rambling article on the purpose of the Gospel, in which he brought into the argument for the first time the famous *Birkat ha-Minim* (on which more later), a rabbinic text that was to figure prominently in subsequent debate. Aberle, like Bretschneider, realized that there could be no answer to the question of the purpose of the Gospel without some explanation of the opposition of "the Jews." But again like Bretschneider, he made no detailed examination of the Gospel text (apart from several pages on the Logos). He concluded his article with these words: "John's Gospel is the letter of repudiation [*Absagebrief*] addressed to restored [that is, post-70 CE] Judaism, which was already beginning to direct against the young Church all the weapons with which it was later to attempt to arrest her victorious march through the centuries."[5]

For the next significant contribution to the debate we are indebted to the much better known William Wrede (whom we have already met). While recognizing that the Gospel was actually addressed to the Christian community, Wrede insisted that "to achieve an historical understanding of the Gospel *we must see it as a writing born out of and written for conflict* [*aus dem Kampfe . . . und für den Kampf*]. And further that "what really allows us to discern the true lever of the Gospel is an acknowledgement of its polemical thrust. In a word, from being a timeless meditation, the Gospel becomes a writing that belongs to a particular period, has a particular situation in view, and is written for a particular purpose."[6] Like Bretschneider and Aberle before him, Wrede highlighted a historical problem that most others ignored, but he too failed to expatiate further on the particular situation of the evangelist and his community.

There followed a period of more than sixty years during which Johannine scholars (with one important exception, which we shall consider in a moment) paid scarcely any attention at all to the kind of questions Wrede had asked. Why so? The answer to this question is not altogether clear. In the early period, at least part of the reason must have been the surprisingly long-lasting obsession with the problem of the authorship of the Gospel. For the later period,

---

5. Moriz von Aberle, "Über den Zweck des Johannesevangeliums," *Theologische Quartalschrift* 42 (1861): 37–94. Emphasis in the original.

6. William Wrede, *Charakter und Tendenz des Johannesevangelium* (Tübingen: J. C. B. Mohr [Paul Siebeck], 1903), 40, 67.

the dominance of Rudolf Bultmann meant, I suspect, that other scholars too concentrated mostly on the questions that he had raised. His dominance lasted for some forty years. In 1925, two major articles appeared, laying out the broad lines of Bultmann's theories concerning the origins of the Gospel and its basic ideas. His magisterial commentary was published in 1941, and his survey article for the third edition of *Religion in Geschichte und Gegenwart* in 1959. Meanwhile, the leading British scholars at this time, C. H. Dodd and C. K. Barrett, took no more interest than Bultmann in properly historical questions, Barrett because he thought of the Gospel as a possession for all time, and Dodd because of his conviction that the Gospel should be interpreted in the light of the higher religions of Hellenism.[7] One of the first scholars since Wrede to take an interest in the historical situation out of which the Gospel rose was Raymond E. Brown. In the first volume of his great commentary, which appeared in 1966, he anticipated Martyn by suggesting that the Gospel was written as a response to the expulsion of Christians from the synagogue that was brought about by the publication of the Twelfth Benediction of the *Shemoneh Esre*.[8] According to Dwight Moody Smith, Brown's work appeared too late to influence Martyn, whose book appeared two years later,[9] but the two men were soon to become friends and colleagues who continued to share an interest in the history of the Johannine community.

In fact, Martyn's most important discovery had been anticipated more than quarter of a century earlier in a most unexpected quarter. For, surprising as it may seem, it is first of all to Rudolf Bultmann that we owe the most penetrating insight ever made into the immediate circumstances of the Gospel's composition. Generally speaking, Bultmann was convinced that the main concern of the fourth evangelist was to offer answers to the deep existential

7. Two scholars who realized very early the importance of the Gospel's Jewish background were Hugo Odeberg and Adolf Schlatter, whose commentaries were published respectively in 1929 and 1930. But they had little impact at the time.

8. Raymond E. Brown, *The Gospel according to John*, vol. 1, *I–XII*, Anchor Bible 29 (New York: Doubleday, 1966), lxxiv–lxxv. Perhaps it should be added that Brown had also noticed interesting affinities between John and the Dead Sea Scrolls as early as 1958 in an article entitled "The Qumran Scrolls and the Johannine Gospel and Epistles," in *The Scrolls and the New Testament*, ed. Krister Stendahl (New York: Harper, 1958), 183–207.

9. D. Moody Smith, "The Contribution of J. Louis Martyn to the Understanding of the Gospel of John," in *The Conversation Continues: Studies in Paul and John in Honor of J. Louis Martyn*, ed. Robert T. Fortna and Berverly R. Gaventa (Nashville: Abingdon, 1990), 285. Even so, Martyn was able to refer to an article of Brown on the Paraclete, published in 1967, the year after the appearance of the first volume of Brown's commentary (Martyn, *History and Theology in the Fourth Gospel* [New York: Harper & Row, 1968], 135 n. 198).

questions confronting all mankind, and he usually paid little attention to more mundane difficulties concerning the particular conflict between the Johannine community and "the Jews." In one striking passage in his great commentary, however, he uncharacteristically remarks on the immediate situation reflected in the two miracle stories in chapters 5 and 9.

> Manifestly, [these two stories] "must be understood against the same historical background. Both reflect the relation of early Christianity to the surrounding hostile (in the first place Jewish) world; in a peculiar way they reflect, too, the methods of its opponents, who directed their attacks against men who did not yet belong to the Christian community, but who had come into contact with it and experienced the power of the miraculous forces at work in it. These men were interrogated, and in this way their opponents attempted to collect evidence against the Christian community.

And then, sliding smoothly and uninterruptedly from historical conjecture into theological reflection, he continues:

> Such stories provided the Evangelist with an external starting-point, and at the same time they were for him illustrations alike of the world's dilemma, as it was faced by the revelation, and of the world's hostility. The world attempts to subject to its own κρίσις [judgment] the event which is, in fact, the κρίσις of the world; it brings the revelation, as it were, to trial.[10]

Tucked away as it is on a single page of this big book, it is perhaps not surprising that Bultmann's acute historical observation escaped the attention of most of his contemporaries, and even, rather later, that of J. Louis Martyn, who reached the same conclusion independently and made it the keystone of his pioneering work, *History and Theology in the Fourth Gospel* (1968).[11] One scholar, however, who did come to realize the importance of Bultmann's historical aside was C. K. Barrett. It receives no mention in the first edition of his commentary (1955),[12] but in the second edition (1978) he remarks that

---

10. Bultmann, *The Gospel of John: A Commentary* (Oxford: Basil Blackwell, 1971): 239.

11. I too had missed it in spite of what I thought of at the time as a close reading of Bultmann in preparation for my rather bigger book on John (1991). Wayne Meeks, however, did refer to Bultmann's historical observation on p. 293 of his pioneering study, *The Prophet-King: Moses traditions and the Johannine Christology*, Supplements to Novum Testamentum 14 (Leiden: Brill), published in 1968, the same year as Martyn's book.

Bultmann had "cautiously anticipated" almost the whole of Martyn's theory.[13] The theology alluded to in Martyn's title, however, has nothing to do with the universal significance attributed by Bultmann to the opposition between the early Christians and their Jewish adversaries. Martyn focuses instead on the history of this conflict, and his book really does strike a new note. His friend and fellow Johannine scholar, Dwight Moody Smith, while acknowledging that "in setting John against a Jewish, rather than a Christian, background, Martyn had predecessors," continues, "but he rightly gets credit for a sea-change in Johannine studies for somewhat the same reason that the Wright brothers got credit for the airplane. Others may have gotten off the ground, but Martyn—like the Wright brothers—achieved sustained flight."[14]

Because Martyn's thesis has a direct bearing on my whole argument I need to explain what is new in it. Like Bultmann, Martyn recognized the relationship between the evangelist's handling of the two healing miracles in chapters 5 and 9; but I will concentrate on his treatment of the story of the cure of the blind beggar in John 9, a story that focuses on the man's excommunication from the synagogue to which he belonged, and the reason for it. The purpose of the story within the Gospel, like the cure of the lame man in chapter 5, is chiefly, on the face of it, to underline Jesus' achievement as a miracle-worker. But it is oddly different from the traditional accounts of miracles familiar to us from the other Gospels. At its heart is a report concerning the refusal of the blind man's parents to confront those who are questioning them concerning the cure of their son: it was "because they feared the Jews, for the Jews had already agreed that if anyone should confess him [Jesus] to be the Messiah, he was to be put out of the synagogue" (9:22). Provided that we are willing to look beyond the occasion of the story in the career of Jesus so as to see here some reference to the situation of the evangelist (as even Bultmann was prepared to do), it takes only a moment's reflection to recognize the significance of such an agreement on the part of the synagogue authorities. Effectively it means that anyone who refuses to disown

12. Commenting on 9:22, however, he had already raised the possibility of a link between the Gospel and the *Birkat ha-Minim.*

13. C. K. Barrett, *The Gospel according to St. John: An Introduction with Commentary and Notes on the Greek Text,* 2nd ed. (London: SPCK, 1978), 250.

14. D. M. Smith, "Contribution of J. Louis Martyn," 279. In a useful footnote (p. 292 n. 14) Moody Smith lists a number of works along similar lines that appeared about the same time as Martyn's *History and Theology.* It is particularly interesting to compare Martyn's book with Ernst Käsemann's *Testament of Jesus: A Study of the Gospel of John in the Light of Chapter 17* (London: SCM), for the English edition of this book appeared in the same year (1968). Käsemann was eager to pursue an argument with Bultmann that he had begun some years earlier (1957). (I shall be commenting further on this disagreement in my final chapter.)

Jesus is to be barred from the synagogue forever. Martyn puts it like this: "what had been an inner-synagogue *group of Christian Jews* now became—against its will—a separated *community of Jewish Christians*."[15]

I must emphasize here that this conclusion on Martyn's part takes us a long way outside the setting of the Gospel story itself: having just left the temple precincts (8:59), Jesus notices a blind beggar by the wayside, and his disciples ask him whether the man's affliction is a consequence of his own sin or that of his parents. Once healed, he is told to go and wash in the pool of Siloam. The story concerns an event that took place in the Jerusalem of Jesus' own day, when the temple was still standing. But Martyn is interested in a much later period, the period of the composition of the Gospel, when the temple had been destroyed, and Jews and Christians had already parted and were in continuing conflict. The questions he addresses to the text are those of a historian, and it is instructive to compare his approach with that of Xavier Léon-Dufour, which I discussed in chapter 2. Léon-Dufour also distinguishes two levels (*temps*) of understanding; but whereas for him the second level is that of *the Christian readers of the Gospel*, at any time and in any place, for Martyn the second level is that of *the evangelist himself and his own community*. Martyn states in the introduction to his book that his first task "is to say something as specific as possible about the actual circumstances in which John wrote his Gospel," and he goes on to ask, "May one sense even in its exalted cadences the voice of a Christian theologian who writes *in response to contemporary events and issues* which concern, or should concern, all members of the Christian community in which he lives?" He follows up this question with the bold suggestion that in seeking to answer it we must "make every effort to take up temporary residence in the Johannine community. . . . We must sense at least some of the crises which helped to shape the lives of some of its members."[16] Although, as I have already remarked, he is pursuing the line taken by Bretschneider and Wrede very much earlier, Martyn is advancing beyond them in, to use his own word, specificity. This really is a new question.

What is more, the way he chooses to search for answers to this question is not just novel but extraordinarily imaginative. He suggests that each of the various players in this little drama "is actually a pair of actors playing two parts simultaneously." So there are really two stages: the lower stage, which is where the story we are reading is taking place, and the higher stage, on which is portrayed the dramatic interaction between the synagogue and the Johannine

15. This important conclusion was added in the second edition of *History and Theology* (1979), 66.

16. Martyn, *History and Theology* (1968), xviii. Emphasis in the original.

group within it. "To observe the sequence of scenes," adds Martyn, "one needs only to be aware of the two-level stage."[17] But in his search for specificity Martyn goes even further: the beggar, he suggests, is a Christian convert; the Sanhedrin, the local Jewish city council (for which he employs the Greek term *gerousia*). Jesus himself represents a latter-day prophet speaking in Jesus' name. What takes place on the upper stage, of course, is told indirectly, and to have any chance of seeing it we have to replay for ourselves Martyn's imaginative projection.

Now it may be objected that not one person in a hundred, not one person in a thousand, is likely to read the Gospel in this way. With a little nudging we might be persuaded to accept Léon-Dufour's two levels of understanding, for while the evangelist is recording actions and discourses that took place a half-century earlier, he himself is addressing readers in his own present. (In this respect he is no different from most historians.) But what is all this nonsense about a latter-day prophet? There is not a shred of evidence that such a person ever existed. The Gospel is telling us about Jesus, nobody else. Martyn attempts to stave off any possible objection to what he calls the *doubling* of Jesus with an early Christian preacher by the aid of a subtle exegesis of 9:4: "It is necessary for *us* to work the works of him who sent *me* while it is day." "Immediately surrounding this verse," he points out, "is the original healing story in which Jesus works the works of God (vss. 1-7). But this occurrence is not terminated in Jesus' earthly lifetime, as the expansion of the simple healing narrative in verses 8-41 makes clear.. . . The Risen Lord," he concludes, "continues his earthly ministry in the work of his servant, the Christian preacher."[18] No doubt Martyn would add that we should use our imagination to picture the dramatic events that led to the bitter divorce toward the end of the first century between the traditional believers within the synagogue and those of its members who professed belief in Jesus. For he is also picturing the response of John's first readers, all members of his own community, as they applaud the beggar's crushing response to the Pharisees—just the sort of people they have encountered many times, people whom they think of as blind and bigoted—as he says to them, "I was blind and now I see," and as they deplore, however sympathetically, the refusal of the man's parents to stand up to those same people because of their fear of being ostracized themselves. Martyn points out that the word ἀποσυνάγωγος employed by John really means a person excommunicated from the synagogue, adding that the same word occurs also

---

17. Martyn, *History and Theology* (1968), 17.
18. Martyn, *History and Theology* (1968), 9.

in two other contexts. One of these is the Farewell Discourse, where Jesus predicts to his disciples that "they [that is, the Jews] will cause you to be excommunicated from the synagogue" (16:2). The other is a passage in which Jesus, speaking of the rulers (ἄρχοντες), says that many of them believed in him, "but on account of the Pharisees made it a practice not to confess him, lest they be excluded from the synagogue" (12:42). This is Martyn's conclusion:

At some time prior to John's writing an authoritative body within Judaism reached a formal decision regarding messianic faith in Jesus, Henceforth, whoever confesses such faith is to be separated from the synagogue. Many Jews, even "rulers," do in fact believe, but they manage to conceal their faith, lest they be excluded from the company of their brethren. Others, like the blind beggar, clearly reveal their commitment and are cast out. Indeed, John's church has a number of members who have personally experienced the operation of the awesome agreement. They are Jewish excommunicates [ἀποσυνάγωγοι].[19]

So much for the evidence from the Gospel itself. I confess that I am not fully persuaded that Martyn is right in every detail. For his picture of what happens in the upper stage to be fully coherent he needs to posit a second blind beggar in John's own day, cured of his blindness by the latter-day prophet—surely a rather unlikely supposition. But such reservations as I have do not extend to his general argument that most of the story is directly relevant to the controversies between two groups in the synagogue toward the end of the first century. Conclusive for this position, as he himself observes, is the contemptuous dismissal of the man born blind in 9:28: "You are that man's disciple [μαθητὴς ἐκείνου], but we are disciples of Moses," a statement that, as he says, "is scarcely conceivable in Jesus' lifetime, since it recognizes discipleship to Jesus not only as antithetical, but also as somehow comparable, to discipleship to Moses. It is, on the other hand, easily understood under circumstances in which the synagogue views the Christian movement as an essential and more or less clearly distinguishable rival."[20] This point deserves to be underlined. Moses is by far the most important single figure for Judaism, as Jesus is for Christianity and Muhammad for Islam. When the earliest followers of Muhammad ranked him ahead of Jesus, whom they continued to honor as a prophet, they were setting up a new religion. The

---

19. Martyn, *History and Theology* (1968), 21.
20. Martyn, *History and Theology* (1968), 19.

same is true of those who ranked Jesus ahead of Moses, although the fourth evangelist, at least, leaves less of a place for Moses than Muhammad did for Jesus.

So in this first part of his argument, headed "Exclusion from the Synagogue according to the Fourth Gospel," Martyn has already made his case.[21] But there is a second and longer part to his argument too, entitled "Exclusion from the Synagogue according to Other Sources." In this part (already anticipated in the reference to "an authoritative body within Judaism") Martyn argued that the expulsion from the synagogue testified to in the Gospel should be understood in the light of the euphemistically named "Benediction of the Heretics" (*Birkat ha-Minim*), a reformulation—turning a blessing into a curse—of the twelfth of eighteen benedictions recited as a prayer (*Amidah*) in early synagogue worship. This argument aroused a storm of controversy, but Martyn has never retracted his view that the *Birkat ha-Minim* was issued under Gamaliel II, who, in Martyn's opinion headed the Jamnia Academy from about 80 to about 115 CE. While admitting that some objections of Wayne Meeks to his arguments in the first edition had a certain cogency, he nevertheless reiterated his opinion that the *Birkat ha-Minim* "is in some way reflected in John 9:22."[22] The most that can be said for this position is that it cannot be conclusively disproved; but since I would endorse Meeks's observation that the *Birkat ha-Minim* "has become a kind of red herring in Johannine research,"[23] I will say no more about it here. There is already enough to justify the widespread support Martyn received for his main thesis.

Before proceeding, I wish to stress two features of the passage in the Gospel we have been considering: its complexity and its urgency. The trouble is that the complexity may well veil the urgency, because this is not immediately evident to us as we read the Gospel nearly two millennia after it was composed: the urgency has somehow to be teased out from the text. I have compared the

21. Commenting upon Martyn's book in the first edition of *Understanding the Fourth Gospel* (p. 109 n. 102), I made the point that his reading of chapter 9 "is not *built upon* his interpretation of the Eighteen Benedictions; at most it is buttressed by it." Moody Smith, in his "Postscript for the Third Edition of Martyn, *History and Theology*," observed that this was also *historically* true, in the sense that Martyn first added this argument when his original doctoral dissertation of 1957 was revised and published as a book. See *History and Theology*, 3rd ed. (2003), 20.

22. Martyn, *History and Theology*, 2nd ed. (1979), 54 n. 69.

23. "Breaking Away: Three New Testament Pictures of Christianity's Separation from the Jewish Communities" in *"To See Ourselves as Others See Us": Christians, Jews, 'Others' in Late Antiquity*, ed. Jacob Neusner and Ernest S. Frerichs, (Chico, Calif.: Scholars Press, 1985), 93–115; quotation from 102. For further discussion of this issue, see Dwight Moody Smith, "Contribution," 280–81 and n. 17; Ashton, *Understanding the Fourth Gospel*, 2nd ed., 31–33.

evangelist's approach with that of Giuseppe Verdi in his early opera *Nabucco* (a.k.a. Nebuchadnezzar), which tells of the suffering of the exiled Jews in Babylon. Was he aware, I have sometimes wondered, that the prophet Daniel had preceded him in deliberately telling two stories at the same time? The book of Daniel purports to tell of the iniquities (and horrifying punishment) of the Babylonian Nebuchadnezzar, whereas the subtext refers to the crimes (and, hopefully, the subsequent punishment) of the tyrant Antiochus Epiphanes, who had provoked the Maccabees into armed resistance some four centuries after the Babylonian exile. Similarly, the anger and the hope that ring out in the chorus of the Hebrew slaves may be thought of as projecting the anger and hope of the Italians, as they looked forward to finally ridding themselves of their Austrian oppressors. The fear and anger of the Johannine community, as they see themselves exiled from the synagogue by those they call the Jews, is similarly projected back upon the life of Jesus. But they had a burning conviction that they had been given the truth (led into all truth) and that through this truth they would come to enjoy a freedom that would release them from the constraints to which they were subjected by their fellow Jews: "the truth will set you free."

In the next chapter I will be considering the nature of this new truth and inquiring into the source of the evangelists' ideas concerning it.

6

The Apocalyptic Background

In this chapter, I have two aims in mind. I want to refer back to the Essenes, because I believe that a greater knowledge of this sect will help us to arrive at an understanding of the relationship between John's Gospel and its author's Jewish contemporaries. But I will be focusing particularly on the Gospel's affinity to a manner of thinking, left unmentioned until now, that emerged relatively late in the long history of Judaism but is clearly discernible in the Qumran corpus. This way of thinking, which rests on the conviction succinctly expressed by the prophet Daniel that "there is a God in heaven who reveals mysteries" (2:28), is what we call *apocalyptic*. This word is commonly used to mean something ominous, portentous, or doom-laden. But I use it here, in a sense much closer to the Greek word from which it is derived, to mean *revelatory*: having to do with the disclosure of mysteries. Applied to the thought and writing of Jewish seers and scribes, it refers to their belief that God's revelation did not cease with the Law and the Prophets or with what more generally was accepted as Scripture (which would have to include the Psalms, and also wisdom writings such as Proverbs and the book of Job). God continued to be "a God who reveals mysteries."

Accordingly, I propose to take a fresh look at a topic I discussed more than twenty years ago in a chapter of my book *Understanding the Fourth Gospel* entitled "Intimations of Apocalyptic." I argued in my earlier work that there were notable affinities between the Gospel of John and apocalyptic literature. Since that book was written I have considerably revised my views on this topic; but still believing that the comparison is illuminating, I will discuss it, as I did before, under four headings, starting with the Two Ages.

THE TWO AGES

The topic can be usefully addressed through the Dead Sea Scrolls, in particular through one very significant text: the Habakkuk pesher. The prophet's complaint to God, right at the beginning of this little book (consisting of three short chapters), that "the wicked [singular] besets the righteous" (1:4), gives the author of the pesher the immediate opportunity of identifying the wicked as "the Wicked Priest" and the righteous as "the Teacher of Righteousness." This is the rivalry, or rather enmity, that really concerned him, although it had nothing to do with what the prophet is actually saying. In the following verse, God, through the mouth of the prophet, responds: "I am doing a work in your days that if told you would not believe" (1:5), and goes on (1:6-11) to speak of the Chaldeans, whom he is rousing up to perform acts of terrible violence. The commentator, however, takes these two verses separately, interpreting the Chaldeans, or Neo-Babylonians, the big threat during Habakkuk's lifetime, around the end of the seventh century BCE, to mean the Kittim (that is, the Romans, who controlled the whole of the Near East throughout the duration of the Qumran settlement),[1] and the incredulous in v. 5 (actually the people the prophet was addressing centuries earlier) to refer to those among the contemporaries of the Teacher of Righteousness who refused to listen to the word received by him from the mouth of God. Underlying and justifying what to a modern reader looks like a blatant disregard for the real meaning of the text is the conviction that the prophet's message is not for the people of his own time but for what the commentator calls "the final generation," that is to say his own contemporaries.

The reason for this conviction is clarified later, in a comment on Hab. 2:1-2:

and God told Habakkuk to write down that which would happen to the final generation, but he did not make known to him when time would come to an end. And as for that which he said, *That he who reads may run with it (read it speedily)*: interpreted this concerns the Teacher of Righteousness, to whom God made known all the mysteries of his servants the prophets. (1QpHab 7:1-5)

". . . to whom God made known all the mysteries of his servants the prophets." A similar boast occurs in one of the *Hodayot* (Songs of Praise), where the author speaks of himself as "a discerning interpreter of marvelous mysteries" (1QH 10:13). It is worth pausing to reflect on the word *mystery*. A mystery (which in Latin may be *mysterium*, but also *secretum*) is a truth that no amount of searching will disclose but remains hidden until it is revealed. In fact the words *mystery*

---

1. The word *kittim* occurs several times in the Hebrew Bible. The first time it is used to refer to the Romans is in Dan. 11:30, which is no doubt the source of its usage in the pesharim.

and *revelation* are correlatives, for it makes no sense to speak of a mystery unless there is at least the theoretical possibility that the truth it hides may at some point become known—as the mysteries of the prophets were made known to the Teacher of Righteousness. To refer to prophecies as mysteries is effectively to regard them as hidden truths whose meaning will be revealed later.[2] And it should be observed that this is also how the apocalyptic writers thought of their own dreams and visions. After receiving one of his strange visions, the prophet Daniel was told that the vision was true, but that he should "seal up the vision, for it pertains to many days hence" (8:26; cf. 12:4, 9). Similarly *1 Enoch*: right at the beginning of the book comes the assertion that in recounting his vision of the Holy Ones and of heaven, he is speaking "not for this generation, but concerning one that is distant" (1:2). In Daniel and *1 Enoch* these assertions are easily understood, because the books that bear the names of these two seers were actually written long after they themselves were supposed to have lived. There would be no point in pretending that the relevance of the message was restricted to the time when the events of the story, as it is told, took place. But the instructions or assertions regarding the future relevance of the visions they record correspond so closely to the way the words of the prophets are treated in the Qumran pesharim that it is reasonable to suppose that they directly influenced the author or authors of these commentaries, permitting and indeed promoting their extraordinary conviction that the prophets were speaking not for the people of their own time but for the members of this new community. The number of copies of Daniel and of *1 Enoch* found at Qumran shows that both of these books were especially popular there.[3] So we see that notions

2. On this topic, see now Samuel I. Thomas, *The "Mysteries" of Qumran: Mystery, Secrecy, and Esotericism in the Dead Sea Scrolls* (Society of Biblical Literature Early Judaism and Its Literature 25 (Atlanta: Society of Biblical Literature, 2009). Martin Heidegger was probably right to say that the root of the word ἀλήθεια is the verb λανθάνειν ("conceal"), preceded by an alpha-privative. "*The most primordial phenomenon of truth*," he says, "*is first shown by the existential-ontological foundations of uncovering*," and "only with Dasein's *disclosedness* is the *most primordial* phenomenon of truth attained" (Martin Heidegger, *Being and Time* [Oxford: Basil Blackwell, 1973], 263). If Heidegger is right to argue that the very concept of truth implies uncovering (*Entdecken*) and uncoveredness (*Entdecktheit*), then truth must also be linked with apocalyptic. Rudolf Bultmann (a friend and colleague of Heidegger at the University of Marburg) refers to this section of Heidegger's *Sein und Zeit* in part of a long inquiry into Ἀλήθεια ("Untersuchungen zum Johannesevangelium A. Ἀλήθεια," *Zeitschrift für die neutestamentliche Wissenschaft* 27 [1928]: 134), but he makes no connection with apocalyptic.

3. Julio Trebolle-Barrera, "Qumran Evidence for a Biblical Standard Text and for Non-Standard and Parabiblical Texts,'" in *The Dead Sea Scrolls in Their Historical Context*, ed. Timothy H. Lim et al. (Edinburgh: T&T Clark, 2000), 89–106; James C. VanderKam, "Apocalyptic Tradition in the Dead Sea Scrolls and the Religion of Qumran," in *Religion in the Dead Sea Scrolls*, ed. John J. Collins and Robert A.

perfectly appropriate to writings supposedly composed in the distant past, such as Daniel and *1 Enoch*, were transferred to the works of prophets like Habakkuk, who were actually addressing their own contemporaries. And since the lessons of the Torah too, as we have already seen, could not be comprehended without a special revelation reserved to the members of the sect, first and foremost the Teacher of Righteousness, then all Scripture, it is fair to conclude, the Law and the Prophets, was conceived at Qumran as held in reserve until eventually its truths were made known to "the discerning interpreter of marvelous mysteries" and to the community as a whole.

Virtually the same idea is expressed in the concluding doxology of Paul's letter to Romans: "Now to him who is able to strengthen you according to my gospel and the preaching of Jesus Christ, according to the revelation of the mystery which was kept secret for long ages but has been disclosed and through the prophetic writings made known to all nations, according to the command of the eternal God, to bring about the obedience of faith" (Rom. 16:25-26; cf. 1 Cor. 2:6-9; Col. 1:26; Eph. 3:4-5, 9). Since knowledge of the mystery is transmitted through the writings of the prophets—the Scriptures—it must have been somehow contained in these beforehand.

Paul speaks of a mystery kept secret for long ages. Compressing this, we may speak rather of *two* ages, the age of concealment and the age of disclosure, a fundamental element in the pesher method of interpretation used at Qumran, and an essential feature of what came to be called apocalyptic. So the motif of mystery and disclosure is shared among Paul, the Qumran Essenes, and apocalyptic in general. Yet we should not exaggerate the resemblances. The mystery revealed to Paul did not emerge from his study of the Old Testament: it came to him in a blinding flash. Only later did he realize that this new revelation was already somehow hidden in the Bible. There is no possibility that the Qumran community could have transformed itself, like Christianity, from a new sect to a new religion, for in spite of their new understanding of the prophets that found voice in the pesharim they continued to insist above all on the strict observance of the law. Paul, on the other hand, and (much later) John saw the Christian gospel not as the fulfillment of a prophecy but as the revelation of a mystery. Their appropriation of the essentially apocalyptic concept of the two ages of revelation was not the exception but the norm for Christian believers.

Since this is so, what reason is there for claiming a particular debt to apocalyptic on John's part? Any early Christian writing, one might say, must

Kugler, Studies in the Dead Sea Scrolls and Related Literature (Grand Rapids: Eerdmans, 2000), 113-34.

either affirm, or at least imply, that the old order has passed, and the new, in some sense the fulfillment of the old, has begun. Some answer is to be found in John's exceptional emphasis on the significance of Jesus' death. The other three evangelists, in recording the rending of the temple veil, certainly see Jesus' death as an event charged with meaning. John, however, is the only one of the four to recognize its full cosmic significance. "Now," declares Jesus, "is the judgment of this world, now shall the ruler of this world [that is, the devil] be cast out" (12:31; cf. 14:3; 16:11). Unlike his three predecessors, the fourth evangelist does not record any actual encounter between Jesus and the devil during his lifetime—no exorcisms and no temptation narrative. But John's assurance that Jesus' death meant a final and absolute judgment upon the ruler of this world must derive, either directly or indirectly, from the dramatic portrayal, in several apocalypses, of the destruction of the forces of evil. The most terrifying of these is to be found in the opening chapter of the oldest apocalypse of all, *1 Enoch:*

> The Great Holy One will come forth from his dwelling . . . he will appear with his mighty host from the heaven of heavens. All the Watchers [that is, the rebel angels] will fear and quake. . . . All the ends of the earth will be shaken, and trembling and great fear will seize them. . . . The high mountains will be shaken and fall and break apart. . . . The earth will be wholly rent asunder, and everything on the earth will perish, and there will be judgment on all. (*1 Enoch* 1:4-9)

Here is an example of the kind of properly eschatological prediction that used to be thought of as the hallmark of apocalyptic in general, and by some as actually synonymous with it. Jesus' statements in the Fourth Gospel concerning the total defeat of the ruler of this world are a clear indication of his debt to the apocalyptic tradition.[4] Elsewhere in Jewish and early Christian literature the prince or ruler of this world is given a variety of names: Satan, of course, but also Shemihazah, Asael or Azazel (*1 Enoch*), Beliar (*Ascension of Isaiah*), Belial (the *War Scroll*), Ornias and Beelzebul (*Testament of Solomon*). In the Gospel of John he is given no name except in the short and sinister remark at the end of the Last Supper, where we are told that *Satan* entered into Judas (13:27); but the message is the same as in the properly apocalyptic writings, no less momentous and impressive for its brevity, and involving a dramatic victory over the forces of evil very different from the usual deployment of the theme of judgment in

---

4. See Judith Kovacs, " 'Now Shall the Ruler of This World Be Driven Out': Jesus' Death as Cosmic Battle in John 12:20-26," *Journal of Biblical Literature* 114 (1995): 227–47.

this Gospel, where people pass judgment upon themselves as they opt for or against the message of Jesus.

VISIONS AND DREAMS: THE TWO STAGES

Turning now to the second aspect of apocalyptic that I want to discuss in this chapter, I start with a book that, judging from the number of manuscripts of it found there, was, as I have already said, very popular at Qumran. The book of Daniel falls into two parts. The first part shows us Daniel at the court of Nebuchadnezzar and his son Belshazzar, kings of Babylon. Daniel is summoned by these two kings to interpret for them a series of nasty dreams, all of which, in one way or another, concern the future of their kingdom. The tales in which these dreams are recorded are well known and have been handed down in picture, song, and story: the statue with the feet of clay, Daniel in the fiery furnace and (later) in the lions' den, the writing on the wall. Every instance involves a puzzle, often called a "mystery," whose solution is hidden from the dreamer and requires an interpreter. The successful interpreter always turns out to be Daniel himself, since the king's team of hired magicians proves to be not up to the job. In the second part of the book, from being a skilled interpreter Daniel now emerges as a dreamer, or rather a visionary seer, who has a series of alarming visions of heavenly happenings that he cannot understand without help. In Daniel's own case, help comes from an angel, sent by God to enable him to understand the significance of what he has just seen. This angel, not always the same, is generally referred to as an *angelus interpres*, an angel interpreter.

Accordingly, whether we have to do with a dream or a vision, every episode in the book involves a puzzle or a mystery told in two stages, the stage of concealment and the stage of disclosure, when the meaning of the dream or vision is revealed. There is a particular Aramaic and/or Hebrew word that is commonly used in the book to denote the act of interpretation or explanation, a word rendered by Theodotion, who translated Daniel into Greek, as ἀναγγέλλειν. At one point, for instance, the angel Gabriel approaches Daniel while he is at prayer, to tell him that as he began his supplications, "a word went forth, and I have come to explain [RSV: tell] it to you; therefore consider the word and understand the vision" (Dan. 9:23).[5]

---

5. In John 16:12-15, the word ἀναγγέλλειν is used of the Paraclete, who, like the interpreting angel of the apocalypses, enables the apostles to reach a full understanding of what up to then they had been incapable of understanding properly. See above p. 40 and n. 14.

Insiders and Outsiders

A common theme in the Gospels, as everyone knows, is the hostility shown to Jesus by many of his own people. In John's Gospel, where Jesus' adversaries are usually referred to simply as the Jews (οἱ Ἰουδαῖοι), this hostility is particularly marked. In this contrast between insiders and outsiders (as in other respects), the members of the Johannine community are comparable to the Essene sect, which I discussed in my fourth chapter. In fact this sect is a classic example of a breakaway group claiming to represent the true, authentic tradition of the larger, parent body from which it has seceded. Bryan Wilson, in his influential book *Magic and the Millennium*, argues convincingly that the withdrawal of social groups from the world "leads to the establishment of a separate community preoccupied with its own holiness and its means of insulation from the wider society."[6]

I should add at this point that I was mistaken, in the first edition of *Understanding the Fourth Gospel*, to argue for a direct connection between the Fourth Gospel and the Qumran community simply on the basis of the dualistic language (especially the opposition between light and darkness) that the Gospel shares with many of the sectarian writings of the Dead Sea Scrolls, above all the Two Spirits section of the *Community Rule* (1QS 3:13–4:26). I am now fully in agreement with Philip Esler's rejection of my earlier argument; in a chapter entitled "Introverted Sectarianism at Qumran and in the Johannine Community," he argues, rightly I now think, that the introverted sectarianism found in both groups is best explained by the fact that "the fundamental social reality for both groups was a marked division between themselves and the outside world. In such a context dualism comes naturally";[7] so there is no need to posit a direct debt. Although I have returned to the view that there may well be a connection between the two groups, it is for different reasons.

Now although I have counted the insiders/outsiders distinction as one typical feature of apocalyptic writing, it should be pointed out that it has no place in John J. Collins's classic definition of an apocalypse (quoted further on in this chapter). The reason for this is that it cannot be said to characterize the apocalyptic genre as such, from any formal or literary perspective. The distinction occurs quite noticeably in the majority of apocalypses (and we will shortly see some typical examples) simply because these mostly represent the

---

6. Bryan R. Wilson, *Magic and the Millennium: A Sociological Study of Religious Movements of Protest among Tribal and Third World Peoples* (London: Paladin, 1935), 23–24.

7. Philip F. Esler, *The First Christians in Their Social Worlds: Social-scientific Approaches to New Testament Interpretation* (London: Routledge, 1994), 90–91.

views of men and women opposed to people in their own milieu whom they regard as alien and hostile.

What is more, it would be wrong to suggest that the distinction is restricted to apocalyptic. Here is a quotation from the Gospel of Mark that actually uses the language of insiders and outsiders with specific reference to the mystery of the kingdom of God: "To you has been given the mystery [μυστήριον] of the kingdom of God, but for those outside everything is in riddles [ἐν παραβολαῖς], that they may indeed see but not perceive, and may indeed hear but not understand; lest they should turn again, and be forgiven" (4:11-12). (The confusion arises from the fact that the Greek word παραβολαί, besides meaning parables, as it commonly does, can also mean riddles, as in this passage in Mark.)

We in our turn may be forgiven for failing to understand this mysterious saying, for neither, apparently, did one of Mark's earliest readers, the evangelist Matthew, who altered the purpose clause and transformed it into an *explanation*: Jesus spoke to the crowd in parables not with the intention of veiling his meaning from them in riddling sayings but *because they needed parables*, conceived as figurative explanations, to assist their comprehension (Matt. 13:13). If Matthew understood what Mark's Jesus was saying (and I rather suspect he did not), then he completely disagreed with him. But it is Mark, not Matthew, who effectively conveys the sense that his readers or hearers belong to a privileged minority and differ from everyone else in their ability to comprehend the mystery that has been entrusted to them. Those outside, in the nature of things, are unable to penetrate mysteries. It might be added that Mark's conception of a mystery hidden from outsiders—Matthew and Luke use the plural form, μυστήρια, at this point—brings him quite close to the apocalyptic view of the Christian message I associate with John. Indeed, what is often called the messianic secret may be better conceived as the hidden phase of an apocalyptic revelation of the true meaning of the kingdom of God, the primary object of Jesus' assertion that "there is nothing hid, except to be made manifest; nor is anything secret, except to come to light" (Mark 4:22).

If Mark's Jesus, in the reference to "those outside" in the passage I have just quoted, seems to be looking for enemies, John's Jesus literally demonizes his own regular adversaries, the Jews: "Why do you not understand what I say?" he asks them: "It is because you cannot bear to hear my word. You are of your father, the devil, and your will is to do your father's desires. He was a murderer from the beginning, and has nothing to do with the truth, because there is no truth in him. When he lies, he speaks according to his own nature, for he is a liar and the father of lies" (8:43-44).

In apocalyptic writings outsiders are frequently identified as "the foolish," in contrast to the wise, and as "the wicked," in contrast to the righteous. Since they are both foolish and wicked, they refuse to listen to words of wisdom; but it is often implied that even if they did they would be unable to comprehend them. In the book of Daniel this is spelled out clearly in the last chapter: "none of the wicked shall understand, but those who are wise shall understand" (Dan. 12:10). I have already insisted on one crucial difference between the Essenes and their opponents, "the Seekers of Smooth Things," namely, the conviction of the former that any reliable interpretation depends on a special revelation. Even the Torah is mysterious, insofar as it cannot be properly understood without divine aid. The same holds, as we have already observed, of the words of the prophets, who were often thought of as authors of Scripture (see, for instance, Rom. 1:2; 3:21). The net result of all these revelations is *knowledge*, not the ordinary sort of knowledge, however, that is primarily the outcome of study and learning, but a very special kind of knowledge reserved for members of the sect and setting them apart from all outsiders. The oath exacted from incoming members was a promise to return wholeheartedly to the Torah "*in accordance with all that has been revealed of it* to the sons of Zadok, the Priests, keepers of the covenant and seekers of his will, and to the multitude of the men of the covenant who together have freely pledged themselves to his truth" (1QS 5:9-10). The Master, accordingly, was entrusted with the important task of instructing his members "in the mysteries of marvelous truth" (1QS 9:18). But this duty was accompanied by a corresponding negative responsibility: those whom he saw as outsiders "are not included in his covenant since they have neither sought nor examined his decrees in order to learn the hidden matters in which they err" (1QS 5:11) and have no entitlement to know the truth. Consequently, the Master is instructed to conceal the teaching of the Law from these men (1QS 9:17), that is, the men of injustice, or sin (*'wl*), who have just been called the men of the pit (*šḥt*) (1QS 9:16). They are to be completely shunned, not even argued with.

Behind these peremptory commands we can detect an anxious apprehension. In revealing his secret knowledge to the members of his community the Master is running the risk that some renegade might pass this knowledge on to others who are not entitled to it. Nevertheless, "the Interpreter shall not conceal from them through fear of an apostate spirit any of those things hidden from Israel which have been discovered by him" (1QS 8:11-12). His anxiety, however well grounded, does not give him the right to keep his fellow covenanters in the dark.

I have already pointed out that the charge leveled against the enemies of the sect that they have failed to examine God's decrees so as to "learn the hidden matters in which they err" looks grossly unfair, because it is said at the same time that God denied them the kind of special revelation without which the necessary awareness was simply not available. The sectarians are anxious to blame "the Seekers of Smooth Things" for looking for loopholes and easy answers, but at the same time they lay exclusive claim to special revelations that are an essential element in the new covenant that entitles them to arrogate to themselves the proud name of Israel.

In the *Damascus Document* the hidden things in which all Israel strayed are spelled out as "his holy sabbaths, his glorious appointed times [that is, feast-days], his righteous testimonies, his true ways, and the desires of his will, which a person shall do and live by them" (CD 3:14-16). The specified sins concern the cultic calendar, but the vague expression "the desires of his will" must refer to bitter disputes over other interpretations of the law that we can only guess at. It is obvious that the breakaway of the new sect was preceded by acrimonious arguments between the two groups concerning these. But much more was at stake than the need to win debates over the correct interpretation of detailed items of legislation. The primary concern of the leaders of the community was to ensure that the novices in their charge were imbued with a sense of the exceptional nature of the privileged existence to which they were about to commit themselves. And one way to do this was to convince them that their Instructor was himself the recipient of divine revelations regarding the specific interpretation of the Scripture on which their rule was based.

Very much later in the history of religious thought, one of the first tasks of those entrusted with the instruction of the young votaries of the Christian religious orders that began to emerge when Christianity had become the dominant religion of the Western world, was to persuade them that the heavenly vocation of each of their founders (Benedict, Dominic, Francis, and Ignatius are the most important names here)—a vocation that was nothing short of a personal revelation from God—legitimized and indeed sanctified the astonishingly strict rule of life to which they were submitting themselves. The rules of the new orders show nothing of the bitter recriminations of the sins of their parent body so typical of the key writings of the Essenes. But in other respects, such as their layered organization, whereby priests formed the upper layer with a Master or Superior at the very top, with their vows of poverty and chastity, and above all with the felt need for the inspiration provided by a dominant foundation myth, the later Christian religious orders bore an uncanny resemblance to the only Jewish religious order known to us—which preceded them by several centuries.

Now we must take a further step. The sense that the community had privileged access to the truth extended beyond the traditions hidden in the Scriptures and reached out to include other mysteries besides. This meant that, unlike many if not most Jews, even in the Second Temple era, they were open to the possibility that God had not yet had his final say—that the Mosaic Torah was not the definitive revelation it was thought to be by many or most of their contemporaries.

The documentary evidence for this openness among the Dead Sea Scrolls is of two kinds. I have already remarked on the popularity of two particular books at Qumran: Daniel and *1 Enoch*. These books are apocalypses in a more technical sense than the sense in which I have been using the word *apocalyptic*, for their revelations are of a particular sort. Here I cite the definition of apocalypse given by John J. Collins. He begins by outlining what he calls "a common core of constant elements." This permits

> a comprehensive definition of the genre: An apocalypse is defined as a genre of revelatory literature with a narrative framework, in which a revelation is mediated by an otherworldly being to a human recipient, disclosing a transcendent reality which is both temporal, insofar as it envisages eschatological salvation, and spatial insofar as it involves another, supernatural world.[8]

I want now to discuss in turn two books found at Qumran that indisputably fit this definition. Concerning Daniel, however, the first of these, we must start with a qualification. Strictly speaking, only the second half of the book is apocalyptic in the narrow sense of the word, for it is not until chapter 7 that Daniel, the eponymous hero of the book, begins to have the kind of visions or dreams that are at the heart of any true apocalypse. Up to that point he himself is the interpreter: as an honored guest at the court of Nebuchadnezzar, he is repeatedly asked to "expound the interpretation" of the king's dreams.

Early on in Daniel we find the king seeking an explanation of his first dream, which concerned a succession of great kingdoms, subsumed under the image of a formidably large statue, variously composed. Its head was of gold, its breast and arms of silver, its belly and thighs of iron, and its feet partly of iron and partly, famously, of clay. Daniel tells the king what he knows already: none of his own hired team of clever men can expound to him "the mystery which

---

8. "Introduction: Towards the Morphology of a Genre," *Semeia* 14 (1979), 9

he has asked." But, Daniel assures him, "there is a God in heaven who reveals mysteries" (2:28). Thus, very early in the book, in an assertion that could easily be missed, comes the crucial distinction that, as I observed earlier, marks out Jewish apocalypses in the full sense from "the Law and the Prophets." "There is a God in heaven who reveals mysteries," Daniel tells the king, and he has made known to him "what will be in the latter days" (2:28). The Teacher of Righteousness, as I argued in the previous chapter, must have reflected deeply on the idea that prophecies could have a relevance long after the time when they were first uttered, as well as on the notion that they contained mysteries; and indeed there is a strong likelihood that this was the inspiration behind the passage in the Habakkuk pesher asserting that God had told him (the prophet) to write what was going to happen to the last generation (1QpHab 7:2).

Anyone reading the book of Daniel for the first time will be startled by the abrupt shift of emphasis in the second half of the book, and above all by the difference between the first dream of Daniel himself and those of the king recounted in the opening chapters. For now, in chapter 7, we are suddenly transported into heaven. Daniel himself, hitherto so confident and assured, is dazzled and bewildered by what he now sees: the four winds of heaven stirring up the sea, four great beasts emerging from the sea, one like a lion with the wings of an eagle, one like a leopard, and a third like a bear. The fourth beast, different from the rest, had ten horns. But these were less significant than the little horn that appeared among them, for in it "were eyes like the eyes of a man and a mouth speaking great things" (7:8). At this point came a scene that captured the imagination not just of Daniel, but also of Jesus, of the four evangelists, and of other Jewish apocalyptic seers. The vision of the so-called Ancient of Days seated on a throne was inspired by a much earlier vision of the prophet Ezekiel, but the figure "like a man" that was presented before God and given an enduring dominion over all the peoples of the world, had never been seen before. So much has been written about this figure by one learned professor after another that he has virtually been swallowed up in scholarship, and his true importance lost sight of. In a later chapter I will speak of the crucial role he plays in the development in the fourth evangelist's thinking of the person of Jesus. Here I simply want to emphasize that in any branch of Judaism, the appearance of an angelic figure, soon to be called "*the* Son of Man," seated on a throne alongside that of God himself, is truly astonishing. And whatever conclusions we reach concerning Jesus' own understanding of this figure, his importance in the final eschatological prophecies attributed to Jesus in the Synoptic Gospels is beyond question.

This great vision is the first of several in the book of Daniel that had to be interpreted for the seer as hidden prophecies of the fate of a series of different kingdoms. As he watched, the little horn that had attracted his attention earlier in the course of his rapidly evolving vision "made war with the saints and prevailed over them, until the Ancient of Days came and judgment was given for the saints of the Most High" (7:22). Certain elements in one of the subsequent prophecies make it plain that the little horn is to be identified with the villainous Antiochus Epiphanes, whose decrees prohibiting particular practices enjoined by the Jewish law triggered the Maccabean rebellion.

It is not part of my purpose here to give a detailed exegesis of these later visions. What I want to stress is that, although they are all apocalyptic in the strong sense, they could be accepted without cavil by all of Judaism. Interestingly, Daniel was not placed among the prophets in the Hebrew Bible but among the so-called Writings, after Qohelet (Ecclesiastes) and Esther.[9] Nonetheless the book of Daniel was fully integrated into the Hebrew Bible, and his new revelations, mostly historical in character, were not thought at the time to present any challenge, or even to contribute any significant addition, to the Law and the Prophets. This is not the case with the second apocalyptic writing that I propose to consider now, a writing that stands well outside the Hebrew canon.

For a long time the remarkable writing that we now call *1 Enoch* was known simply as *Ethiopic Enoch*, because until the discoveries at Qumran the only extant copies were in this language, the reason for this being that it was recognized as canonical by the Ethiopian church and included in its Bible. Although quoted once in the New Testament (Jude 14-15) and quite often by the Greek and Latin fathers of the church, the book in its entirety was not known in the West until early in the nineteenth century, when a complete copy that had been brought to England in 1773 from what was then Abyssinia was translated into English. Fragments of four of the five parts into which it is now generally divided were found at Qumran. These are all in Aramaic, the language in which it was originally composed. (The Ethiopic text is a translation of a Greek translation of the Aramaic original.) So although the Qumran community represented a particularly severe form of Judaism and lived a life in strict conformity with the Torah, nevertheless it kept and treasured a book that contains revelations very different from those of the Hebrew Bible.[10]

9. In placing Daniel among the prophets, translators of the Bible are following the Septuagint.

10. Another book of which significant (Hebrew) fragments were found at Qumran is the book of *Jubilees*. This too is complete only in Ethiopic, for the same reason as Enoch: it was recognized as canonical by the Ethiopian church.

Even more significant is the fact that these new revelations were conceived as surpassing those of Moses.

While not directly critical of the law, the author of these writings, who identifies himself with the antediluvian Enoch, deflects the attention of his readers from it, because he is much more concerned with his own revelations. In the so-called Animal Vision (chapters 85–90), a figurative and highly compressed version of the history of Israel up to the reign of the Seleucids, the writer is evidently fascinated by the early part of Genesis, which contains his own story, but shows relatively little interest in the patriarchs. Moreover, when he comes to the great events of the book of Exodus he omits any reference to Sinai. From these six chapters alone one might conclude that the author is distancing himself from any tendency to restrict the traditions of Judaism to the law and from attaching too much significance to the figure of Moses. In the even briefer Apocalypse of Weeks, in which the whole of the history of Israel is told in seventeen verses, the author does mention the Sinaitic covenant ("a covenant for all generations"; 93:6); but at the end of the Epistle of Enoch (chapters 92–105), which starts with the Apocalypse of Weeks (93:1-10 91:11-17), he speaks of two mysteries, first "that sinners will alter and copy the words of truth, and pervert many," and second "that to the righteous and pious and wise *my books* will be given for the joy of righteousness and much wisdom" (104:9-12). The joy of "the righteous and pious and wise" will come not from the words of the law (though these, admittedly, are called "the words of truth") but from Enoch's own writings ("my books"), which, having been written ages earlier (even before the Flood), took precedence over the Torah.

Now there is considerable disagreement among scholars on the question whether there was a distinct, Enochian group in Second Temple Judaism that rejected the traditional belief in the overriding importance of the Torah.[11] In the passage we have just been considering, the Torah is summed up as "the words of truth"—which shows that even though the writer regarded his own revelations as superior he continued to respect the Torah and to accept its injunctions. But the fact that some modern scholars have inferred from the evidence that there was an ongoing polemic and competition between the Enochic and Mosaic traditions shows that it is possible to read it in this way. The author of the Fourth Gospel may have been among those who saw Enoch as challenging the

11. The debate is fully and fairly set out by Anthea E. Portier-Young, *Apocalypse against Empire: Theologies of Resistance in Early Judaism* (Grand Rapids: Eerdmans, 2004), 292–305. She herself concludes that "there is no evidence that the early Enochic literature rejects the Pentateuchal laws as such. . . . Nor is the figure of Moses vilified. . . . But he is not presented as the mediator of revelation or of the covenant. Instead, the role of mediator is transferred to Enoch."

central position of Moses in the Jewish tradition. If so, it is easier to understand how he himself might have ranged himself against those in his own community who announced themselves to be "disciples of Moses," and declared allegiance to Jesus instead. (This will be a central topic in the remaining chapters of this book.)

George Nickelsburg, the author of what is now the standard commentary on *1 Enoch*, has pointed out the importance for Enoch of the concept of wisdom, mentioned at key points in the book as a designation for the whole corpus. This is how Enoch addresses his son Methusaleh, in what is really the conclusion to the Book of Watchers (chapters 1–34, the first of the five parts of *1 Enoch*):

> All these things I recount and write for you, and all of them I have revealed to you, and I have given you books about all these things. Keep . . . the books of the hand of your father, that you may give them to the generations of eternity. Wisdom I have also given to all the generations until eternity, this wisdom that surpasses their thought. (*1 Enoch* 82:1-2; cf. 104:12-13)

At the beginning of the *Community Rule*, in a passage that I have already quoted more than once, the Master is instructed to admit into the community ("the Covenant of Grace") "all those who have freely devoted themselves to the observance of God's precepts, that they may be joined to the counsel of God and may live perfectly before him *in accordance with all that has been revealed concerning their appointed times*, and that they may love all the sons of light, each according to his lot in God's design, and hate all the sons of darkness" (1QS 1:8-10; trans. Vermes). This brutal opposition between light and darkness is equally characteristic of apocalyptic, especially of the so-called Epistle of Enoch, the last of the five books of Enoch. It is also, of course, quite explicit on the very first page of the Fourth Gospel. Yet perhaps the most distinctive image in the Gospel of the gulf separating insiders from outsiders is the opposition between above and below, which is the theme I wish to turn to now.

Correspondence: Above and Below

The fourth and last feature of apocalyptic writings to be investigated is what I have called *correspondence*. Of the four it is the most elusive and intangible, but arguably no less important than the others. One scholar who saw its importance and introduced it into his interpretation of the Fourth Gospel was J. Louis

Martyn, who used it to illustrate the two levels, or, as he puts it, the two stages of understanding. Here is what he says:

> John did not create the literary form of the two-level drama. It was at home in the thought-world of Jewish apocalypticism. The dicta most basic to the apocalyptic thinker are these: God created both heaven and earth. There are dramas taking place both on the heavenly stage and on the earthly stage. Yet these dramas are not really two, but rather one drama. For there are corresponding pairs of actors; a beast of a certain description in heaven represents a tyrannical king on earth, etc. Furthermore, the developments in the drama on its heavenly stage determine the developments on the earthly stage. One might say that events on the heavenly stage not only correspond to events on the earthly stage, but also slightly precede them in time, leading them into existence, so to speak. What transpires on the heavenly stage is often called "things to come." For that reason events seen on the earthly stage are entirely enigmatic to the man who sees only the earthly stage. Stereoptic vision is necessary, and it is precisely stereoptic vision which causes a man to write an apocalypse.[12]

Interestingly, what Martyn singles out as "the dicta most basic to the apocalyptic thinker" are ignored altogether in John J. Collins's widely accepted definition of the apocalyptic genre. [See above, p. 107]. But Martyn is not wrong. He recognizes that one distinctive feature of apocalyptic writing is the subsequent projection down to earth of the heavenly events watched and recounted by dreamers and seers. A good example is what Daniel says about the feet of the statue in Nebuchadnezzar's first dream. Having interpreted the upper parts of the statue to represent three successive kingdoms, he then turns to the kingdom that interests him most: the fourth. "As you saw the feet and toes," he tells the king, "partly of potter's clay and partly of iron, it shall be a divided kingdom; but some of the firmness of iron shall be in it, just as you saw iron mixed with the miry clay . . ." (2:41). And so on: the particular characteristics of the fourth kingdom closely correspond to the detailed composition of the statue's feet. After his vision of the statue, the king saw "a stone cut by no human hand," which "smote the image on its feet of iron and clay, and broke them in pieces" (2:34). The interpretation that follows introduces a new, indestructible

---

12. J. Louis Martyn, *History and Theology in the Fourth Gospel* (New York/Evanston: Harper & Row, 1968), 127.

kingdom, founded by God himself, which "shall break in pieces all these kingdoms and bring them to an end . . . just as you saw that a stone was cut from heaven by no human hand, and that it broke in pieces the iron, the bronze, the clay, the silver, and the gold" (2:44-45). So Martyn's suggestion that events on the heavenly stage not only correspond to events on the earthly stage but also, as it were, lead them into existence is a perfectly reasonable one. It would be borne out by a close examination of the other dreams and visions recorded in Daniel's text.

Yet we should not fail to notice that when we apply this analogy to the Gospel the focus shifts quite radically. Martyn is clearly thinking of the relation between the dramatic conflict between Jesus and the Jews portrayed on the story level of the Gospel, and the conflict the evangelist himself had lived through between the Jesus group and the hardliners in the synagogue. What is basically the same conflict, Martyn argues, is resumed at a different time and in a different place. But of course both of these episodes take place on earth, and Martyn nowhere suggests that one of the two stages on which the Johannine drama is enacted is really situated in heaven. The correspondence evident in the apocalyptic literature between the dramatic events in heaven and their counterparts on earth is *spatial*: the temporal element is of secondary importance. In the Gospel, on the other hand, the correspondence is essentially *temporal*. (The confusion is assisted by the ambiguity of the word *stage*, which can be used either of time or of place.) Stereoptic vision (a term that, it should now be clear, must be very loosely understood) may be necessary in both cases, but in an apocalypse we are looking first up to heaven and then down to earth, whereas with the special kind of vision required to appreciate the Gospel we are directed to follow events that happened some time ago and then, with a knowledge of what transpired later, to read them in a new way. So it is now no longer a question of first looking up and then down, but of looking first backwards and then forwards (or, more accurately, of comprehending both past and present in a single vision).

As a consequence of this shift in perspective I have been forced to abandon one more important strand in my argument. Convinced that there must be something in the Gospel to justify a comparison with the correspondence motif that appears in many apocalyptic writings, I struggled to find a similarity that, I am now convinced, is not there. Seduced by the brilliance of Martyn's reflections on the need for stereoptic vision, I failed to realize the importance of the fact that, whereas in the true apocalypse this meant the realization that the events seen to occur in heaven were mirrored by events occurring later on earth, in the Gospel, very differently, the parallel is between the events of Jesus' life and the later experiences of the Johannine community.

Concluding Remarks

Up to this point I have been retracing a program set out twenty years ago in a chapter in *Understanding the Fourth Gospel* entitled "Intimations of Apocalyptic," which was left virtually unchanged in the second edition (2007). But anyone reading what I have written so far in this chapter might reasonably conclude that I have been forced to abandon one by one what I once thought of as four stout planks that could be used to build a platform sturdy enough to support my thesis of a fundamental affinity between the Fourth Gospel and apocalyptic. The motif of the two ages is shared with other early Christian writers, and to some extent with the Qumran community. That of the two stages can equally well be regarded as no more than a reflection of the two levels of understanding, whereby Jesus' deeds and words came to be properly understood only after the resurrection. The clear opposition between insiders and outsiders, though also prominent in many apocalypses, arises from a conflict perceptible in any society in which the members of a breakaway group are attempting to convince themselves that they alone possess the truth. And the theme of correspondence between heaven and earth is missing altogether.

In fact I never went so far as to suggest that the Gospel is an apocalypse in any ordinary sense of the word. But must I now admit that I was wrong to conclude that "the fourth evangelist conceives his work as an apocalypse—in reverse, upside down, inside out"?[13] No, not wrong, because even though I am now obliged to confess that many of the arguments I used to support my thesis were mistaken, or at best misleading, I still believe that I was right to detect in the Gospel a fundamental affinity with apocalyptic that had not previously been observed. Let us take another look at John Collins's widely accepted definition of *apocalypse*:

> a genre of revelatory literature with a narrative framework, in which a revelation is mediated by an otherworldly being to a human recipient, disclosing a transcendent reality which is both temporal, insofar as it envisages eschatological salvation, and spatial insofar as it involves another supernatural world. [See above, p. 107].

---

13. Ashton, *Understanding the Fourth Gospel*, 328–29.

Up to the phrase "eschatological salvation" (which is one way of understanding John's "eternal life") it is hard to deny that the Fourth Gospel fits this definition tolerably well. Of course it does not look like an apocalypse: no human seer is recorded to have had a heavenly dream or vision or to have been transported up to heaven to receive one. Nevertheless, Jesus is certainly thought of as an otherworldly being, and his revelations are mediated within a narrative framework. It is only the conclusion that poses problems, for although Jesus does at one point in the Gospel (3:12) claim to have spoken of "heavenly things," these are nowhere specified, and the evangelist gives no more than the merest hint that Jesus was enabled to speak of these (things that belong to "another supernatural world") by virtue of an ascent into heaven (3:12-13).[14]

Yet almost every page of the Gospel deals with mysteries and heavenly truths. Let us take a fresh look at a few of these pages. What are we to make of the Gospel's frequent allusions to heavenly realities? Toward the beginning of the Gospel, when Nathanael, the "Israelite without guile," confesses his faith ("You are the Son of God! You are the King of Israel!"), he is promised that he "will see heaven opened, and the angels of God ascending and descending upon the Son of Man" (1:49-51), a saying that, on the face of it (this is the first mention of the Son of Man in the Gospel), refers to the angelic Son of Man in Daniel's great vision. And although a moment's reflection tells us that this immediate response cannot be right, and that the Son of Man in question can be none other than Jesus himself, the saying is nevertheless a baffling one, not least because the promise is left unfulfilled. In the book of Revelation the seer tells us that he looked, "and lo, in heaven, an open door" (4:1). In the Gospel of Mark, after Jesus' baptism, when he was coming up out of the water, "immediately he saw the heavens split open and the Spirit descending upon him like a dove" (1:10). In the Gospel of John, where Jesus' baptism is not recorded, there is no open door and no vision of the opening of the heavens—simply the promise of such a vision. It is hard to believe that such a promise, made by Jesus himself, is altogether empty; yet we are left wondering what it can mean and why it was made.

Commentators are agreed that the promise to Nathanael alludes to Jacob's dream at Bethel (the house of God): Jacob dreamed "that there was a ladder set up in heaven and the top of it reached to heaven; and behold the angels of God were ascending and descending on it (Gen. 28:12). In fact, the Hebrew allows an alternative interpretation, according to which the angels were said to be ascending and descending not upon the ladder but upon Jacob himself! This interpretation, which was adopted by some rabbinic commentators, is

14. I will be commenting further on this passage in chapter 8.

the one that lies behind the saying in the Gospel, with the major difference that in the Gospel version of the story the patriarch Jacob—and his ladder—are replaced by the Son of Man. In Genesis, Jacob's ladder fulfills the function of the Babylonian ziggurat (satirized in the story of the Tower of Babel), which was to establish a link between earth and heaven. In the Gospel this function is taken over by the Son of Man. This being so, we can see that part at least of what Jesus is saying is that he himself, in his role as Son of Man, is the true intermediary between heaven and earth. Kick away the ladder! A little further on in the narrative he asserts that "no one has ascended into heaven but he who descended from heaven, the Son of Man" (3:13): there is no further mention of the angels of Jacob's dream, and the ascent/descent motif from now on is associated exclusively with the Son of Man.

A little later, concluding his conversation with Nicodemus, Jesus asserts, "we speak of what we know, and bear witness to what we have seen" (3:11). What exactly, though, *did* he see? He claims to have seen "heavenly things" (v. 12), and implicitly, therefore, to be speaking of them. But just as the promise to Nathanael (that he will see the heavens opened) is never fulfilled, neither, apparently, is Jesus' claim to be speaking of heavenly things. Both of these claims are, in the strong sense, *apocalyptic*. They amount to assertions involving the revelation of heavenly mysteries. But such a revelation never seems to be given. Rudolf Bultmann, time and again, insisted that Jesus' revelation has no content: all that he reveals is that he is the Revealer—no what, just a naked that. Wayne Meeks, in the same context, speaks of "empty revelation forms."[15] But to leave the matter there seems curiously unsatisfactory. For who can read this Gospel without a pervasive sense that somehow or other heavenly things are spoken of on virtually every page? I believe that the evangelist himself would endorse this comment. The concluding paragraph of chapter 3, which represents the evangelist's own reflections on the preceding dialogue with Nicodemus,[16] insists upon Jesus' heavenly status:

He who comes from above is above all; he who is of the earth belongs to the earth, and of the earth he speaks; he who comes from heaven is above all. He bears witness to what he has seen and heard, yet no one receives his testimony; he who receives his testimony sets his seal to this, that God is true. For he whom God has sent utters the words of God, for it is not by measure that he gives the Spirit; the

15. Wayne A. Meeks, "The Man from Heaven in Johannine Sectarianism," *Journal of Biblical Literature* 91 (1972): 44–72.

16. Reasons for reading the passage in this way are given in *Understanding the Fourth Gospel*, 277–80.

Father loves the Son and has given all things into his hand. He who believes in the Son has eternal life; he who does not obey the Son shall not see life, but the wrath of God rests upon him. (3:31-36)

This is not the first time in this Gospel that something affirmed in one sentence is seemingly contradicted in the next (see 1:12). No one receives the testimony of the one from above; no one listens to what Jesus has to say. No: wrong—at least one person *does* receive his testimony. I take that person to be the evangelist himself. How, though, does he set about stating this message, affirming it in the strongest possible way, by setting his seal to it? He says first, very simply: God is true. What does he mean? He means that when he himself, the evangelist, records the testimony that he and he alone has accepted from the man from heaven, what he is really recording is the message of God himself; *for he whom God has sent* [namely, Jesus] *utters the words of God.* By adding a comment concerning his own work toward the end of a passage especially rich in theological content, the evangelist is singling it out and drawing his readers' attention to it, something he does quite rarely. And despite the fact that the whole story is set on earth, the one who delivers the message, the Jesus of the Gospel, does not belong on earth at all. If he did he would speak of earthly things, but the truth is that he belongs to heaven; he "comes from above" and "is above all."

A further explanation is added: it is not by measure that he gives the Spirit. The subject of this verb, the one who gives the Spirit, is probably God; but the best-attested manuscript reading of this verse leaves open the possibility that the subject is the one who utters the words of God, namely, Jesus. But of course the whole thrust of the passage tells us that this would make no difference: whether sent by God (14:26) or by Jesus (16:7), the Spirit is the one who makes it possible for those who receive the testimony to comprehend it. (Had this passage been properly understood by the future champions of East and West, who were to argue interminably over who sent the Spirit, the church might have been spared centuries of schism and discord.)

I have not space to comment fully on the whole of John 3, one of the richest chapters in the Gospel. But no one reading this passage will wish to leave out heaven altogether. Jesus unquestionably asserts that his message, what he has seen and heard, is a heavenly message. Yet "the heavenly things" of which he spoke earlier in the chapter (3:12) *are nothing more than the record of Jesus' words and deeds in the Gospel that John is writing,* words and deeds that are poles apart from the kind of heavenly events recounted by visionaries like Daniel and Enoch in the books that bear their names. Yet these words and deeds are no less truly revelations—revelations concerning a human life made by the one that lived it. Conveyed as they are by the evangelist, speaking as a witness of what Jesus said and did in the presence of his disciples before his resurrection, they have been transformed, reshaped, and re-envisioned through the special understanding bestowed by the Paraclete. The Paraclete is also a witness, but his witness is not something added to or separable from the witness of the evangelist and his community. Throughout the Gospel, whoever is doing the witnessing, whether it is John the Baptist, Moses and the Scriptures, the Paraclete, the disciples, and finally the evangelist himself, the object of the witness, what they are witnessing to, is none other than Jesus himself, not in his preexistence or in his eventual abode in heaven, but in his earthly life, recollected and newly conceived. So the new revelation is the Gospel itself, a story set on earth—which is why it may be called an apocalypse in reverse.

Yet in spite of the Gospel's affinities with the Jewish apocalypses, it would be wrong to ignore the differences. The basic conviction the evangelist shared with the apocalyptic writers who preceded and followed him was that God had further mysteries to reveal above and beyond the Torah. And as in the Jewish apocalypses, these were communicated by one known to be a heavenly being. But unlike the angels of the apocalypses, the Revealer of the Fourth Gospel had descended to earth from heaven. Above all the fourth evangelist differs from his predecessors in insisting that his own new revelation altogether supersedes the earlier revelation given through Moses. Those who accept this new revelation are in possession of a wonderful truth that, it is no exaggeration to say, is the central message of Christianity. The Gospel of John contains this message in its purest form.

Excursus III. The Changing Gospel

How you read the Gospel will depend largely on the importance you attach to the problem spots, or aporias, as scholars call them, from a Greek word meaning "impasse," points at which the continuity of the Gospel, read carefully, is open to question. Most readers, of course, are blithely unaware of these problem spots and would no doubt endorse the suggestion of David Friedrich Strauss (famous for his skepticism about the historical reliability of the Synoptic Gospels), who wondered whether the Gospel itself might be said to be that seamless robe—*ungenähter Leibrock*, χιτὼν ἄραφος—of which the Gospel itself speaks (John 19:23)[1] But once you study the Gospel more closely you notice that at various points there is indeed a lack of continuity, most obviously at the end of chapter 14, where Jesus concludes a long discourse by saying, "Let's move away from here," and then carries on talking for a further three chapters. With a little ingenuity all these aporias can be explained, or at least explained away. C. H. Dodd, who insists on reading the Gospel "as it has come down to us," says about this one that "the movement is a movement of the spirit, an interior act of will, but a real departure nevertheless."[2] But like most of the other difficult conjunctions, the easiest and the best solution to this puzzle is the quite straightforward hypothesis that the author has introduced new material at this point—which means that the Gospel was not composed at a sitting but over a long period of time. This is not a new idea: it is well expounded in a little book by Barnabas Lindars called *Behind the Fourth Gospel*,[3] and also, less systematically, by Martin Hengel in *The Johannine Question*: "the Gospel was not written down quickly in a few weeks or months, but grew quite slowly, over what period and in how many stages we do not know."[4] Nevertheless

---

1. David Friedrich Strauss, *Gesammelte Schriften* 7 (Leipzig, 1877), 556. (Better translated as "robe" than as "tunic." Is there any such thing as a seamless tunic?).

2. C. H. Dodd, *The Interpretation of the Fourth Gospel* (Cambridge: Cambridge University Press), 1953), 290, 409.

3. Barnabas Lindars, *Behind the Fourth Gospel*, Studies in Creative Criticism 3 (London: SPCK, 1971).

4. "The different 'strata', breaks, supposed 'contradictions', inconsistencies and explanatory glosses," he adds, "are best explained as a result of this slow growth of the Gospel" (Martin Hengel, *The Johannine Question* [Philadelphia: Trinity Press International, 1989], 94–95). "Who of us," he asks later, "has not inserted additional sentences into his or her own manuscript, thus breaking the sentence sequence without noticing? In an author unused to literary work like the head of a school it would be remarkable if this did not happen here and there" (p. 100).

the majority of commentators, compelled by the nature of the commentary genre to start at the beginning and carry on to the end, pay no attention to suggestions of this kind; and many, like Dodd, express what amounts to a moral disapproval of any reading that deals honestly with the aporias. So although some of the most perceptive of Johannine scholars (Raymond Brown and Barnabas Lindars among them) have argued persuasively that the Gospel cannot be properly understood as a continuous composition, most scholars nowadays, certainly in the English-speaking world, refuse to allow what is sometimes called a *diachronic* (as opposed to a *synchronic*) approach to the text, and treat the Gospel as if it was a fully coherent piece of writing, structured from the outset with care and deliberation.

In principle there is no contradiction between the synchronic and the diachronic approach. These terms are ultimately derived from a series of lectures by the famous student of linguistics Ferdinand de Saussure, first published in 1916 under the title *Cours de linguistique générale*. De Saussure recognized that the synchronic study of a language at a particular point in time could not be combined with the (diachronic) study of its historical development, but he acknowledged the validity of both approaches and lectured on each of them separately. It is true that works of literature are more complex than languages in one important respect, because any significant addition to or rearrangement of, say, a novel or a play is bound to affect its meaning. The difficulty is most acute when we have to do with classical writings such as the Bible or the works of Homer, because long tradition has hallowed not just the books themselves but the order in which they have been read over many centuries. The obvious solution, then, is to admit both kinds of reading. Dodd argues for the synchronic reading of John's Gospel on the grounds that "the present order is not fortuitous, but deliberately devised by somebody—even if he were only a scribe doing his best—and that the author in question (whether the author or another) had some design in mind, and was not necessarily irresponsible or unintelligent."[5] This is a rather lame and halting advocacy of the synchronic approach. Better, surely, to admit the difficulties, and try to account for them. The resulting (diachronic) view of the text, once its implications have been properly recognized, can give way later to a full, synchronic, holistic reading. In this way we have some chance of arriving at an understanding of the aims and methods of the final redactor—who may well be the author himself, not just

---

5. Dodd, *Interpretation*, 290.

"a scribe doing his best." This is the best way of approaching the *Iliad*;[6] and it is how Germanists approach Goethe's *Faust*.[7]

Since my general argument rests on the hypothesis that there were at least two editions (or rather stages)[8] of the Gospel, I need to offer some defense of that hypothesis here. (There may have been more than two, but I leave that question aside.) I will argue that the Gospel was not written at a sitting, or in a matter of days, or even (probably) in a matter of months. Like the community within which and for which it was composed, it changed: it had a history. Although I am confident that this thesis can be proved with tolerable certainty, I do not want claim an equal certainty for my own version of the Gospel's many additions and alterations, which must have been made gradually over several months, possibly years. The evangelist (and I am confident that most of what we now call the Gospel of John was the work of a single individual) did not deliberately plant clues to these changes at various points in his book so as to be sure they would be picked up by clever readers years later, when he was no longer there to help them. On the other hand, he was not concerned to smooth over the difficult junctures consequent upon his alterations and insertions. These clumsy transitions, or aporias, whose very awkwardness makes them evident to an alert reader, are discernible in several places and will form the main stepping-stones of my argument. Like a number of other scholars, I perceive them as standing proud from the surface of the Gospel text; though of course to many others (such as C. K. Barrett) they seem at the very most no more than negligible bumps or blemishes. Disagreements about the relative significance of all or any of them are inevitable. The most significant aporia (if we leave aside the problem of chapter 21 and the puzzle of the end of chapter 14, both of which I have dealt with previously)[9] comes between chapters 5 and

---

6. M. L. West, in a recent study of the *Iliad*, sums up his hypothesis in his preface: "that the poet progressively amplified his work, not just by adding more at the end but by making insertions in parts already composed" (*The Making of the Iliad* [Oxford: Oxford University Press, 2011], v). My sentiments exactly! In an *envoi*, West quotes from J. Enoch Powell's preface to a similarly inspired work on Herodotus, published in 1939: "I make myself no illusions about the unpopularity to which a work of dissection is doomed—in England especially." Powell concludes, "The moment anyone attempts to trace out such a process in one particular case, he finds himself face to face with the whole forces of prejudice and thoughtlessness" (quoted in West, *Making of the Iliad*, 431).

7. Germanists benefit from the survival of an *Urfaust*. Classical and biblical scholars are not so lucky: any *Ur-Ilias* or *Ur-Johannes* can be nothing more than a postulate.

8. The term *edition*, which suggests publication, is misleading, because the author may well have made most of the changes in his manuscript before publishing it. I have retained *edition* here because it is the word used by Brown and Lindars, the authors whom I am following at this point.

6. Since this provides important evidence that the Gospel underwent at least two editions, it requires further comment here.

If the great scholars of previous generations, chief among them Julius Wellhausen,[10] Eduard Schwartz,[11] and Rudolf Bultmann,[12] had been told that the time would come when their successors would dismiss as of no importance or significance the problems they themselves had sweated over for so long, they would probably have responded with incredulity. Some sort of turning point, I think, is marked by the work of C. K. Barrett, who in 1978 published a second, much expanded, edition of his careful and scholarly commentary.[13] Barrett, very much aware of the earlier labors of Bultmann, whom he obviously respects, mentions a half-dozen of the most obvious difficulties in a section of his introduction headed "Theories of Displacement and Redaction." Rightly, I think, he finds Bultmann's own displacement theory to be unsatisfactory, but instead of attempting an alternative explanation of his own, he concludes, "Neither displacement theories nor redaction theories are needed to explain the present state of the gospel, in which certain roughnesses undoubtedly remain, together with an undoubted impression of a vigorous unity of theme."[14] So what is his explanation of what he calls "roughnesses"? He has none to give. Yet he has just summarized, in a footnote, the excellent suggestion of Barnabas Lindars that the Gospel underwent two editions, a suggestion that involves an astute and, in my view, plausible solution to the problem spots or roughnesses that Barrett himself is content to leave unexplained. He must have looked at

9. John Ashton, *Understanding the Fourth Gospel* (Oxford: Clarendon, 1991), 30–32; 2nd ed. (2007), 42–44. In this context, see the sensible observation of Martin Hengel (using the term *interventions*, where I would prefer *insertions*): "That these interventions were made sparingly and cautiously is evident from the fact that such disruptive breaks and 'contradictions' have been left without being attended to. How easy it would have been to omit the offensive [*sic*] demand in 14.31b! No one would then have supposed that this was the 'original ending' of the farewell discourse" (*Johannine Question*, 106–7). I interpret *offensive* here to mean "problematic."

10. Julius Wellhausen, *Erweiterungen und Änderungen im vierten Evangelium* (Berlin: Georg Reimer, 1907).

11. Eduard Schwartz, "Aporien im vierten Evangelium," in *Nachrichten von der Königlichen Gesellschaft der Wissenschaft zu Göttingen: Philologisch-historische Klasse* (1907): 342–72; (1909): 115–48, 497–650. (Well over two hundred pages!).

12. Throughout his commentary Bultmann offers solutions for dozens of aporias. See too his review of two books by Emanuel Hirsch: "Hirsch's Auslegung des Johannesevangeliums," *Evangelische Theologie* 4 (1937): 115–42.

13. C. K. Barrett, *The Gospel according to St. John: An Introduction with Commentary and Notes on the Greek Text*, 2nd ed. (London: SPCK, 1978).

14. Barrett, *Gospel*, 26.

Lindars's work with some care, but having done so he immediately looked away again. Although he discusses each of the difficulties in turn when he comes to them in the body of his commentary,[15] he always finds some kind of justification for leaving the text as it has been transmitted, and he ends by opting for the conservative solution.

Worth pointing out is the difference between Barrett's approach and that of some of his contemporaries, especially Lindars (whom I have just mentioned) and Raymond Brown. Both of these scholars, whose commentaries are among the very finest of a score or more that one could name, recognize that the best explanation of the Gospel's aporias is that it went through at least two editions. Understandably they shy away from the daunting task of organizing their work (as Bultmann did) in a sequence corresponding to their compositional theories.[16] But, unlike Barrett, they acknowledge that commentators should take account of the different stages in their interpretation of the Gospel.

In this respect Lindars and Brown, along with J. Louis Martyn (the importance of whose contribution to Johannnine studies is widely acknowledged) are poles apart from most of their successors. R. Alan Culpepper's *Anatomy of the Fourth Gospel*, published in 1983, which can be seen in retrospect to have been the first of a whole fleet of new "literary critical" studies of the Gospel, contains the following pronouncement: "dissection and stratification have no place in the study of the gospel and may confuse one's view of the text."[17] As we have already noted, C. H. Dodd, in his *Interpretation of the Fourth Gospel*, had championed a similar, equally intransigent strategy of interpretation thirty years earlier; but Culpepper is the first scholar, as far as I know, to base his opposition to what he terms "dissection and stratification" on literary critical principles. (Richard Bauckham's appeal to "literary criticism's sensitivity," which we noticed in Excursus II, relies for its apparent plausibility on the work of Culpepper and the many studies of the Gospel that followed in its wake.)

---

15. See, for example, p. 219 (on 3:22-30), p. 272 (on the transition between chapters 5 and 6), p. 317 (on 7:15), p. 367 (on the lack of a link between chapters 9 and 10), p. 377 (on whether 10:19 should follow 9:41), and pp. 454 and 470 (on the conclusion of chapter 14).

16. Apart from Bultmann the only commentators to attempt some such reorganization are Jürgen Becker, *Das Evangelium nach Johannes*, 2 vols. (Gütersloh: Gütersloher Verlagshaus Mohn, 1979/81), and Marie-Emile Boismard and Arnaud Lamouille, *Synopse des quatre évangiles en français*, iii. *L'Évangile de Jean* (Paris: Éditions du Cerf, 1977).

17. R. Alan Culpepper, *The Anatomy of the Fourth Gospel: A Study in Literary Design* (Minneapolis: Fortress, 1983), 5.

Fernando F. Segovia, in a short but illuminating article in which he charts his own changing loyalties to one method after another in the study of the Gospel, distinguishes three different approaches: first, historical criticism (the method of study I myself continue to favor); second, literary criticism (the approach of Culpepper and his successors); and, third, "cultural studies," a movement he himself had recently joined and whose acceptance by biblical scholars he ascribes to "the influx into the discipline of individuals who had never been part of it before and who were now [he is writing in 1996] making their voices heard for the first time, Western women, non-Western readers and critics, and racial/ethnic minorities in the West."[18] (This movement is one manifestation of what is more generally called postmodernism.)

Commenting on the change from historical to literary criticism, Segovia has this to say:

> One can readily see how the established discourse and practice of tradition criticism would be directly and severely affected by such a different interpretive framework, given the shift away from textual disruption to textual smoothness, from a problematic and unintelligible text to a unified and coherent text, from a reading in search of stages of composition to a reading in search of arrangement and development, from a text that reflected/engaged the situation of the community to a text that became an object of attention in its own right. . . . The focus would lie no longer on the historical process of composition and its various stages of formation but rather on the literary process of composition with its artistic devices, strategic concerns and aims, and intertextual echoes or references.[19]

What puzzles me in these remarks is the way Segovia slips easily from the method of study to the text itself, as if the distinction between these was of no significance. In the text itself there is no shift from textual disruption to textual smoothness or from unintelligibility to coherence: what has changed is not the text but the angle of vision. You can choose to notice what Barrett calls the roughnesses in the text, or you can choose to ignore them; but you cannot simply wish them away. One may question too whether the change of focus from the historical process of composition to the literary process of composition

18. Fernando F. Segovia, "The Tradition History of the Fourth Gospel," in *Exploring the Gospel of John: In Honor of D. Moody Smith*, ed. R. Alan Culpepper and C. Clifton Black (Louisville: Westminster John Knox, 1996), 183–84.

19. Segovia, "Tradition History," 182–83.

can be carried through as smoothly as Segovia appears to suggest. Two very different and surely irreconcilable ways of explaining the bumps and blemishes in the Gospel text may have to be settled by rational discussion; but advocates of the newer methods often seem reluctant to engage in the kind of argument required to decide who is right and who is wrong in this matter. A discontinuity in the text resulting from an awkward and badly concealed insertion cannot reasonably be explained *at the same time* as an example of a carefully planned and executed artistic device. Reflecting on the change in his own understanding of the Gospel, Segovia says this:

> I find myself less and less favorably disposed towards those approaches to the Gospel that highlight the disruptive character of the text and use perceived aporias as a key point of departure for reading the text. In fact, the more liberally such a technique is invoked, the less receptive I become. Why? I would respond that by and large I find that the proposed aporias can be readily explained in other—and, I would add, simpler ways.[20]

Readers who, instead of ignoring the aporias, prefer to look and see what can be learned from them about the composition of the Gospel, will find themselves frustrated by the unsubstantiated assertion that there are simpler ways of explaining them. On the previous page Segovia had accused historical criticism (or tradition history) of being "predisposed towards aporias," instead of being "oriented towards unity and coherence, or interested in questions of strategies and 'texts.' "[21] But it is not so much a matter of being "predisposed" toward aporias, as of a readiness to recognize them for what they are and a reluctance to brush them under the carpet. The truth is that we all start out by looking for unity and do not give up on it without good reason.

Segovia makes a further admission:

> My argument is not that I have unveiled the real meaning of the text (its actual structure, arrangement, and development) or discovered the intention of the author (whether real or intended), but that I can advance such a reading of the text in the light of the evidence, the textual features and constraints, that I find in it. . . . My proposed

---

20. Segovia, "Tradition History," 186. Nonetheless, at two points (chapters 15–16 and chapter 21) Segovia admits that he finds himself "reluctant to give up altogether on the presence of disruptive aporias."

21. Segovia, "Tradition History," 185.

reading of the Gospel ultimately says as much about me as about the Gospel, if not more.[22]

In that case, one is tempted to say, why should we bother to read Segovia if what really interests us is the Gospel of John?

Some thirty years ago, in a half-dozen pages of a chapter entitled "The Community and Its Book" in the first edition of *Understanding the Fourth Gospel*, I set out clearly and concisely my own conclusions concerning the composition of the Gospel, conclusions repeated sixteen years later, with a few minor corrections, in the second edition. Nothing I have seen since in the work of those Johannine scholars, the large majority, who have abandoned traditional historical criticism,[23] has persuaded me to change my mind. I will not repeat those conclusions in full, but, because the thesis of the present book is so intricately bound up with parts of this general theory, I will briefly summarize them before proceeding to some more detailed arguments.

1. Underlying the present text of the Gospel is what German scholars call a *Grundschrift*, often named a Signs Source, but which I prefer to think of as a missionary manifesto, written to promote faith in Jesus as the Messiah and as the prophet foretold by Moses.[24]

2. This manifesto was accepted by some members of a Jewish synagogue, but not by all. The disagreements that ensued between the traditionalists and the partisans of Jesus (the Jesus group) went on for a long time, culminating in a breakdown of communications and finally in the complete separation of the two parties.[25]

---

22. Segovia, "Tradition History," 186.

23. Introducing a collection of narrative-critical essays that he edited under the title of *The Gospel of John: An Anthology of Twentieth Century Perspectives,* New Testament Tools and Studies 17 (Leiden: Brill, 1993), Mark Stibbe calls attention on the first page of the book to a loss of historical consciousness among his contributors, leading to the rejection of historical criticism in "nearly all the books which study the final form of John's Gospel."

24. I have attempted a reconstruction of this in *Understanding the Fourth Gospel*, 185–94 (Excursus IV: A Call to Faith). Martyn thinks that "a recoverable literary stratum," constituting "part of a very early sermon which must have lain at the origin of the Johannine community," can be found behind John 1:35-49. For him, this sermon belongs to "the Early Period" of the community: see his essay "Glimpses into the History of the Johannine Community," in *The Gospel of John in Christian History: Essays for Interpreters* (New York: Paulist, 1979), 90–121. In my view it belongs rather to the prehistory of the community, and originally, though it came to be used to introduce the Gospel, it was more likely to have been a missionary manifesto than a sermon.

3. Many of the arguments that preceded the breakdown are remembered in controversy stories that figure importantly in the first edition of the Gospel, which also contained revelatory sayings and longer discourses of a prophetic nature.

4. The second edition of the Gospel contained a new introduction (the Prologue), an extra chapter (chapter 6), an expansion of the Farewell Discourse (chapters 15–17), and a different explanation of the decision to put Jesus to death (chapter 11), which led to the displacement of the temple episode to its present position in chapter 2.[26]

I will conclude with a thorough examination of the awkward conjunction between John 5 and 6, one of the two most significant problem spots justifying the conclusion that there must have been (at least) two editions of the Gospels.[27]

Between John 5 and John 6

This problem has traditionally been seen as one of *order*. It has appeared to many students of the Gospel that chapter 6 should come not after chapter 5 but before. This is how Bultmann states and solves the problem:

> The present order of chs. 5 and 6 cannot be the original one. Since in 6.1 Jesus goes "to the other side" (πέραν) of the lake, he must have been at the lake-side beforehand; but in ch. 5 he is in Jerusalem. Thus ch. 6 has no connection with ch. 5. On the other hand it would follow on ch. 4 very well [because Jesus is in Galilee at the end of that chapter]. Correspondingly, 7.1 assumes that Jesus had been staying in Judaea (Jerusalem) up till then, and ch. 7 would thus link up with ch. 5. So the original order must have been 4, 6, 5, 7. This is confirmed by the fact that this order makes good sense of 4.44, which otherwise makes no sense at all, and also by the fact that 6.2 (τὰ σημεῖα . . . ἐπὶ τῶν ἀσθενούντων ["the signs he performed on those who were diseased"]) is now seen to be a reference back to the exemplary story

---

25. Martyn assigns both of these disagreements and the eventual rupture to what he calls "the Middle Period" of the community ("Glimpses," 102–7).

26. Both the first and the second edition of the Gospel belong to what for Martyn is "the Late Period" ("Glimpses," 107–21).

27. The other problem spot, the ending of chapter 14, I discuss in *Understanding the Fourth Gospel*, 1st ed., 30–32. The argument concerning John 6, already set out in *Understanding*, 2nd ed., 44–48, is repeated here because it is so important for the thesis of the present book.

of 4.46–54. It also enables us to see the chronological order which the Evangelist had in mind. The festival which was imminent in 6.4 has started in 5.1. Finally 7.1 states that Jesus left Judaea because the Jews wanted to kill him, which is appropriate only as a reference back to 5.18 provided ch. 5 immediately preceded ch. 7. Moreover the themes which are discussed in chs. 5 and 6 make the order 6, 5 more probable. Ch. 6 shows that the revelation is the κρίσις of man's natural desire for life, ch. 5 that it is the κρίσις of his religion. In ch. 6 we have the dispute with the people, in ch. 5 with their leaders.[28]

Bultmann rightly sees that the primary difficulty is *contextual*. There can be no doubt, I think, that if the problems he highlights so effectively could be solved simply by rearranging the material his solution would work very well, and it is not surprising (as he himself says in a note) that he was not the first to propose it (nor the last). (It had been put forward in fact as early as the fourteenth century[29] and is also the preferred solution of Rudolf Schnackenburg and Jürgen Becker.) But if one is relying on the dislocation hypothesis, it is too good to be true. For if the Gospel had in fact been composed not on a scroll but on a codex and its leaves had somehow become lost and jumbled up in the way the theory requires, then it becomes hard to credit that once they had been gathered together again the evangelist (or anyone else already acquainted with the material) would have reassembled them in the wrong order.

The synchronists, however, have a different problem, because they have to make sense of chapters 5 and 6 as they stand. How do they manage to do this? Dodd gets around the problem by ignoring it. He does, to be fair, discuss many of the other aporias (though never convincingly), but not this one. He correctly observes an important break between chapters 4 and 5, which starts with a journey to Jerusalem. But the difficult transition, as Bultmann notes, is between chapters 5 and 6, where without warning we suddenly find Jesus in Galilee again, at the lakeside. Dodd contents himself with observing that "the introductory sentences, vi.1–3, bring together motives which belong to the common substance of the Gospel tradition."[30] Not a word about the

---

28. Rudolf Bultmann, *The Gospel of John: A Commentary* (Oxford: Basil Blackwell, 1971), 209–10.

29. By Ludolph of Saxony; see J. H. Bernard, *A Critical and Exegetical Commentary on the Gospel according to St. John*, ed. A. H. McNeale, 2 vols., International Critical Commentary (Edinburgh: T&T Clark, 1928), 1:xvii n.1. Much earlier if you count Tatian, who puts John 6 (in chapters 18–20 of the *Diatessaron*), before John 4–5 (in chapters 21–22).

30. Dodd, *Interpretation*, 333.

sudden shift of location, nor about the difficulties that have induced many commentators to transpose chapters 5 and 6.

A solution from the literary critical or narratological camp has been proposed by Mark Stibbe. Following up an observation that the plot, characterization, and vocabulary of the Gospel seem designed to evoke a sense of elusiveness, mystery, excitement, and suspense, he continues by quoting a remark of H. E. Edwards concerning the itinerary of chapters 5 and 6: "It is as if you were reading a letter from a friend in which he was telling you about salmon fishing in Scotland, and then, as you turn the page, the letter went on, 'After this I went over London Bridge.'"[31] "It is not impossible," comments Stibbe, "that the author intended this sequence in order to heighten the sense of Jesus' ability to move about so quickly and so elusively." Not impossible, perhaps, but surely not very likely. Is this, I wonder, one of those simple solutions to the aporias of the kind favored by Bauckham and Segovia?

Craig Keener disposes of the difficulty toward the beginning of his exegesis of chapter 5:

To keep the Gospel's geography neater, some have argued that chs. 5 and 6 have been transposed, but this approach does not take into account what John simply assumes, namely major chronological as well as geographical gaps (e.g. 7:2; 10:22; 11:55). While such transposition is conceivable for pages in a codex, it is difficult to conceive such an accident for the earliest version, on scrolls;[32] and no manuscripts attest the alleged transposition. It is possible that 6:28-29 depends on the prior description of the works of Father and Son in 5:20, 36. Further, . . . the closing paragraph of ch. 5 presents Jesus as one greater than Moses, which becomes a central theme in ch. 6. 'After these things' (μετὰ ταῦτα) is a common chronological transition device.[33]

---

31. H. E. Edwards, *The Disciple Who Wrote These Things: A New Inquiry into the Origins and Historical Value of the Gospel according to St. John* (London: J. Clarke, 1953), 53.

32. This seems to be a sheer assumption on Keener's part. The papyrologists Colin H. Roberts and T.C. Skeat conclude on the basis of the number and spread of the second- and third-century papyrus fragments of the Gospels, and the early date of some of them, that "all in all, it is impossible to believe that the Christian adoption of the codex can have taken place any later than *circa* AD 100 (it may of course have been earlier)" (*The Birth of the Codex* [London: Oxford University Press for the British Academy, 1983], 61).

33. Craig S. Keener, *The Gospel of John: A Commentary*, 2 vols. (Peabody, Mass.: Hendrickson, 2003), 634.

Since "the major chronological as well as geographical gaps" are among the Gospel's salient aporias,[34] to assume that John assumes them, in an otherwise continuous narrative, is to beg the question. It comes as no surprise to find that Keener, like all partisans of synchronicity, gets around many of the Gospel's aporias (in his case 14:31 as well as 7:2 and 10:22) by ignoring them.

Nevertheless his concluding observation concerning the presentation of Jesus as one greater than Moses is worth following up. A similar comment is made by Andrew Lincoln, for whom the transposition theory "may well be over-concerned with geographical issues at the expense of thematic links."[35] Peder Borgen has a short study of John 6 in which, after excusing himself from the task of dealing with the relationship of that chapter with chapter 5, he observes that "the final part of the discourse in 5:19-47 might serve as the thematic background of ch. 6: Jn 6.31-58 serves as an illustration of the searching of the Scriptures mentioned in Jn 5.39-40. The phrase ἐραυνᾶτε τὰς γραφάς in Jn 5.39 is even a Greek equivalent of the technical term for performing a midrashic exegesis."[36] Borgen follows this observation up with further arguments to the same effect but fails to note that Barnabas Lindars had made exactly the same point in 1972 in support of his suggestion that chapter 6 is *a later insertion.*[37] Unwilling to consider how this chapter follows on from what precedes, Borgen sidesteps the real difficulty: if the evangelist wished to illustrate his point about Jesus as the fulfillment of Scripture, why nevertheless did he not add a verse or two in explanation of his sudden return to Galilee?

Unlike Martin Hengel, not one of these authors—Bultmann, Dodd, Stibbe, Keener, Borgen—even considers the possibility that the Gospel was not composed at a single sitting but over a period of years. Yet it is surely much more likely that the evangelist *added* an extra chapter at this point without taking the trouble to make the adjustments that a smooth transition would require than that he neglected to provide a link while engaged in the process of a continuous composition.[38] Elsewhere in his Gospel, when Jesus moves from

34. John 7:2, which places Jesus in Judea (when at the end of ch. 6 he is still in Galilee) belongs, as Bultmann saw, to the same complex of problems as the one under discussion. John 10:22 is connected with the puzzling transition between chapters 9 and 10. See my essay, "The Shepherd," in *Studying John: Approaches to the Fourth Gospel* (Oxford: Clarendon, 1994), 114–40: 11:55 is irrelevant in this context—it is not a problem but a parenthesis.

35. Andrew T. Lincoln, *The Gospel according to St John,* Black's New Testament Commentaries 4 (Peabody, Mass.: Hendrickson, 2005), 210.

36. Peder Borgen, "Observations on the Midrashic Character of John 6," *Zeitschrift für die neutestamentliche Wissenschaft* 54 (1963): 233–34.

37. This is the more surprising because he actually refers to Lindars's suggestion (and to my support of it) on the preceding page.

one place to another the evangelist says so.[39] Why not here? The Gospel records in 6:1 that Jesus crossed the Sea of Galilee but says not a word about how he got to Galilee in the first place. Why not? Lindars's answer, elegant and economic (and effectively supported by Borgen) is surely the best of the many solutions on offer. If it has not been considered seriously by subsequent commentators this can only be because they have not entertained the proposal that the composition of the Gospel was interrupted, perhaps more than once, while the Jesus group was experiencing major changes in its relationship with the synagogue.

It should be observed that the relationship between Jesus and "the Jews" is very different in chapters 5 and 6. As happens so often, internal dissension is accompanied by a slackening of hostility toward enemies from without. The implacably resentful persecutors of the previous chapter have given way to groups of people divided among themselves. Jesus' interlocutors, though often referred to by the vague term *crowd*, [40] continue nevertheless to be called οἱ Ἰουδαῖοι (6:4, 41, 52). In this chapter, however, their "grumbling" (γογγυσμός, v. 41) is prompted more by bewilderment than by a real antagonism. The best explanation of this change of attitude is that the two chapters represent different periods of the community's relationship with "the Jews."

38. See n. 9 above, on the end of ch. 14.

39. See John 2:2, 12, 13; 3:22; 4:3, 43, 46; 5:1; 7:10; 10:22, 40; 11:54; 12:1, 12-14. The fact that the Gospel says nothing about any change of time and place between 7:10 and 10:22 constitutes another aporia, one I have treated in detail in "Shepherd," 114–40.

40. The word ὄχλος occurs four times in this chapter, eight times in chapter 7 (where the controversies belong to an earlier stage in the history of the Johannine group), seven times in chapters 11–12, and only once elsewhere in the Gospel (5: 13).

7

The Mission of the Prophet

QUESTIONS IN CONTEXT

In the preceding six chapters I have been setting the scene for the remaining three. I now want to focus directly on the three strong streams of Jewish tradition that flowed into the Christology of the Fourth Gospel. One of these will be dealt with in this chapter (the mission of the prophet) and two in the next (the Incarnation of Wisdom and the Son of Man). Finally, in the concluding chapter, I will tackle the problem that prompted me to write this book—the problem of John's switch of allegiance from Judaism to Christianity. But first I need to place my book in the larger context of the questions that have been addressed to the Gospel since Adolf Harnack, in 1886, declared the origin of the Johannine writings to be "the most marvelous enigma [or riddle] that the history of early Christianity presents."[1] Rudolf Bultmann, taking up this riddle in his first major statement on the Gospel, gave it an extra twist by placing the Gospel in an exclusively Christian context. For him the riddle was "where John's Gospel stands in relation to the development of early Christianity"[2] (actually a misleading way of putting the question, because he was already confident that the Gospel did not belong to any of the three main branches of Christian doctrinal development). First proposed in 1925 and carried through with enormous consistency in his commentary of 1941, the solution he offered (a revelation discourse source) effectively isolated the Gospel from all other (particularly Jewish) sources, except insofar as these had already impacted upon the Gnostic texts he uses.

---

1. Adolf von Harnack, *History of Dogma,* 7 vols. (New York: Russel & Russell, 1958), 1:96–97 (first German ed., 1886).

2. Rudolf Bultmann, "Die Bedeutung der neuerschlossenen mandäischen und manichäischen Quellen für das Verständnis des Johannesevangeliums," *Zeitschrift für die neutestamentliche Wissenschaft* 24 (1925): 100.

Four years after the appearance of Bultmann's commentary came the end of the Second World War, and two years after that the discovery of the first Dead Sea Scrolls, after which, largely due to the pioneering efforts of, among others, Raymond E. Brown, it became impossible to ignore the Jewish origins of the Fourth Gospel. Benefiting from the work of Brown, whose commentary was complete by 1968, I myself added a different twist to Bultmann's formulation of the problem. In a book published in 1991, exactly fifty years after the appearance of his commentary, I proposed that for Bultmann's "Christian" we should substitute "Jewish," asking instead "what is the position of the Gospel in *Jewish thought*."[3]

Meanwhile, however, another significant shift of direction had taken place. After the collapse of Bultmann's Mandaean hypothesis, no one had been bold enough to suggest an equally comprehensive alternative. The reasons for this universal hesitation are laid out clearly and concisely in the introduction to Wayne Meeks's *Prophet-King*.[4] Bultmann had assumed that the key features of John's Christology (or rather of the Gnostic myth that lies behind it) requires a single large explanation, that of the Gnostic redeemer myth. In a monograph of 1961 proving that this assumption rests on false premises, Carsten Colpe demolished the whole huge hypothesis.[5]

Colpe's demolition job, Meeks pointed out in relation to his own work,

supports the validity of the present investigation of a narrow aspect of John's christology in the face of Bultmann's elaborate theory that had seemed to account so cogently for the total christological picture in John. . . . It is appropriate in a study of the Fourth Gospel to focus attention upon a single phenomenon or group of closely related phenomena."[6]

Meeks was issuing here what amounted to a scholarly manifesto, calling for a radically new approach to the Gospel; and in fact in the remaining years of the twentieth century many fine monographs were published along the lines Meeks recommended.

---

3. John Ashton, *Understanding the Fourth Gospel* (Oxford: Clarendon, 1991), 124.

4. Wayne A. Meeks, *The Prophet-King: Moses Traditions and the Johannine Christology*, Supplements to Novum Testamentum 14 (Leiden: Brill, 1967).

5. Carsten Colpe, *Die religionsgeschichtliche Schule: Darstellung und Kritik ihres Bildes vom gnostischen Erlösermythus*, Forschungen zur Religion und Literatur des Alten und Neues Testament 78 (Göttingen: Vandenhoeck & Ruprecht, 1961).

6. Meeks, *Prophet-King*, 16.

Yet we should observe that, however many such studies were published and whatever their quality, they could never altogether compensate for the loss of a comprehensive explanation. Only a single source as wide-ranging as the one Bultmann thought he had found could prove an adequate substitute. Unless, that is, the evangelist himself could plausibly be shown to have deliberately set out to weave together the various strands that might be examined separately in a series of scholarly monographs so as to form a coherent christological pattern consistent enough to persuade at least some of his readers that his Gospel was indeed an indivisible unity. Does it follow, then, that anyone who finds such a suggestion in the highest degree improbable must abandon any attempt to find an answer to Harnack's great riddle?

Perhaps not. We should first take another look at Bultmann's solution. Detecting a striking resemblance between the strange documents he had been perusing and the elaborate Christology of John's Gospel, he was overwhelmed by the conviction that, rightly read, these could account for the combination of seemingly disparate elements in John's picture of Christ that were otherwise, he thought, impossible to explain. In a certain sense, then, he may be said to have formulated his question to fit the answer he had already discovered.

This means that if we discard Bultmann's *solution*—as we must—we are not necessarily obliged to accept his *question*, at least not in the way he thought it had to be put. We still have to account for the whole picture (as I will attempt to do in the final chapter), but we should also be prepared to recognize the possibility that the various elements of John's Christology may have reached him at different times and come to him from different sources. Since this is what I think myself, I propose to tackle one by one what I believe to be the three main streams (streams rather than strands) of Jewish tradition that were the source, or sources, of John's picture of Christ. The first of these, the Mosaic prophet, was already present hidden deep in the origins of Johannine Christianity. The second, wisdom, reached him indirectly, having first been developed, as I shall show, by someone else, probably a member of his community, before he took it over to form the Prologue to his Gospel. The third source, the Danielic Son of Man, must be considered independently of the other two.

THE PROPHET LIKE MOSES

On the assumption that John was eager to work out a comprehensive and coherent theory about Christ, the themes I am about to discuss—the mission of the prophet, the story of wisdom, and the descent of the Son of Man—are often treated under the heading of Christology. It is rather the case that ideas classed by later commentators as theological came to the evangelist (who was not a theologian) mostly in either pastoral or polemical contexts.

This is not quite true, however, of the first of these three traditions. Jesus himself was conscious from the outset of his career that he was sent by God and spoke on God's behalf. And there can be no doubt that this is how he was perceived by his earliest disciples. The Jesus group in the synagogue took this for granted. Subsequently, however, their conviction that Jesus was a not only *a* prophet but *the* prophet led to the separation of the two parties in the synagogue—seen by the evangelist as an expulsion or excommunication.

The first clear indication of the big disagreement comes at the moment of irreversible breakdown. The point at issue, the acid test, the shibboleth, we are told, was the affirmation on the part of the Jesus group that Jesus was the Messiah (9:22). Here, however, two problems arise that J. Louis Martyn, in his otherwise very perceptive discussion of this passage, fails to recognize. In the first place, right from the beginning it was their belief that in Jesus they had found the Messiah that distinguished the newcomers from the other members of the synagogue. So their confession of faith in Jesus as Messiah cannot have come as a surprise. In the second place, there was nothing blasphemous in proclaiming the advent of a Messiah (for the Messiah was never thought to have been anything other than an exceptional human being—and we know that many putative Messiahs were to arise in the long history of Judaism).[7]

Because of Nathan's famous prophecy to King David (2 Samuel 7) the Messiah was called "the son of God." David himself was given this title, and it was passed on to his descendants. We know from Qumran that in some circles a priestly Messiah was expected too: ". . . until the prophet comes, and the Messiahs of *Aaron* and Israel" (1QS 9:11), but whenever mention is made of the Messiah in the New Testament, certainly in the Gospel of John, it is the Davidic Messiah that is meant: "Has not the scripture said that the Messiah is descended from David, and comes from Bethlehem, the village of David?" (7:42).

Jesus was recognized as the Messiah quite early on in the Christian movement. So much is clear from the Synoptic Gospels. And (as I indicated both in chapter 1 and in Excursus III) I myself favor the view that an early missionary document written to proclaim Jesus' messiahship was adopted and

---

7. As we noted in chapter 1, Martyn believed that there is strong evidence for what he called a "Moses-Messiah" in the Jewish tradition. He even speaks of "the 'office' of Mosaic Prophet-Messiah" (*History and Theology in the Fourth Gospel,* 3rd ed. [Louisville: Westminster John Knox, 2003], 108). Possibly, though he does not say so, he considered confessing Jesus as Messiah to be much the same as confessing him as the Mosaic Prophet.

built upon in the Gospel of John.[8] Certain members of the synagogue mentioned in John 9 had accepted Jesus as Messiah long before there had been any open conflict within the synagogue and before such tension as there was had built up to breaking point. When "the disciples of Moses" eventually took the decision to expel any of the members of the synagogue who confessed Jesus as Messiah, they did so either because the title itself had gathered a new and greater significance or, more probably, for other quite different reasons, not made explicit in the text of the Gospel. One of the major aims of Martyn's little book was to highlight the immense significance of the existence of a cohort of practicing Jews, now self-proclaimed followers of Jesus, who had reached the conviction that he offered a new revelation, one that challenged Moses' position at the center of the Jewish faith. How did this come about? How did the supporters of Jesus come to see him as much more than the Davidic Messiah that he had been believed to be soon after his death and possibly, as some think, even during his lifetime?

Martyn raises this question in one of his programmatic essays,[9] suggesting that some Jews will have responded to the claim that Jesus was the Messiah by submitting it to close midrashic examination, and noting too that the evangelist found it necessary to deny claims made for Moses, such as the claim that he had ascended into heaven on Sinai to receive heavenly secrets. But his earlier book did not touch on this question; and Raymond Brown, aware of a major gap in the argument, attempted to bridge it by stressing the fresh impetus given to the Christian Jews by the accession to their ranks of a largish number of converts from Samaritanism. The special interests of this group will, he thinks, have precipitated a new wave of theological reflection eventually resulting in the high Johannine Christology we know so well. Moreover, according to Brown, "the acceptance of the second group by the majority of the first group is probably what brought upon the whole Johannine community the suspicion and hostility of the synagogue leaders. After the conversion of the Samaritans in chap. 4, the Gospel concentrates on the rejection of Jesus by 'the Jews.'" Brown goes on to point out that "immediately after chapter 4 we get the picture of a very high christology and sharp conflict with 'the Jews' who charge that Jesus is being deified (5:16–18)."[10] Against this I argued that it would be straining credulity too far to suppose that the sequence of events recorded in

---

8. Ashton, *Understanding the Fourth Gospel*, 1st ed., 185–94.

9. J. Louis Martyn, "Source Criticism and Religionsgeschichte in the Fourth Gospel," in *Jesus and Man's Hope*, ed. D. G. Buttrick, 2 vols. (Pittsburgh: Pittsburgh Theological Seminary, 1970), 1:247–73; reprinted with slight abridgments in *The Interpretation of John*, ed. John Ashton, 2nd ed., Studies in New Testament Interpretation (Edinburgh: T&T Clark, 1997), 121–46.

the Gospel directly reflects the catalytic effect Brown attributes to the accession of a number of Samaritan converts to the original group. Nonetheless, we will have to consider very carefully the suggestion that in the synagogue to which the Johannine group belonged speculation about the figure of Moses was rife (though we should not assume that this was confined to the Samaritan converts).

My own first answer to the problem came in the chapter of my book entitled "Son of God." Postponing (as I do now) consideration of the traditions of preexistent Wisdom and the Son of Man, I confined myself in this chapter to the prophecies concerning the two titles of Messiah and Prophet that are signaled early on in the Gospel at the point where John the Baptist explicitly disavows them both (1:20-21). As we have seen, this disavowal was followed two days later by the delight first of Andrew, who reports to his brother Simon Peter that "we have found the Messiah" (1:41), and, second, of Philip, who tells Nathanael that "we have found him of whom Moses in the law and also the prophets wrote" (1:45).

Some might want to suggest that questions regarding Jesus' claims to be the Messiah and the Mosaic prophet could have arisen during his lifetime. Well, no! However much Jesus' own words and actions may have prompted others to see in him much more than a man of God with a mission to heal and to preach the kingdom of God, he did not claim the title of Messiah himself, except just possibly at his trial before the high priest immediately before this death, when it was too late to question him. The various episodes that fill John 7, although easily read on the first level of understanding as part of the *story* of Jesus, reflect controversies that took place much later.

Now the concept of Jesus' messiahship was not one that fully engaged the evangelist's own interest. It is true that the word *Messiah*, translated into Greek, gives us *Christos,* the name by which Jesus eventually came to be known by believers and unbelievers alike, the name that now identifies the Christian religion. But at the time the title of Prophet was more important. Two distinct (and incompatible) challenges to the messianic claims of Jesus focus on the tradition of his Galilean origins: the first asserting that "we know where this man comes from; and when the Messiah comes no one will know where he is from" (7:27), and the second asking, "Is the Messiah is to come from Galilee? Has not the scripture said that the Messiah is descended from David, and comes from Bethlehem?" (7:41-42). Neither of these challenges takes us very far; but in reply to the first of them Jesus seizes the opportunity to affirm and emphasize

10. Raymond E. Brown, *The Community of the Beloved Disciple: The Life, Loves, and Hates of an Individual Church in New Testament Times* (New York: Paulist, 1979), 36 (cited in Ashton, *Understanding the Fourth Gospel*, 1st ed., 295).

his prophetic status: "You know me, and you know where I am from.[11] But I have not come of my own accord; he who sent me really did,[12] and you do not know him. I know him, for I come from him, and he sent me" (7:28-29).

Jesus undoubtedly claimed prophetic status during his lifetime: it was implicit in his career as a preacher and teacher. The Gospel, however, goes much further by making it clear from the very first chapter that he was perceived by others to be "the one of whom Moses in the law and the prophets wrote." There seems to be an important distinction between *a* prophet, that is to say, anyone who can legitimately claim to speak on behalf of God, and "*the* prophet who is to come into the world*" (John 6:14), a particular individual who will fulfill the promise of Moses that "the Lord your God will raise up for you a prophet like me from among you" (Deut. 18:15), a promise repeated to Moses a few verses later: "I will raise up from among them a prophet like you . . . and I will put my words in his mouth, and he shall speak to them all that I command them" (18:18).

It might be argued that this promise is quite specific, in that it concerns a particular prophet distinguished from all others by his close resemblance to Moses; but it is fair to ask whether this is to read too much into it. Moses is unquestionably the archetypal prophet, but anyone who speaks legitimately on behalf of God already resembles him in that respect: a line toward the beginning of the *Community Rule* refers to "Moses and all his servants the prophets" (1QS 1:3; see 1QpHab 7:5). Another document from Qumran, however, shows that the expectation of a particular prophet was not restricted to Christian circles. The *Community Rule* refers to a time when "there shall come *the* Prophet and the Messiahs of Aaron and Israel" (1QS 9:10); 1 Maccabees too testifies to the expectation of a new prophet. When the stones of the altar had been defiled by Antiochus, Judas Maccabeus set them aside "until there should come a prophet to tell what to do with them" (4:46; cf. 14:41). There is no direct allusion to Deuteronomy in either of these instances, but proof comes in another important manuscript from Qumran (4Q175) entitled by Geza Vermes "Testimonia or Messianic Anthology."[13] This consists of a succession of passages from three books of the Bible.[14] The first of the these is drawn from the Samaritan book

---

11. There is no need for a question mark at the end of this sentence, which is best interpreted as an ironic admission by Jesus that his interlocutors are right in what they say, even though they have a very partial understanding.

12. ἀλλ' ἔστιν ἀληθινὸς ὁ πέμψας με. The word ἀληθινός means "true" in the sense of real or genuine, not in the sense of honest. God is a true sender, as Jesus is the true vine (15:1) and God is the true God (17:3).

13. Geza Vermes, *The Complete Dead Sea Scrolls in English* (London: Penguin, 2007), 495–96.

of Exodus and combines two texts from our Deuteronomy, 5:28-29 and 18:18 (quoted at the end of the preceding paragraph); the second cites the oracle of Balaam: "A star shall come out of Jacob and a scepter shall rise out of Israel" (Num. 24:15-17); the third is the blessing of Levi in Deut. 33:8-11. So here is a firm attestation of the expectation of three eschatological figures, a Moses-like prophet, a messianic star, and a Levitical priest.[15]

In the Gospel, of course, the three titles disowned by John the Baptist differ from this list insofar as the third of them, Elijah, is not a priest but another prophet, and in any case in the Gospel as we have it Jesus is not recognized as Elijah.[16] Moreover, even though there now can be little doubt that the reference in John 1:21 and 45 is to the Moses-like prophet, there cannot so early have been any suspicion that Jesus had already superseded Moses or would eventually do so.

The first sign in the Gospel that problems had arisen concerning the two titles of Messiah and Prophet comes once more in chapter 7. Besides questions about Jesus' messiahship, this chapter reflects a rejection of the claim that he was the expected prophet. On the last day of the feast (of Tabernacles) Jesus issued the extraordinary invitation, "If anyone is thirsty, let him come to me and drink," whereupon "some of the people said, 'this is really the prophet.' Others said, 'This is the Messiah' " (7:37-41). A denial of the second claim comes immediately: "Is the Messiah to come from Galilee?" The denial of the first claim is deferred to the last verse of the chapter (giving a chiastic structure to the whole episode), in a sardonic reply to Nicodemus: "Search and see that the prophet does not arise from Galilee" (7:52).[17] No further comment is made at this juncture about the role of this new prophet. Perhaps there was already a

14. Plus a fourth, from the so-called *Psalms of Joshua*, quoting Josh. 6:16, a curse on anyone seeking to rebuild Jericho, probably directed against John Hyrcanus. See John J. Collins, *The Scepter and the Star: The Messiahs of the Dead Sea Scrolls and Other Ancient Literature*, Anchor Bible Reference Library (New York: Doubleday, 1995), 94.

15. See Rudolf Schnackenburg, "Die Erwartung des 'Propheten' nach dem neuen Testament und den Qumran Texten," *Studia Evangelica 1* (Berlin: Akademie-Verlag, 1959); Meeks, *Prophet-King*, 22 and n. 3. See also Martyn's discussion in *History and Theology*, 3rd ed., 104–6, plus references in n. 158. Martyn sees in Deut. 33:8-11 a reference to the Priestly *Messiah* (= the Messiah of Aaron), but there is nothing in the text itself to justify this inference.

16. Though Martyn makes a strong case for the view that in the earliest version of the Signs Source, besides the Messiah and the Prophet, Jesus was also accepted as the eschatological Elijah. See Martyn, *The Gospel of John in Christian History: Essays for Interpreters* (New York: Paulist, 1978), 9–54.

17. Most manuscripts have the singular προφήτης in this verse. But the Bodmer papyrus P66* reads ὁ προφήτης, and Meeks has argued persuasively that in any case v. 52 should be understood as a contradiction of the claim in v. 40 that "this is really *the* prophet" (*Prophet-King*, 33–34).

perceived risk that the Moses-like prophet who was to come would eventually take Moses' place and actually supersede him, but this is not indicated here, and the full significance of the claim that Jesus is the prophet has yet to emerge. In chapter 6, which belongs to the second edition of the Gospel,[18] the claim becomes explicit in the response of those who have just witnessed the miracle of the loaves and fishes: "This is indeed the prophet who is to come into the world" (6:14).

This response stands in stark contrast to the reception of the blind beggar in chapter 9. "What do you say about him [Jesus]," demanded the Pharisees, "since he has opened your eyes?" He said, "He is a prophet" (9:17), a reply that provoked an angry rejoinder: "Give God the praise; we know that this man is a sinner" (9:24). It is this exchange that led to the key distinction already mentioned more than once, between the disciples of "that fellow" and the disciples of Moses. For although the assertion of the blind beggar was no more than a simple recognition that Jesus was *a* prophet, the inference drawn by the Pharisees was that he was now challenging the position of Moses as *the* prophet of God, the bringer of the law. The Jesus group in the synagogue had now come to be regarded as "the disciples of that fellow" [Jesus], *as opposed to* "the disciples of Moses." Once this had happened there was no conceivable chance that the two groups could remain together. This is surely the crucial point, very much more significant than the ostensible reason for the dismissal of the followers of Jesus—their claim that he was the Messiah. For regardless of whether they were aware of it at the time, the group that split off from the synagogue was now no longer Jewish in the religious sense of the word, but Christian.

The upshot of my argument is that the Johannine community came to see Jesus as having ousted Moses from his position at the heart of the Jewish religion so as to take his place as the bearer of grace and truth. This is stated clearly in the Prologue, which cannot therefore have been composed before the final rift between the two parties in the synagogue. Moreover, such an extreme statement of absolute opposition must have been preceded by a long buildup of festering antagonism. As it happens, there is quite a lot of evidence in the Gospel itself of the extraordinary bitterness with which the Johannine community came to turn against its Jewish traditions. I treat it now under the rubric of "Family Quarrels."

---

18. See excursus III above.

Family Quarrels

Taken together, this evidence points to a sustained attack on all that traditional Judaism most valued. It may be divided into four categories, relating to (1) family or ancestry, (2) sacred space, (3) feasts or festivals, and (4) the law.[19]

Briefly, then, under the first category, family or ancestry, the main evidence concerns Abraham, the first and the most revered of the patriarchs. There is nothing in the Gospel, or anywhere else in the New Testament for that matter, to match the virulence of the dispute between Jesus and the Jews in chapter 8, where Jesus denies that his adversaries, though in fact descendants of Abraham, have any right to call themselves his children, and insists that their true father is not God, as they claim, but the devil (8:37-44). Such a terrible accusation amounts to a complete denial of family and national identity. In 1:51 the Son of Man—Jesus himself—takes the place of Jacob, whose other name is Israel, as the true intermediary between heaven and earth. Later in the Gospel, asked by the Samaritan woman whether he is "greater than our father Jacob, who gave us this well," Jesus responds by contrasting the water from that well with the water he will provide himself, "a spring of water welling up to eternal life" (4:12-14). He does not actually answer the woman's question, "Are you greater than our father Jacob?" (4:12), or the question of the Jews, "Are you greater than our father Abraham?" (8:53), but we have to infer that, had he answered, the answer must have been yes. In fact the Jews are denied the parentage of Abraham, and in two separate passages, by taking on the role of Jacob, Jesus dismisses more of their most valued traditions.

Next what I have called sacred space. We have already seen that, as early as John 2, Jesus asserts that he will build, or rather raise, a different kind of temple, which he specifies as his own body. At the time the Gospel was composed, of course, the temple had already been destroyed; but Jesus' promise of a completely different temple effectively reduces it to insignificance and brushes aside any hopes they may have had of a later restoration of the sacred edifice that had been at the heart of their religious practice for centuries. In chapter 4, what comes under attack is not just the temple but the city of Jerusalem itself: "the hour is coming," Jesus tells the Samaritan woman (for whom the mountain near where they were standing, Mount Gerizim, was truly holy), "when neither on this mountain nor in Jerusalem will you worship the Father: the hour is coming when true worshipers will worship the father in spirit and truth" (4:21, 23).

---

19. "Family Quarrels" is the heading of a short section in *Understanding the Fourth Gospel,* 2nd ed., 78–81, in which this topic is given a more thorough discussion.

Most of the great Jewish festivals are also threatened. Pentecost, the Feast of Weeks, is never mentioned in the Gospel, but in one way of another all the other major festivals come under attack: the Feast of Sukkoth (Tents or Tabernacles), above all a *water* festival, is appropriated by Jesus at the feast itself: "if anyone thirst, *let him come to me* and drink" (7:37). Next Hanukkah, the Feast of Dedication: when Jesus declares, in the context of this feast, that *he* is the one consecrated by the Father (10:36), he is effectively challenging the significance of the renewed dedication of the altar of the temple. Still more remarkably, when Jesus is taken down from the cross, his body still unbroken, a verse from Exodus insisting on this is quoted to prove that *he and he alone* is the true Paschal Lamb (19:36; Exod. 12:46). Thus, the greatest Jewish feast of all, the Passover, is also superseded.

Finally, the law. As elsewhere in early Christian circles, the law continued to be valued by John as testimony to the truth brought by Jesus: "You search the scriptures," he tells the Jews, "because you think that in them you have eternal life; but they really bear witness to me" (5:39). And again, in the same discourse: "If you believed Moses you would believe me, for he wrote of me" (5:46). But from John's perspective (which differs from that of Paul or of Matthew) Moses is good for nothing else. The verse from the Prologue that I have already quoted more than once deliberately belittles the law: "grace and truth came about through Jesus Christ" (1:17). So in one way or another all that the Jews held most dear, all that entitled them to be proud of their own identity, has been swept aside. They have been denied a family, a city, and a sacred space. The great festivals that marked their year in the way that Christmas, Easter, and Pentecost came to do in Christendom, have been dismissed. The very heart of their religious belief, the law, has been torn out. Why should they not be angry?

Conclusion

In the present chapter I have focused on just one of Jesus' titles, that of the Prophet. The conviction grew that he was indeed the Moses-like prophet whose coming had been announced and was expected, culminating in a belief that he had actually superseded Moses. But this conviction did not and could not imply a belief that he was thereby claiming equality with God. A prophet is one who speaks on behalf of God and who by the very nature of his calling is subordinate to God. Moreover when Jesus is accused of claiming equality with God he firmly denies this, as the Gospel makes clear, and talks instead of the prophet's duty to speak *on behalf of* God. When charged with ditheism, he is quick to reply: "Truly, truly, I say to you, the Son can do nothing of his own accord, but only what he sees the Father doing; for whatever he does, that the Son does likewise" (5:19; cf. 8:28). It is true that in this passage Jesus explicitly recalls the Father/Son relationship. But he does so to emphasize that it is God, the Father, who is in control. His assertion that he does nothing of his own accord is repeated in different terms several times in the Gospel. He does not speak on his own authority (7:17-18; 12:49; 14:10), and he does not seek his own will (5.30; 6.38). He has not come of his own accord (7:28). Stated positively, he does the will of the Father, does his work, fulfills his commandments (4:34; 5:36; 10:37-8; 17:4). The Father works through him (14:10).[20]

Clear as they are, these emphatic assertions by Jesus of his own subordination to God leave us wondering how and why they were so misunderstood by his adversaries. Something has been left unsaid. If the claim to be a prophet, or even the prophet of God par excellence cannot even come close to a claim to equality with God, then the challenge remains to find something in the Gospel to account for the murderous hostility of "the Jews" that finds expression so often in its pages.

Part of the answer is to be found in the close association between prophecy and mission. While recognizing the prophet's subordinate role, we should also remember that Jesus' relationship with God is thought of throughout the Gospel in terms of the Jewish law of agency, whereby the agent is virtually identified with his master, just as an ambassador, by a legal fiction, is identified with the country he represents. In the simple formula of the Mekilta, "an agent is like the one who sent him."[21] Finally, in certain contexts, there appears to be a recognition by the evangelist that Jesus' relationship with God was that of a son and heir: "the Father loves the Son and has given everything into his hand" (3:25; cf. 10:18; 13:3; 17:2).[22] Yet even in combination the themes of mission, agency, and sonship do not fully account for the Gospel's high Christology. We should now ask whether the Jesus of the Fourth Gospel was thought to be truly divine in the sense that he was subsequently defined to be by the Christian church. This question will be addressed in the next chapter.

20. Cf. Rudolf Bultmann, *The Gospel of John: A Commentary* (Oxford: Basil Blackwell, 1971), 240 n. 1.

21. *Mekilta* on Exod. 12:3. This, along with a number of other tannaitic texts, is quoted by Peder Borgen in what is now recognized as the standard discussion of the subject: "God's Agent in the Fourth Gospel," in *Religions in Antiquity: Essays in Memory of Erwin Ramsdell Goodenough*, ed. Jacob Neusner, Supplements to Numen 14 (Leiden: Brill, 1968), 137–48.

22. See *Understanding the Fourth Gospel*, 211–31, part of the chapter entitled "Son of God," where all these points are fully argued.

Excursus IV. The Prologue: God's Plan for Humankind

As long ago as 1986 I published an article on the Prologue[1] in which I adopted and developed a thesis put forward much earlier (1964) by Paul Lamarche that the subject of John 1:3 is not creation, as is widely assumed, but that this verse "is essentially concerned with the realization of the divine plan."[2] Apart from the briefest of notes by Craig Evans,[3] my article lay disregarded until it was eventually picked up in 2006 in a book devoted to the Prologue by Peter M. Phillips.[4] Phillips does not discuss all my arguments, and his treatment of those he does discuss is unconvincing. Since the issue is clearly an important one, affecting not just the interpretation of the Prologue itself but (as I will show in chapter 8) that of the Gospel as a whole, it must be covered properly. I will first cite Lamarche's arguments as set forth in my translation of his original article;[5] then, after following these up in each case with further reasons of my own, I will deal with Phillips's attempted rebuttal.

1. Lamarche challenges the standard interpretation of John 1:3:

"Does v. 3 really speak of creation? The word here is not κτίζω ("create") as in Colossians (1:15) or in Revelation (4:1; 10:6), nor even ποιῶ ("do/make"), but γίνομαι, which means not "to be created" but "to become/to happen." If the central perspective of the Prologue is indeed God's universal plan, it is clear that the very wide meaning of this verb can perfectly express God's activity by means of his Logos throughout the history of the world, starting, of course,

---

1. John Ashton, "The Transformation of Wisdom: A Study of the Prologue of John's Gospel," *New Testament Studies* 32 (1986): 161–86; reprinted in *Studying John: Approaches to the Fourth Gospel* (Oxford: Clarendon, 1994), 5–35 (references here are to the reprint).

2. "As early as 1958," Lamarche adds, "T. F. Pollard had arrived at the same conclusions" (Pollard, "Cosmology and the Prologue of the Fourth Gospel," *Vigiliae Christianae* 12 [1958]: 147–63).

3. Craig A. Evans, *Word and Glory: On the Exegetical and Theological Background of John's Prologue,* Journal for the Study of the New Testament: Supplement Series 89 (Sheffield: Sheffield Academic Press, 1993), 112 n. 1.

4. Peter M. Phillips, *The Prologue of the Fourth Gospel: A Sequential Reading,* Library of New Testament Studies (London/New York: T&T Clark, 2006).

5. Paul Lamarche,"The Prologue of John," in *The Interpretation of John,* ed. John Ashton, 2nd ed., Studies in New Testament Interpretation (Edinburgh: T&T Clark, 1997), 47–65.

from the creation, right up to the Incarnation, and including Israel's election and the natural law of the Gentiles. Everything that has happened—the history of salvation as well as the creation—happened through the Logos.

Arguments in support of the very wide meaning that must be given to γίνομαι include the following:

a. The use of this verb in the Prologue as a whole ought to shed light on its meaning in v. 3. No doubt in v. 10 the world has "become," that is, has been "created," unless this refers rather to the world of human beings, which has just come about in history. But in any case this is just one aspect of "becoming" in the Prologue. In fact, the same verb is used for John the Baptist, who "comes"; for Christ, who "came" before John and who "becomes" flesh; for the grace and truth that "come" through Jesus Christ; and for the faithful, who "become" children of God.

b. The same (historical) use of the word is found in the first verse of Revelation: "The revelation of Jesus Christ, which God gave him to show to his servants what must soon take place [γίνεσθαι]" (cf. Rev. 1:19; 4:1; 22:6).

c. The same usage is found in the Septuagint, particularly in a passage in the book of Judith: "For you have brought all this about [ἐποίησας] and everything that preceded and followed; you have planned [διενοήθης] both present and future. and all that you planned has come to pass [ἐγενήθησαν ἃ ἐνενοήθης]" (Jdt. 9:5-6).[6]

Let me now deal with Phillips's attempted refutation both of Lamarche's arguments about the meaning of the verb γίνεσθαι, and of the support I gave them in my own article: "Ashton notes," he says, "that καὶ ἐγένετο is used in the standard Greek phrase as a reflection of the Hebrew narrative conjunction ויהי— 'and so it came to pass that. . .'." "The use in this verse [1:3]," he admits, "could act in a similar way—'all things came to pass through him.' " He goes on to point out, however, that where the word ἐγένετο is used in this sense in the Gospel (and he instances John 1:6, 28; 2:1; 3:25; 5:9; 6:16, 21; 7:43) it is used without καί. So, he concludes, there are clearly problems with the suggested rendering of John 1:3, "since the relevant conjunctive particle is missing and ἐγένετο is not found at the beginning of the phrase."[7]

6. Lamarche, "Prologue," 51–52.
7. Phillips, "Prologue," 160–61.

I find this argument very puzzling indeed, not least because I did not write the sentence he attributes to me. What I wrote was this: "the verb γίνεσθαι, without contextual support such as it finds in Genesis 1 [where indeed the Hebrew ויהי is always rendered by the Greek καὶ ἐγένετο] does not naturally refer to creation." The opening of John 1, Ἐν ἀρχῇ, is unquestionably a reference to the opening of Genesis, but subsequent translators were mistaken when they concluded that what follows must also concern creation. (Lindars, commenting on the words *were made* in John 1:3, says that "the verbs in this sentence are the historic past 'was,' or 'came into being',," yet in his subsequent comments he retains the "were made" of the RSV.)[8] In twelve of the twenty instances of καὶ ἐγένετο in Genesis 1 it is found (twice in each case) in the standard phrase used to indicate the end of each of the six days of creation: καὶ ἐγένετο ἑσπέρα καὶ ἐγένετο πρωί. In the other eight instances, although the reference to creation is obvious, the English translation is not "And it was made" but simply "And it was so"—or, in the first occurrence, v. 3, "And there was (light)." What Phillips calls "the relevant conjunctive particle [καί]" (present in all the references to creation in the Genesis story) does not occur either in John 1:3 or in any of the other Gospel instances that he cites (nor does ἐγένετο come at the beginning of the phrase). Most if not all of these instances, such as 6:16, Ὡς δὲ ὀψία ἐγένετο ("When evening came") tally nicely with what I believe to be the correct rendering of 1:3: "everything came to pass through him." So Phillips's observation, far from counting against my argument, actually supports it.

2. Another of Lamarche's arguments concerns an ancient Gnostic text that loosely paraphrases the Prologue—the Valentinian writing known as the *Gospel of Truth*:

"Nothing happens without him, nor does anything happen without the will of the Father" (37:2ff.). Here is the context of this passage: "Each one of his words is the work of his one will in the revelation of his Word. While they were still in the depth of his thought, the Word which was first to come forth revealed them" (37:4ff.).[9]

In this passage the Coptic is variously rendered "happens" or "comes into being." There is nowhere any suggestion of creation.

To Lamarche's point about the Coptic *Gospel of Truth* may be added an argument from the Syriac (Curetonian) translation of the actual text of John

8. Barnabas Lindars, *The Gospel of John* (London: Marshall, Morgan & Scott, 1972), 84–85.
9. Lamarche, "Prologue," 52.

1:3, which reads, in F. C. Burkitt's rendering, "Everything came to pass in Him, and apart from Him not even one thing came to pass."[10] The translator of this version, unlike some others, including that of the Old Latin, followed by Jerome, was not misled by the allusion to Genesis in the first verse; *facta sunt* in v. 3 means something very different from "came to pass," and it may well be that not only the translators of the King James Bible but others too had an eye on the Latin when they missed the real meaning of ἐγένετο (rendered accurately by the Syriac "came to pass") and chose something closer to *facta sunt*—the English "were made" being a case in point.[11] An interesting parallel is to be found in *4 Ezra* 6:6: "then I planned these things and they came into being through me and not another," for where the Syriac (in Michael Stone's translation) has "came into being," the Latin, just as in John 1:3, has *facta sunt*.[12]

3. My next argument (not used by Lamarche and ignored by Phillips) concerns the crucial difference between πάντα and τὰ πάντα. Ignace de La Potterie had already pointed out that in New Testament times the regular expression for the created universe was τὰ πάντα.[13] Commenting on John 1:3, Bultmann said that "the concept κόσμος is here represented by πάντα—everything that there is—whereby *no account is taken* of the fact that this can be summarized as τὰ πάντα (τὸ πᾶν), whether it be as a whole over against God, or as the unity of the divine cosmos in itself."[14] As parallels he cites Rom. 11:36; 1 Cor. 8:6; Col. 1:16-17; Heb. 2:10. In the last of these instances, which all have τὰ πάντα, the author takes up a phrase from Ps. 8:7 quoted a couple of verses earlier: πάντα ὑπέταξας ὑποκάτω τῶν ποδῶν αὐτοῦ ("you have placed all things under his feet"), but then proceeds to *correct* it, speaking of him "for whom and through whom *the universe* (has its being)": δι' ὅν τὰ πάντα καὶ δι' οὗ τὰ πάντα, a deliberate reference to the whole cosmos. Clearly aware that the

---

10. *Evangelion da-Mepharreshe: The Curetonian Version of the Four Gospels*, ed. F. C. Burkitt, 2 vols. (Cambridge: University Press, 1904), 1:423. (Phillips makes no attempt to deal with this argument.)

11. This is certainly true of the translators of the King James Version, which had such a strong influence on its successors.

12. Michael Edward Stone, *Fourth Ezra: A Commentary on the Book of Fourth Ezra*, Hermeneia (Minneapolis: Fortress Press, 1990), 143. G. A. Box, translating the Latin rather than the Syriac, has "and through me alone and none other *were they created*" (*The Ezra-Apocalypse* [London: Sir Isaac Pitman & Sons, 1912], 67).

13. Ignace de La Potterie, *La vérité dans saint Jean*, 2 vols., Analecta biblica 73, 74 (Rome: Biblical Institute Press, 1977), 1:162–66.

14. Rudolf Bultmann, *The Gospel of John: A Commentary* (Oxford: Basil Blackwell, 1971), 36–37 (my emphasis). Bultmann is aware of the difference but seems to think of it of no significance.

psalmist was thinking of all creation in submission to God, the writer used the phrase he knew (τὰ πάντα) to express this. With this in mind we can recognize that Col. 1:16, ὅτι ἐν αὐτῷ ἐκτίσθη τὰ πάντα ("because the entire universe was created in him"), far from being a genuine parallel to John 1:3, has probably contributed to a continuing misunderstanding.[15]

The evidence from the Septuagint is complex but points in the same direction.[16] In Gen. 1:31, which tells how God surveyed the now completed creative work ("God saw everything that he had made") the Greek is τὰ πάντα, one of more than a dozen examples of the use of this term in the Septuagint to refer to the created universe; whereas Ps. 8:7, which I have just quoted, is one of only a very few instances where the simple πάντα has the same reference. A telling example of the felt difference between the two comes in Wis. 7:27, where it is said of wisdom that μία δὲ οὖσα πάντα δύναται καὶ μένουσα ἐν αὐτῇ τὰ πάντα καινίζει. Here, unfortunately, the English translator of the RSV failed to notice the difference: "Though she is but one, she can do all things, and while remaining in herself, she renews all things." A better translation would be: "Even alone she is omnipotent, and quite unaided she restores the entire universe."

Added to Lamarche's first two arguments, this evidence, from both parts of the Bible, is decisive. The standard rendering of John 1:3, "all things were made through him," is simply wrong.[17]

4. Lamarche, however, has one more argument, based on texts from the Dead Sea Scrolls:

The community rule at Qumran has a number of passages quite close to John 1:3; and these, often quoted, but rarely used to cast light on the Prologue, concern not so much creation as all that happens in

---

15. A similar argument can be developed from a misquotation of the Prologue by the Gnostic Ptolemy, the pupil of Valentinus, who, as reported by Irenaeus, did indeed believe that in the Prologue John was concerned with the genesis of the universe (τῶν ὅλων): "he (the apostle) λέγει εἶναι τά τε πάντα δι'αὐτοῦ γεγονέναι καὶ χωρὶς αὐτοῦ γεγονέναι οὐδέν (cited by Epiphanius, Panarion 33.3.6). Ptolemy recognized that the article was required before πάντα to give him the sense he wanted.

16. I dealt with it fully in "Transformation," 20 n. 37.

17. Michael Theobald, Das Evangelium nach Johannes Kapitel 1–12, Regensburger Neues Testament (Regensburg: Pustet, 2009), acknowledges the difference and translates 1:3 as "Alles wurde durch ihn, und ohne ihn wurde auch nicht eines" (p. 106), but later (p. 113) asserts that πάντα here refers not to the cosmos as such but to "die Dinge." He continues to think in terms of creation, asserting that 1:4 is all about "creatio continua" (p.114). But what can creatio continua mean except the working out of God's plan for the world?

the history of salvation. In fact they occur in the content of human action (1QS 11:10), of the working out of God's plan (1QS 11:18-19) and of the revelation of his mysteries: "For without thee no way is perfect, and without thy will nothing is done . . . all things come to pass by thy will. There is none beside thee to dispute thy counsel or to understand thy holy design, or to contemplate the depth of thy mysteries and the power of thy might" (1QS 11:17-19).

And at this point Lamarche adds an important explanatory note:

> The words used in these passages (היה and עשה), far from being confined to the idea of creation (ברא) (cf. 1QS 3:17, 25), signify everything that happens and takes place through the initiative of God. This can be confirmed by comparing these passages with other texts from the Community Rule, e.g. 1QS 3:15, the beginning of the section on the two spirits: "From the God of Knowledge comes all that is and shall be (כול הווה ונהייה)." See further 8:4, 12 and 9:3: "When these things happen (בהיות) in Israel"; also 9:24: "All that happens to him (כול הנעשה בו)" and 9:26: "he shall bless his Maker (עושיו) and declare [his wondrous deeds] in all that happens (יהיה)."[18]

Lastly, a little further on, Lamarche adds a final clinching quotation from 1QS 11:11:

> "All things came to pass (הווה) by his knowledge; he establishes all things by his design and without him nothing is done (יעשה)." In this sentence, so close to John 1:3, what takes the place of the Johannine Logos is God's plan (מחשבה); cf. Jer. 29:11; 51:29; Mic. 4:12; Ps. 33:10f.[19]

Commenting on this passage, I observed that a better parallel than the texts cited by Lamarche is to be found in the famous epilogue to the prophecy of Second Isaiah: "For as the heavens are higher than the earth so are my ways higher than your ways and my thoughts (מחשבותי) than your thoughts" (Isa. 55:8-9), which is directly followed by the declaration concerning every word that goes forth from my mouth (דברי). This declaration harks back to the introduction to this prophet's message, "the word of the Lord abides for ever"

18. Lamarche, "Prologue," 63 n. 16.
19. Lamarche, "Prologue," 54.

(Isa. 40:8), and forms a literary inclusion. "The whole of the prophet's message," I concluded, "is bracketed by these two statements concerning the word of God, which may fairly be said therefore to signify the divine plan Second Isaiah is anxious to promulgate, a plan which involves the superimposition of creation upon history."[20]

Phillips questions whether 1QS 11:11 is a genuine parallel to John 1, arguing that "the contexts are entirely different. The text from the Community Rule comes from a section dealing with the iniquity of humankind, whilst the Prologue discusses the transcendence and immanence of the divine." Yet he admits that 1QS 11:11 "provides a straightforward acknowledgment that God's intention is behind everything that happens"[21]—close enough to the meaning Lamarche and I find in John 1:3 to make it surprising that he refuses to admit the parallel.

The case for the relevance of 1QS 11:11 and of the other passages that Lamarche cites from the *Community Rule*, especially the beginning of the section on the Two Spirits, 1QS 3:15, can now be reinforced by appealing to Carol Newsom's brilliant discussion of this section and its allusions to the first chapter of Genesis. Introducing her discussion, she observes that the source of all is expressed in 1QS 3–4 not simply as "God" but as אל דעות, "God of knowledge." "What endows the world with meaning is not the impulse of an acting/reacting deity but that set of structured relationships called מחשבות כבודו, 'His glorious plan.' "[22] She goes on to point out, as I remarked in an earlier chapter, that "where Genesis 1 is concerned with creation, 1QS 3–4 is concerned with the מחשבה [i.e. the plan, literally thought, of God] that grounds creation."[23]

It is true that the allusion to Genesis 1 in John's Prologue is restricted to the opening words, "In the beginning"; but Newsom's analysis of the passage from the *Community Rule* shows how easy it was for a Jewish author to suggest that the creator God of Genesis should be seen rather as a God of knowledge, carefully planning the future of humankind as a whole and of human beings individually. Her remark that "what endows the world with meaning is . . . that set of structured relationships called מחשבת כבודו, 'His glorious plan,' " could equally well have been said of the Logos in the Johannine Prologue.

20. Ashton, "Transformation," 22.

21. Phillips, *Prologue*, 137.

22. Carol A. Newsom, *The Self as Symbolic Space: Constructing Identity and Community at Qumran*. Studies on the Texts of the Desert of Judah 52 (Leiden: Brill, 2004), 84.

23. Newsom, *Self as Symbolic Space*, 86.

In the light of all this evidence, Phillips's conclusion that "Ashton's attempt to move away from the dominance of creation language seems misguided"[24] is unwarranted. A quarter of a century after the publication of my article, Phillips is still, to the best of my knowledge, the only scholar to have argued against my rejection of the standard interpretation of the Prologue as a hymn about creation. Yet of my four arguments he dealt with only two. His dismissal of the first of these, the meaning of the verb γίνεσθαι, is misconceived. Not only does he attribute to me an argument I did not make, but he finds problems in my suggested translation that are simply not there. When he comes to the fourth argument, based on a passage from the Dead Sea Scrolls in which many other scholars besides myself (including Lamarche, Bultmann, Brown, Lindars, and Schnackenburg) have seen a conceptual parallel to the Prologue, he disagrees. Here, as with all such suggested parallels, there is indeed room for disagreement, but this in any case was a supportive argument, buttressing the main case, which is strong enough to stand without it.

The same might be said for the evidence of the Syriac version, which does no more than confirm that some early readers took γίνεσθαι to mean "come to pass" or "happen" (which of course is what it does mean) and were not put off by the early allusion to the opening of Genesis. The fourth argument, however, based on the difference in meaning between πάντα and τὰ πάντα, is substantial enough to merit serious consideration: to ignore it completely is, in current jargon, unacceptable.

A Punctuation Puzzle: John 1:3-4.

This little puzzle has more to do than may appear at first sight with the question we have just been considering. Why do the critical editions of the Greek text refuse to go along with the traditional verse numbering and place the stop not at the end of v. 3 but before its last two words, so that they read (a) [3]πάντα δι' αὐτοῦ ἐγένετο, καὶ χωρὶς αὐτοῦ ἐγένετο οὐδὲ ἕν. ὃ γέγονεν [4]ἐν αὐτῷ ζωὴ ἦν instead of (b) [3]πάντα δι' αὐτοῦ ἐγένετο, καὶ χωρὶς αὐτοῦ ἐγένετο οὐδὲ ἓν ὃ γέγονεν. [4]ἐν αὐτῷ ζωὴ ἦν? It is because the traditional verse numbering was put in at a time when the standard reading of the day was the second of these two alternatives. But the oldest manuscripts (P[75] C* D L W), the early versions (Latin, Syriac, and Sahidic Coptic), and most of the fathers (e.g., Hippolytus, Origen, Eusebius, Athanasius) place the stop earlier—before ὃ γέγονεν. Since modern editors of the Greek text attach great importance to the manuscript

24. Phillips, Prologue, 161.

evidence, it is not surprising that they generally follow the best manuscripts; and in fact the two most recent critical editions are agreed on this point.[25] One notable textual critic, Kurt Aland, who was the leading editor in both of these, has written an important article defending this reading.[26]

Most English translations of the Bible render the variation I have labeled (b). This is no doubt because they derive from the Authorized Version, which worked from the *textus receptus*, the standard text in the seventeenth century. So, for instance, the RSV has, "all things were made through him, and without him was not anything made that was made."

But what about the commentators? Not all of them go into the question in any depth. Those that do are divided. Aland has provided irrefutable evidence that the earliest reading was (a). But he also showed that many of the Fathers were uneasy with this reading, which lends itself readily to heretical interpretations. The attribution of ὃ γέγονεν to v. 3, he tells us, "began to be carried out in the fourth century in the Greek Church. This transfer arose with the Arians, and functioned to guard the doctrines of the church. Its secondary character is unmistakable." Lindars gives an illustration of the danger: "If *all* things came through him, what about the Holy Spirit? Is he one of the creatures? To exclude this interpretation it was necessary to show that verse 3 applied only to that which has been made, as opposed to what is uncreated."[27] Hence the shift of punctuation from (a) to (b).

This is not the only difficulty with (a). As long as we are thinking in terms of creation, it is extraordinarily difficult to find a satisfactory sense for v. 4: "That which has been made was life in him [the Logos]." As Rudolf Schnackenburg pertinently inquires, "what kind of life is that?"— *Was is das für eine ζωή?*[28]

For this reason some commentators, flying in the face of the manuscript evidence, go for (b). Ernst Haenchen is one of them. Arguing against Aland, he declares: "One misconstrues the facts when one connects ὃ γέγονεν to verse 4 by invoking the oldest manuscripts, to say nothing of the fact that one does not thereby achieve a meaningful text."[29] (Just how Aland is misconstruing the facts Haenchen does not say.)

25. *The Greek New Testament*, 4th rev. ed., ed. Barbara Aland, , 2001; Nestle-Aland, *Novum Testamentum Graece*, 27th rev. ed., 1993. Both are published by the German Bible Society (Deutsche Bibelgesellschaft, Stuttgart).

26. Kurt Aland,"Eine Untersuchung zu Joh I 3, 4: Über die Bedeutung eines Punktes," *Zeitschrift für die neutestamentliche Wissenschaft* 59 (1968): 174–209.

27. Barnabas Lindars, *The Gospel of John* (London: Oliphants, 1972), 85.

28. Rudolf Schnackenburg, *Das Johannesevangelium*, 4 vols., Herders theologischer Kommentar zum Neuen Testament 4 (Freiburg: Herder, 1965–84), 1:216.

Barnabas Lindars, working from the RSV, suggests rather hesitantly that (b) might after all be the best reading: "The ancient reading [a] may be a false inference on stylistic grounds, whereby each verse can consist of two balanced clauses." But (like Haenchen) his main reason for preferring (b) is the difficulty of making sense of (a).[30] C. K. Barrett agrees. He offers a couple of stylistic arguments, but, like Haenchen and Lindars, he opts for (b) chiefly because it is the reading that makes the most sense. He says almost nothing about the manuscript evidence, simply remarking that Kurt Aland disagrees with him.[31]

Rudolf Bultmann, almost alone among the major commentators, adopted the older punctuation (a) without discussion, presumably because he could see no reason not to; but he had great difficulty in finding a plausible translation for v. 4a: "the vitality of the whole creation has its origin in the Logos: he is the power which creates life. And it does not matter here whether one understands the text as: 'What has come to be—in him (the Logos) was the life (for it)'; or as: 'What has come to be—in it he (the Logos) was the life.' In both cases it is stated that life was not inherent in creatures as creatures."[32] As Barrett remarks about these suggestions (though without naming Bultmann), they are almost impossibly clumsy.[33] More seriously, the first of Bultmann's alternative translations, despite his disclaimer, attributes life to the created universe, and in my view the second is hardly possible as a rendering of the Greek text.[34]

Every one of these scholars, convinced that the Prologue is about creation, translates the words ὃ γέγονεν as "what has been made," a mistranslation that is at the root of all their difficulties.[35] For once ὃ γέγονεν is understood to refer not to the created universe but to God's plan for humankind and the enactment of this plan in human history, then a perfectly intelligible sense emerges. Here

---

29. Ernst Haenchen, *John: A Commentary on the Gospel of John*, 2 vols., Hermeneia (Philadephia: Fortress Press, 1984), 1:122.

30. Lindars, *Gospel*, 85.

31. C. K. Barrett, *The Gospel according to St. John: An Introduction with Commentary and Notes on the Greek Text*, 2nd ed. (London SPCK, 1978), 156–57.

32. Bultmann, *Gospel*, 39–40.

33. Barrett, *Gospel*, 157.

34. Yet it is defended by Hartmut Gese and Jürgen Becker, both cited approvingly by Michael Theobald, *Im Anfang war das Wort: Textlinguistische Studie zum Johannesprolog*, Stuttgarter Bibelstudien 106 (Stuttgart: Katholisches Bibelwerk, 1983), 20.

35. Raymond E. Brown translates 1:3 correctly, "Through him all things came into being," remarking that "'all things' is a wider concept than 'the world'" (*The Gospel according to John: Introduction, Translation, and Notes*, 2 vols., Anchor Bible 29, 29A (New York: Doubleday, 1966, 1970), 1:3. Yet he too clings to the idea of creation.

is a translation of the Greek text with the correct rendering of ἐγένετο and with the ancient punctuation:

"Everything came to pass through him [δι᾽ αὐτοῦ], and apart from him not even one thing came to pass. What came to pass in him [ἐν αὐτῷ] was life, and the life was the light of men."

Of course this too has to be interpreted; here is my own interpretation, first proposed nearly thirty years ago:

From the very beginning God held his thought (the Logos) close to him, and his thought was a facet of his divinity. All human history, every single thing that has ever happened, took place through the mediation of the Logos, but what has come about *in* the Logos (that is, the special events of God's intervention on behalf of his people), this was life, a life that it was God's prerogative to bestow, a life that was also light—illumination and revelation.

8

Human or Divine?

Before inquiring whether the Jesus of John's Gospel may fairly be called divine (and if so in what sense), let us first ask whether he may fairly be called human. The great majority of scholars, including Rudolf Bultmann, have opted for a human Jesus, but one prominent exception is Bultmann's pupil, Ernst Käsemann, who answered the question with a resounding no. In an early article on the Prologue of the Gospel[1] he had pictured the Johannine Christ as a God walking, or perhaps ambling (*wandelnd*) over the earth, and in his book *The Testament of Jesus*,[2] toward the end of a chapter entitled "The Glory of Christ," he attributed to John what he calls "a naïve docetism." By then his conception of the Johannine Christ had hardened: he was now a "God striding (*schreitend*) over the earth," after which memorable characterization (weakened in the English translation to "God going about on the earth"), Käsemann went on to discuss the declaration in the Prologue that "the Word was made flesh." In what sense, he asked, "is he flesh, who walks on the water and through closed doors, who cannot be captured by his enemies, who at the well of Samaria is tired and desires a drink, yet has no need of drink and has food different from that which his disciples seek?"[3] In the third (German) edition of the book, he responded to

1. Ernst Käsemann, "Aufbau und Anliegen des johanneischen Prolog," in *Libertas Christiana: Friedrich Delekat zum 65. Geburtstag,* ed.Walter Matthias and Ernst Wolf, Beiträge zur evangelischen Theologie 26 (Munich: Kaiser, 1957), 75–99. Did Käsemann get this idea from Wrede, I wonder, who as early as 1903 had described the Johannine Christ as "ein wandelnder Gott" and spoken of his "übermenschliche Hoheit" [superhuman grandeur] (William Wrede, *Charakter und Tendenz des Johannesevangelium* [Tübingen: Mohr Siebeck, 1903], 37), or even from Rudolf Bultmann himself, who in an article of 1930 had described the Jesus of the Gospels as "der über die Erde wandelnde Gottessohn," adding, "zumal [above all] im Johannesevangelium" ("Untersuchungen zum Johannesevangelium B. Θεὸν οὐδεὶς ἑώρακεν πώποτε [Joh 1,18]," *Zeitschrift für die neutestamentliche Wissenschaft* 29 [1930]: 183).

2. Ernst Käsemann,*The Testament of Jesus: A Study of the Gospel of John in the Light of Chapter 17* (London: SCM, 1968).

3. Käsemann, *Testament*, 8–9.

his critics with an uncompromising rebuttal of the charge that his conception of a docetic Christ was anachronistic.[4] (Docetism, the view that Christ may look like a man but underneath is really God is generally classed as a second-century heresy.)

Let me give my own take on the Johannine Jesus, starting with a comparison between the portrait of Jesus painted by the Synoptists (there are of course three, but the differences are relatively small) and the portrait painted by John.

To most modern eyes the synoptic portrait is both simpler and more attractive. We see a man with a special relationship with God, whom he addresses by the intimate name of Abba, Father. He is the promised Messiah, and he has been appointed by God to preach the kingdom, and thereby to fulfil the promise of the Old Testament. His birth was miraculous and his resurrection from the dead, after appalling suffering, unique. But for all that, he was a man of his time; his teaching and preaching, even his healing miracles, can be readily placed in the context of first-century Palestinian Judaism. If he were suddenly to reappear as he really was he would no doubt seem to us, in Albert Schweitzer's phrase, "a stranger and an enigma," but a recognizable human being nonetheless.

Not so the Johannine Christ. He does not belong to this world at all: it is almost true to say that he enters it with the purpose of leaving it, or descends in order to ascend. His real home is in heaven, but he enters an alien world with an unprecedented confidence and assurance, knowing precisely who he is, where he comes from and where he is going. And this too is his message, that he knows both his origin and his destiny, and because of this knowledge he enjoys a special relationship with the Father that verges upon total identification. No doubt he is portrayed as subject to human weaknesses, hunger, fatigue, grief; but these in no way diminish the extraordinary control he exercises upon his own fate. He even orchestrates his own passion; condemned to death, he appears as the judge of the one who condemns him: he can read Pilate's heart, just as he can read the hearts of other men and women. There is in him no trace of that uncertainty, that helpless sense of being flung into the world which Heidegger, with picturesque concision,

4. Käsemann, *Jesu letzter Wille nach Johannes 17*, 3rd ed. (Tübingen: Mohr Siebeck, 1971), 62 n. 69.

calls *Geworfensein*, that incomprehension and bewilderment which ordinary human beings can never entirely escape. . . . Master of his fate, captain of his soul, his head bloody but unbowed, he never had to confront either the fell clutch of circumstance or the bludgeonings of chance.[5]

For this composite portrait I drew on material from all over the Gospel; but it fits at almost every point. It is how the author of the Gospel himself saw Jesus. Nearly a century ago, in 1916, in a book on the Fourth Gospel called *Der Sohn Gottes*,[6] Gillis Petersson Wetter proposed that the category best suited to the Johannine Christ is that of a divine man, defined later by an authority on the subject as "a man with qualities and abilities far beyond the normal, the darling of the gods, and a kind of mediator between the divinity and human beings, at once their counsellor and their champion."[7] Writing in the heyday of the history-of-religions movement, Wetter simply assumed a Hellenistic background for the Fourth Gospel. He added two subtitles to his book, indicating that his attempt to identify the theological bias (*Tendenz*) of the Gospel was at the same time (*zugleich*) a contribution to the knowledge of "savior-figures" in antiquity; and he was confident that the Johannine Christ could be characterized as a divine man (θεῖος ἄνθρωπος). His successors used the term θεῖος ἀνήρ instead, but the meaning was the same. "The existence of this *theios anēr*," wrote Johannine scholar Dwight Moody Smith sixty years after Wetter, "is presently regarded as well-established, the only question being at what traditional level this Christology is to be found."[8]

The qualification is important. Wetter himself pretended to offer a full explanation of the Johannine portrait of Jesus, but his explanation was woefully inadequate. As could be inferred from my own summary picture of John's Jesus, Greek readers might well feel that John's Jesus was just the sort of *theios anēr*

5. John Ashton, *Understanding the Fourth Gospel*, 2nd ed. (Oxford: Clarendon, 2007), 141–42.

6. Gillis Petersson Wetter, *Der Sohn Gottes: Eine Untersuchung über den Charakter und die Tendenz des Johannes Evangeliums. Zugleich ein Beitrag zur Kenntnis der Heilandsgestalten der Antike*, Forschungen zur Religion und Literatur des Alten und Neuen Testaments 26 (Göttingen: Vandenhoeck & Ruprecht, 1916).

7. Ludwig Bieler, Θεῖος ἀνήρ: *Das Bild des "göttlichen Menschen" in Spätantike und Frühchristentum*, vol. 1 (Vienna: O. Höfels, 1935), 20.

8. Dwight Moody Smith, "The Johannine Miracle Source: A Proposal," in *Jews, Greeks, and Christians: Religious Cultures in Late Antiquity. Essays in Honor of William David Davies*, ed. Robert Hamerton-Kelly and Robin Scroggs, Studies in Judaism in Late Antiquity, 21 (Leiden: Brill, 1976), 167. Besides Bultmann and Käsemann, Smith cites Jürgen Becker (1969–70), Helmut Köster and James M. Robinson (1971), Ernst Haenchen (1962–63), and Luise Schottroff (1970).

they were familiar with, a superman with superhuman powers. But Wetter's divine man, having nothing of the rich complexity of the Jesus of John's Gospel, could not compete with the comprehensive explanation attempted less than a decade later by Rudolf Bultmann. Bultmann, seeking a single source for John's elaborate Christology, and failing to find one in any of the three main branches of doctrinal development that can be distinguished in the early church (first, Paul; second, Jewish-Hellenistic Christianity as represented by *1 Clement* or the *Shepherd* of Hermas; and, third, the Synoptic Gospels), had opted instead for a non-Christian (Mandaean) source, one steeped in Gnostic mythology. Wetter too had suggested a non-Christian source, the *theios anēr*; but Bultmann wanted a comprehensive explanation and was pleased to find no fewer than twenty-eight parallels between the Gospel and his chosen documents, including the key themes of revelation, mission, and descent/ascent.[9] Indeed, his Christ was the very embodiment of divine revelation. The Hellenistic *theios anēr*, by contrast, is not a divine being in any metaphysical sense but a superman. As Morton Smith pointed out, it was quite common in the Hellenistic world to describe as divine "any man who excelled in any desirable capacity—beauty, strength, wisdom, prestige, song, fame, skill in speaking, or success in love."[10] (He might have added the gift of healing possessed by Apollonius and Asclepius.)

Looking back at Wetter's book nearly a hundred years after it was published, we may be surprised to see how poorly it accounts for the Johannine Christ, especially when compared with Bultmann's breathtakingly bold hypothesis. The relatively long life of the *theios anthrōpos* may be explained partly, I think, by the fact that the picture it evokes of an exceptional human being, a superman, corresponds quite well to the impression a first-time reader might get of John's Jesus, and partly by Wetter's success in obscuring and to some extent bypassing the larger problem that Bultmann had seen so clearly. Bultmann's fully worked-out Mandaean theory, which had a brief but brilliant career, can now be seen embalmed in the pages of his great commentary, where we may gaze upon it with admiration, and indeed with awe. By contrast, the divine man who stepped out of Wetter's pages had a long life, with numerous avatars, and did not get his final coup de grâce until 1977 (in a book by Carl Holladay published the year after the essay by Moody Smith quoted above),[11] when he found his rightful place in a crowded cemetery alongside numerous

9. The full exposition of the twenty-eight parallels takes up thirty-five pages (104–39) of his famous *Bedeutung* article. For a summary, see *Understanding the Fourth Gospel*, 1st ed., 55.

10. Morton Smith, "Prolegomena to a Discussion of Aretologies, Divine Men, the Gospels and Jesus," *Journal of Biblical Literature* 90 (1971): 174–99.

other impossible proposals whose frailty (their Achilles' heel, one might say) had become evident only on the eve of their demise.

What are we to conclude, though, about the question of Jesus' humanity? Any resemblance of the Johannine Jesus to Hellenistic divine men is not enough to justify a denial of his humanity, for they were not thought of as anything other than exceptional human beings. My own view is that John would have been surprised to be asked whether Jesus was really human. (There may well have been elderly members of his community who knew Jesus personally; anyone sixty years old in 80 CE would have been a teenager when Jesus was alive and active.) Great attention is paid to Jesus' death in the Gospel—and gods do not die. It is just that the evangelist was not greatly concerned with Jesus' human traits: what preoccupied him above all (Käsemann was right about this) was his glory. We shall have to consider this more closely later.

Turning back now to Wetter, I should add that Moody Smith was wrong to speak of the virtual unanimity of Johannine scholars concerning the divine man hypothesis; for Wetter's divine man theory had already been challenged and, I think, effectively refuted, in a single footnote toward the beginning of Wayne Meeks's magisterial *Prophet-King*.[12] What is more, in the following year, 1969, Meeks had made a more wide-ranging criticism of the whole divine man theory in a review of Käsemann's *Testament of Jesus*: "This interpretation," he remarked, "has in recent years been more often ignored than refuted."[13] Meeks went on to summarize his own solution to the problem, one that he had put forward in his *Prophet-King*—"that this portrait of Jesus is drawn largely from a quite special form of the *theios* figure, namely that of the Hellenistic-Jewish (and Samaritan) man of God, a title applied pre-eminently to Moses, but also to the Patriarchs, Enoch, Elijah, and certain of the other prophets."

Meeks's proposal has the great advantage of situating the Gospel more or less where it belongs. It shifts our attention from classical Hellenism to Jewish

11. Carl Holladay, *Theios Aner in Hellenistic Judaism: A Critique of the Use of This Category in New Testament Christology*, Society of Biblical Literature Dissertation Series 40 (Missoula, Mont: Scholars Press, 1977).

12. Wayne A. Meeks, *The Prophet-King: Moses Traditions and the Johannine Christology*, Supplements to Novum Testamentum 14 (Leiden: Brill, 1967), 10 n. 5; further, pp. 22–23. Meeks criticizes especially Wetter's insightless discussion of the question πόθεν εἶ σύ; in John; moreover, Wetter's assertion that the title of Prophet in John was synonymous with "the Son of God" assumes what he wished to prove, "that 'Son of God' is the fundamental title given Jesus in the Fourth Gospel, and that all other titles point to the same notion" (Meeks, 23 n. 1).

13. Meeks, review of *The Testament of Jesus*, by Ernst Käsemann, *Union Seminary Quarterly Review* 24 (1969): 418. With one exception (Haenchen) the works cited by Moody Smith were published after Meeks's review.

and Samaritan sources and focuses in particular on the central figure of Moses. Yet when we look at the rabbinic and Samaritan sources that he scrutinizes with broad and meticulous scholarship in *The Prophet-King* (ruling out Philo, whose abstruse philosophizing is on a different planet), we find that, with a single exception, the *Exagoge* of Ezekiel the Tragedian, they are all are later than the Gospel itself. And if the evangelist did not know the works of Philo, he is surely equally unlikely to have had access to the curious work of Ezekiel (who like Philo hailed from Alexandria).

There remains one author, however, not cited by Meeks, whose writing was probably available to the members of Johannine community. This was Ben Sira, that passionate advocate of the marvels of the Torah. The Johannine group is likely to have given Ben Sira's enthusiastic eulogy of the law a cold reception; and when the author of the Prologue referred to the tabernacling of the Logos, as he did in 1:14, he probably did so in conscious opposition to Ben Sira's tabernacling of the law (Sir. 24:8). In the section of his work beginning, "Let us now praise famous men," after a chapter devoted to the patriarchs—Abraham, Isaac, and Jacob—Ben Sira turned to Moses. This is how he concludes a succinct summary of Moses' achievements: "He [the Lord] made him hear his voice, and led him into the thick darkness, and gave him the commandments *face to face*, the law of life and knowledge, to teach Jacob the covenant, and Israel his judgments" (45:5).

This specific allusion to a direct encounter with God is an early example of Moses speculation and could indeed have prompted some rejoinder from the evangelist. But it is equally possible that he paid it little attention: compared with the rhapsodizing of the rabbis, and above all of the Samaritan *Memar Marqah*, it is a small thing, easily inferred from the account in Exodus, "the Lord called Moses to the top of the mountain, and Moses went up" (19:20). Meeks, however, concludes his very thorough discussion of the rabbinic Haggadah, by asserting that "it can hardly be doubted that *in New Testament times* Moses was regarded by some Jews as one of the great prototypes of the mystic ascent into heaven. As such he seems to have been viewed as the mediator of heavenly secrets of all kinds, which were delivered to him when he went up from Sinai."[14]

In response to this proposal it must first be said that "it can hardly be doubted" is too strong. If Moses was indeed thought of in this way, in New Testament times and in Johannine circles, then of course there would have been a reaction from those who had come to believe that Jesus had superseded Moses as the true intermediary between God and humankind. Coming from their

---

14. Meeks, *Prophet-King*, 115 (emphasis added).

adversaries, this exaltation of Moses would have seemed to the disciples of Jesus a deliberate affront, and could account both for the assertion in the Prologue that "no one has ever seen God" (1:18) and for its qualification, "except him who is from God" (6:46), as well as for the more mysterious saying in 3:13 that "no one has ascended into heaven but he who descended from heaven." (More on this later.) It may well seem unreasonable to suppose that Samaritans and the rabbis began to speculate about Moses only very much later, in the second, third, or fourth century CE. But attractive as it is, and not altogether to be excluded, or placed along with the Hermetica and the Mandaean writings in a box marked *Irrelevant*, this suggestion must be accounted no more than possible. Meeks himself emphatically rejects Käsemann's assertion that the Johannine Christ is docetic—that is to say, not human, although he may appear so, but divine—and at the end of the preceding chapter we decided that the category of prophet rules out any properly divine attribution, because the prophet sent by God to speak on his behalf is both by nature and by definition subordinate to God. But now we can no longer avoid the question opened up by Meeks's researches into the Samaritan and rabbinic sources. We must consider the two other sources that fed into John's Christology: the wisdom tradition and the Danielic Son of Man.

The Wisdom Tradition

Although there are also traces of the wisdom tradition discernible in the body of the Gospel, the debt is especially clear in the Prologue—to which we now turn. After its dramatic opening, the Prologue continues with what looks like an interruption: "There was a man sent from God, whose name was John. He came for testimony, to bear witness to the light, that all might believe through him" (1:6-7). Raymond Brown reports with apparent approval "an interesting suggestion" of M.-E. Boismard and others about the origin of these verses, "that they were the original opening of the Gospel which was displaced when the Prologue was added."[15] I believe that we would be right to adopt this suggestion. Whoever had the idea of using the hymn or poem we call the Prologue as a preface to the Gospel (let us call him the evangelist) recognized

15. Raymond E. Brown, *The Gospel according to John: Introduction, Translation, and Notes*, 2 vols., Anchor Bible 29, 29A (New York: Doubleday, 1966, 1970), 1:35; M.-E. Boismard, *St. John's Prologue* (London: Blackfriars, 1957); similarly, Barnabas Lindars, *The Gospel of John* (London: Marshall, Morgan & Scott, 1972), 82. The first to suggest that 1:6 was the original opening of the Gospel was Friedrich Spitta, *Das Johannes-Evangelium als Quelle der Geschichte Jesu* (Göttingen: Vandenhoeck & Ruprecht, 1910).

the remarkable affinity between his own conception of Jesus and that of the author of the hymn (presumably a member of his own community). He realized how dramatic and powerful an opening this hymn would provide for his own work, but he was also on the lookout for a strong beginning for the body of the Gospel that starts immediately after the Prologue. He would get this with the words: "This is the testimony of John" (1:19). At the same time, he wanted to retain the notice concerning the Baptist. So it occurred to him that by moving the original opening to its present position (as a little parenthesis within the hymn—1:6-7) he could effectively introduce his first witness to Jesus, and at the same time prepare the way for the dramatic dialogue that now follows the Prologue between John (never called *Baptist* in this Gospel) and the priests and Levites. In its present position, the statement concerning John interrupts the thought of the Prologue very abruptly, but these two apparently intrusive verses must have been inserted deliberately. This is also true of v. 15, adopted from 1:31 and put in parentheses in the RSV: "John bore witness to him, and cried, 'This was he of whom I said, "He who comes after me ranks before me, for he was before me."'"

Whatever truth there may be in this admittedly hypothetical restoration is immaterial to the next big question concerning the Prologue—perhaps the biggest of all—which has divided Johannine scholars into two camps. Many, perhaps most, regard it as axiomatic that every word transmitted as *The Gospel according to John* must be taken as the composition of the evangelist unless there is compelling proof to the contrary,[16] and hold that the Prologue in particular was composed precisely in order to furnish a proper introduction to body of the Gospel. C. H. Dodd and Rudolf Bultmann, who agree on this if not on much else, believe that the Prologue should govern our understanding of all that follows. Bultmann declares that "*the theme of the Gospel* is stated in the ὁ λόγος σάρξ ἐγένετο."[17] Dodd says that the "pre-temporal (or more properly, non-temporal) existence of the Son is affirmed with emphasis, and assumed all through the gospel."[18] C. K. Barrett, though he has his own views about how the Prologue should be described, takes a similar line to Dodd: "The Evangelist may have drawn to some extent on existing material—what writer does not? But the Prologue stands before us as a prose introduction which has

16. The story of the woman taken in adultery (7:53—8:11), found only in a mass of very late manuscripts, is one such passage; and the majority of scholars regard chapter 21 as an appendix.

17. Rudolf Bultmann, *The Gospel of John. A Commentary* (Oxford: Basil Blackwell, 1971), 64 (emphasis added). This is a theme to which Bultmann returns, with differing emphases, at several points in his commentary; see pp. 151, 468, 631, 632, 634, 659.

18. C. H. Dodd, *The Interpretation of the Fourth Gospel* (Cambridge: University Press, 1953), 260.

not been submitted to interpolation [!] and was specially written (it must be supposed) to introduce the gospel—and, it may be added, to sum it up."[19] A later scholar states firmly of the Prologue that "the pre-existent state of the Logos is the lens through which the rest of the Gospel and the entire life of Jesus are to be viewed,"[20] and he backs up his statement with a footnote citing the work of several earlier commentators, including Barrett (though not Dodd or Bultmann).

Perhaps the majority of scholars, including some of those just mentioned (not Bultmann), think that the Gospel was composed from beginning to end at a stretch, and they consequently tend to assume that the Prologue was written, like many operatic overtures, with the express purpose of introducing some of the Gospel's great themes. It is true that certain key ideas occur in the first few verses: light and darkness, the world, life, and the widespread (though ultimately ineffective) opposition to Jesus on the part of his own people. On the other hand, the amazing idea that the Logos was somehow to be identified with God's plan for the world and for humanity in general[21] is restricted to these few verses, and the identification of life with "the life of men" involves a very different conception of life from that found in the body of the Gospel, where life is the concomitant reward of faith, and not an attribute of human nature. Moreover the Logos, the undisputed subject of the Prologue, vanishes from sight after the Prologue is over, and never reappears. Barrett, who knows this perfectly well, brazens it out: "If the Prologue was intended to express in eighteen verses the theological content of twenty chapters a good deal of condensation was necessary; and much of John's Christology is condensed in the word λόγος."[22] But this *if*-clause (not argued) represents an assumption, and an unlikely one at that, if only because the word λόγος occurs in this sense nowhere else in the Gospel. How is it possible to move from the use of a single word in the Prologue to the complex Christology of the body of the Gospel, where there is not so much as a hint of incarnation, and Jesus' entry into the world is always referred to either as a descent (as Son of Man) or a mission?

A single sentence in Raymond Brown's commentary shows just how difficult it is to rid oneself of the assumption that the whole Gospel is to be

19. C. K. Barrett, *The Gospel according to St. John: An Introduction with Commentary and Notes on the Greek Text,* 2nd ed. (London, SPCK, 1978), 151.

20. James F. McGrath, *John's Apologetic Christology: Legitimation and Development in Johannine Christology,* Society for New Testament Studies Monograph Series 111 (Cambridge: Cambridge University Press, 2001), 55; cf. 131.

21. As is fully argued in excursus IV.

22. Barrett, *Gospel,* 151.

read in the light of the Prologue. At the very start of his commentary (after more than a hundred introductory pages) he describes the Prologue as "an early Christian hymn, probably stemming from Johannine circles, which has been adapted to serve as an overture to the Gospel narrative of the career of the incarnate Word."[23] Yet, as we have just noted, the remainder of the Gospel says nothing at all about the Incarnate Word. Even though Brown is one of a handful of scholars to recognize that the evangelist did not actually write the Prologue but simply adopted (and adapted) it to serve as a preface to his own work, he continues to read "the career of the incarnate Word" into the body of the Gospel. It is rather the case that the Incarnation is *not* presupposed in the body of the Gospel, and that themes such as exaltation and glorification, and also the descent/ascent of the Son of Man, were worked out and worked into the Gospel before the evangelist had taken over the Prologue and integrated it into his own work. We must accept that if the evangelist was not himself the author of the Prologue, then however readily he accepted it he cannot be credited with its leading ideas. What we *can* say, however, is that, by placing the Prologue at the head of his own work, the evangelist expressed his recognition that God's plan for humankind was embodied in the story of Jesus Christ that he was about to tell. The Prologue is on the same wavelength as the Gospel as a whole and sufficiently in conformity with the thinking of the evangelist to make it easy to see why he might have seized upon it eagerly as an ideal introduction to his own work. Up to that point it had not occurred to him that the Incarnate Word might be an appropriate way of expressing his own conviction that Jesus was "the way, the truth, and the life." But after he was shown a wonderful hymn composed in all probability by a member of his own community, a hymn that brilliantly and succinctly expressed this view, then no doubt he will also have seen how closely the career of Jesus, sought by some, rejected by most, mirrored the fate of Wisdom when she came to earth.[24]

Have I *proved* that the Prologue was not originally composed by the evangelist himself? Have I *proved* that it was added to the Gospel later on in the course of its composition? Perhaps not. I submit, however, that I have made a good case.[25] But there remains one further argument, which in my

---

23. Brown, *Gospel*, 1:1. If we wish to retain Brown's overture metaphor, we should think in terms of the grand concert overtures of Beethoven and Brahms, self-contained and self-sustaining, or the precocious young Mendelssohn's "Overture to a Midsummer Night's Dream," rather than of the lead-in overtures of Mozart, Verdi, and Wagner.

24. On this topic see chapter 9 of *Understanding the Fourth Gospel*, 366-86, "The Story of Wisdom."

25. Martin Hengel takes a similar view: "As with most works, the prologue was added last: perhaps it was composed earlier as a hymn, but this too will have been after careful reflection. John 17 was also

opinion is decisive. "For the law was given through Moses; grace and truth came through Jesus Christ" (1:17). With this sentence Moses has been ousted from his position at the heart of the Jewish religion; his privileged role as God's intermediary has been taken away from him and conferred instead on Christ. This is the announcement of a new religion and could not possibly have been written or uttered by anyone in the Jesus group until a moment in the life of the synagogue when the rebels within it had abandoned the law so completely that they could now see that the teaching of Jesus, not that of Moses, was God's central revelation to humankind. The uncompromising opposition to traditional Judaism expressed in the Prologue would have been inconceivable before the separation of the two parties in the synagogue, and consequently the Prologue must have been composed quite late in the long history of their many disagreements.

Commenting on 1:18 ("no one has seen God"), Brown remarks that it is probably directed against Moses, and adds, "We may well suspect that this theme was part of the Johannine polemic against the synagogue, for it is *repeated* in v 37 and vi 46."[26] He also says that John is holding up the example of the only Son "who has not only seen the Father but is ever at his side." Yet the Prologue does *not* say that the Son has seen the Father: it says that *no one* has seen God. The suggestion that this is part of a polemic against the synagogue is certainly a shrewd one. John 5:37, however ("his voice you have never heard, his form you have never seen"), was probably written by the evangelist before he had become acquainted with the hymn that he eventually adopted as a preface to his own work; and 6:46 ("Not that anyone has seen God except him who is from God; he has seen the Father") is best read as a deliberate qualification of the uncompromising negation in the Prologue—at first sight a surprising idea but one that gains plausibility if it is conceded that chapter 6 belongs to the second edition of the Gospel and was quite possibly written about the time that the Prologue was adapted to form a preface to what follows, forcing a rearrangement of the original opening.[27] In asserting that the

added at a later stage as in inclusion, but not by a redactor: both prologue and ch. 17 clearly show the genius of the author" (*The Johannine Question* [Philadelphia: Trinity Press International, 1989], 93). John 17, yes; but the Prologue is sufficiently different from the body of the Gospel to make it probable that Brown is correct to ascribe its composition to someone other than the evangelist.

26. Brown, *Gospel*, 1:36.

27. For a fuller discussion of the Gospel passages concerning Jesus' vision of God, see my "Reflections on a Footnote," in *Engaging with C. H. Dodd on the Gospel of John: Sixty Years of Tradition and Interpretation*, ed. Tom Thatcher and Catrin H. Williams (Cambridge: Cambridge University Press, 2013), 209–14.

polemical comment against Moses in 1:18 is *repeated* later in the Gospel, Brown has lost sight of his own suggestion that the hymnlike Prologue was not added to the Gospel until the second edition.

We have seen that by using the Prologue as a preface to his own writing, the evangelist proclaimed his own faith in the Incarnate Word. We have also seen (in Excursus IV) that the central motif of the Prologue is not creation, as virtually all commentators simply take for granted, but the revelation of God's plan for humankind as it has been manifested to Christian believers in the life of Jesus. As Paul Lamarche observes, what takes the place of the Johannine Logos in this sentence is the design of God—the divine plan,[28] a conception very different from what we find in a typical apocalypse. God's plan for the world (the Logos) is not revealed by a visionary seer who has seen God and is consequently in a position to pass on his knowledge to others. Rather it is disclosed by a theophany ("we have gazed on his glory"), a form of God's communication with the world found very often in the Bible. The revelation or "exposition" (ἐξήγησις) of God made by Jesus Christ is not, according to the Prologue, made possible by a vision. *That* form of revelation is what the supporters of Moses maintain (it is a constant theme in the Jewish tradition), but they are wrong to do so. Nor is it the case that the Jesus Christ of the Prologue acts as an *angelus interpres*, expounding and explaining a new revelation. No: *he is the embodiment of that revelation.* "Grace and truth," states the Prologue, "came about through Jesus Christ" (1:17), and "it is the only Son, on the Father's lap, who has been his manifestation" (1:18). The reason for rejecting the standard translation ("he has made him known") of the final two words, ἐκεῖνος ἐξηγήσατο, is not only that it inserts an object ("him," that is, the Father) where there is none in the Greek text, but also that it conflicts both with the body of the Gospel (where Jesus conspicuously refrains from giving any account of God at all, except to call him "the one who sent me") and with the Prologue itself, where the mode of revelation is not explanatory but, as we have just observed, theophanic.[29]

---

28. Paul Lamarche, "The Prologue of John," in *The Interpretation of John*, ed. John Ashton, Studies in New Testament Interpretation (Edinburgh: T&T Clark, 1997), 42.

29. I have not managed to find a completely satisfactory translation for ἐξηγήσατο, the only occurrence of the verb ἐξηγεῖσθαι in the Gospel. In classical Greek this word, which almost always has an object in the accusative case, means (1) lead, guide, or govern; (2) dictate, expound, or interpret; (3) tell at length, set forth, explain. None of these meanings fits here. Bultmann (*Gospel*, 79 n. 3) argues that 1:18, in spite of what he calls its "highly mythological language," has been added by the evangelist, because the whole verse is in prose, and because both the use of the pronoun ἐκεῖνος to take up a preceding subject and the way of stressing an idea by preceding it with a negation are characteristic of

The Prologue states firmly (and, one might think, unambiguously) in its opening verse that the Word was God. But this follows the statement, "the Word was with God," or perhaps "close to God" (πρὸς τὸν θεόν), and it soon emerges that the Word is the masculine surrogate of Wisdom, whose presence by God's side is highlighted by one of the earliest and most beautiful hymns to Wisdom in the Hebrew canon: "I was beside him. . . . I was daily his delight, rejoicing before him always, rejoicing in his inhabited world and delighting in the sons of men" (Prov. 8:30-31). But then comes the momentous assertion, "the Word became flesh," proclaiming what was to become one of the cardinal tenets of Christianity; and even if we reject the reading "the only-begotten God" (μονογενὴς θεός) in the last verse (which is read by all the best manuscripts), in favor of the less well attested υἱός ("Son"), it is hard to resist the conclusion that the author of the Prologue thought that Jesus was divine in the strong sense of the word.

We should also no doubt conclude that, since the evangelist fully accepted the Prologue, he too believed that Jesus was divine. Even so, it is worth asking whether this belief is equally evident in the body of the Gospel. And for this we must inquire into the evangelist's use of another Jewish tradition—that of the Danielic Son of Man.

---

his style. If this is right (and Bultmann's arguments are good ones), then the verse must be translated in such a way as to make it clear that it conforms to the evangelist's most cherished ideas. A clue comes in Jesus' response to Philip's plea to "show us the Father": "He who has seen me has seen the Father. . . . I am in the Father and the Father in me" (14:8-11). The word ἐξηγήσατο in this context *may* mean "manifested." It *cannot* mean "gave an account of" or "explained," not only because the verb here has no object but also because these translations do not accord with the evangelist's own practice. There is a use of the Greek middle voice whereby the result of an action is confined to the subject of the verb. If that is the use here, then the meaning is something like "it is he who was the manifestation." See Ignace de La Potterie, *La vérité dans saint Jean*, 2 vols., Analecta biblica 73, 74 (Rome: Biblical Institute Press 1977), 1:220–28. Pointing out that none of the classical meanings fits here, de La Potterie adduces three passages from the Septuagint. The first is 1 Chron. 16:24 (a verse omitted by both Rahlfs and Swete because it is missing from the best manuscripts): ἐξηγεῖσθε ἐν τοῖς ἔθνεσιν τὴν δόξαν αὐτοῦ. The second (from Job 12:7) is inconclusive. The third, Job 28:27, says of God that he saw wisdom καὶ ἐξηγήσατο αὐτήν. Here de La Potterie's translation ("et la manifesta") gives a better sense (at least of the Greek) than the English "and declared it." These are more convincing parallels than Barrett's suggestion (*Gospel*, 170) from Sirach: τίς ἑόρακεν αὐτὸν καὶ ἐκδιηγήσεται;—"Who has seen him and can describe him?" (Ecclus. 43:31). Arguing too that in John 1:17-18, ἀλήθεια and ἐξηγήσατο are "practically parallel," de La Potterie concludes (p. 220) that "perhaps the best" translation of this verse would be: "Le Fils unique, tourné vers le sein du Père, il fut, lui, la révélation." "Revelation," "manifestation"—either will do.

THE SON OF MAN

Although the only occurrence of the name of Moses in John 3 is in v. 14, Moses must be included in any list of an indefinitely large number of Jewish seers of whom it is implied in the previous verse that they did not ascend into heaven: "no one has ascended . . . except the Son of Man."[30]

Hugo Odeberg starts his long commentary on 3:13 by observing, "The wording οὐδεὶς ἀναβέβηκεν etc. immediately suggests that there is a refutation here of some current notions of ascent into heaven. Such notions were, as is well-known, frequent."[31] He continues by drawing on his well-stocked memory and citing a number of possible targets (Enoch, Levi, Isaiah, St. Paul, Rabbi Ishmael, the four who entered paradise), adding the names of Abraham and Moses only much later.[32] Eventually, after several pages of what he admits to be mostly irrelevant citations,[33] he concludes:

> There is only one conception known that can possibly be intended in the controversial utterance, viz, that certain especially gifted or saintly men had ascended or could ascend on high while still on earth. The particular bearing of the theory rejected can be conjectured from the context of Jn 3.13. The preceding context contains two ideas connected with the ascent into heaven; viz. the vision (or entrance into) the Kingdom of God, the highest realm of the celestial world [3.3] and the knowledge of the Celestial realities [τὰ ἐπουράνία; 3.12.] Now the vision of the heavens, especially the highest heaven, the Divine Abode, and the knowledge concerning Divine Secrets of Past, Present and Future derived therefrom, are precisely the central features of the ideas in Jewish Apocalyptic and, at the time of Jn, also in some of the Merkaba-ecstatic circles.[34]

30. In this section I have drawn on two recent articles, "The Johannine Son of Man: A New Proposal," *New Testament Studies* 57 (2011): 508–29; "Intimations of Apocalyptic: Looking Back and Looking Forward," *John's Gospel and Intimations of Apocalyptic*, ed. Catrin H. Williams and Christopher Rowland (London: Bloomsbury T & T Clark, 2013), 3–35.

31. Hugo Odeberg, *The Fourth Gospel: Interpreted in Its Relation to Contemporary Religious Currents in Palestine and the Hellenistic-Oriental world* (Uppsala: Almqvist & Wiksell, 1929), 72, 97.

32. Odeberg, *Fourth Gospel,* 92. One surprising omission is Elijah, whose ascent, along with that of Moses, is denied by the *Mekilta* on Exod. 19:20 (*Baḥodesh* 4). Alan F. Segal, in a significant contribution, adds the names of Baruch, Phineas, Ezra, Adam, and Zephaniah ("Heavenly Ascent in Hellenistic Judaism, Early Christianity and Their Environment," *Aufstieg und Niedergang der römischen Welt* 23.2 (Berlin/New York: de Gruyter, 1980), 1333–94.

33. Two pages from the *Corpus Hermeticum* (73–75), twelve from the Mandaean literature (75–88), and five from rabbinic sources (89–94) concerning the descent and ascent of the Šĕkīnâ.

Crucial here is the observation that Jesus bases his claim of being able to transmit his knowledge of celestial realities ("we speak of what we know and bear witness to what we have seen") on *personal experience*, an experience that came not, as is so often asserted, from some sort of heavenly preexistence but from an ascent into heaven that is denied of all others.[35] We have already observed that the Prologue was not added to the Gospel until the second edition. It is therefore a grave mistake to interpret this passage in the light of the Incarnation, or rather of some supposed preexistent vision. These ideas had not yet entered into the thinking of the evangelist.

"No one has ascended into heaven except. . . ." This is not a total denial of all other revelations. After all, the commonest form of divine revelation in the Bible is that of prophecy, where a named person communicates a message that he or she has received either directly from God or through the mediation of an angel. Specifically, 3:13 denies that anyone apart from Jesus has ascended into heaven (so as to be in a position to transmit directly received knowledge). Odeberg saw that it involved "the refutation of current notion of ascent into heaven," but failed to see that the primary target must have been Moses.

How so, it might be asked, since in the passage in Exodus that describes the reception of the tablets of the law God is said to have descended upon Mount Sinai and to have summoned Moses to meet him (Exod. 19:11, 18-20). Moses is not said to have ascended into heaven. One answer to this question (the one I gave in my Son of Man article) is that in all likelihood the evangelist had in mind a tradition according to which, after climbing Sinai, Moses proceeded to ascend as far as heaven itself. "Not even Moses," runs a midrash on Ps. 106:2, "who went up to heaven to receive the Torah from God's hand into his own, could fathom heaven's depth." This idea, which is also found several times in Philo, goes back at least as far as the *Exagoge* of Ezekiel the Tragedian, in which Moses, enthroned alongside God, receives the obeisance of the stars as they pass in review before him.[36] So it cannot be later than the early first century BCE.

34. Odeberg, *Gospel*, 94–95. Odeberg goes on to discuss what he calls "the positive bearing of this passage," and reaffirms his view of the inclusive sense of the title Son of Man, which involves the incorporation of all believers in a "man" who represents the essence of humanity.

35. Odeberg had previously paraphrased 3:12 as "a world of which I can speak, for I know and have seen it, *having myself come from that world*" (*Gospel*, 49 [emphasis added])—forgetting the key reference to "ascent" in 3:13.

36. See Meeks, *Prophet-King*, 147–49. Meeks quotes the relevant passage and gives a full account of it. I am also indebted to him for the quotation from the midrash just above (p. 205), and for the allusion to Philo (pp. 122–25).

If the fourth evangelist knew of this tradition (and it is just possible that he did), then we could infer from 3:13 that he was concerned not only to emphasize the exclusiveness of Jesus' ascent into heaven but also to deny that any other Jewish seer, first Moses, but also Enoch and Elijah, had either gone up to heaven as an apocalyptic visionary or been translated there at the end of his life.[37] Hidden behind this obscure saying, therefore, could be the beginnings of an attack on the whole Jewish tradition. But in the light of John's general hostility to "the disciples of Moses," he probably did not need any prompting to make this veiled attack upon him. Convinced that the new revelation surpassed the old, he was prepared to push it at every opportunity. Not surprisingly he always accuses "the Jews" of intransigence, and puts the blame on them for their hostility to Jesus. But how could they not have been provoked by his repeated assertions of Jesus' superiority?

For a very long time most scholars were convinced that John derived the descent/ascent motif associated with the Son of Man from Gnosticism. Wayne Meeks, for instance, in his book *The Prophet-King*,[38] expressed the view that this motif still furnished the strongest reason for thinking that the Gospel had a Gnostic background, and this view remained largely unchallenged even after it had been comprehensively demolished by Carsten Colpe in a long article for the *Theologisches Wörterbuch*.[39]

The "figure like a man" who is given dominion by the Ancient of Days in Daniel's first great vision (Daniel 7) was soon to be identified by a title, "*the Son of Man*" (*son of man* being the literal meaning of the Aramaic expression). So much is clear from the eschatological discourses in the Synoptic Gospels, where the reference to "the Son of Man coming in the clouds of heaven" (Mark 13:26) establishes beyond doubt a debt to Daniel's vision, and from the Parables of Enoch. Precisely who is referred to in the Synoptic Gospels every time Jesus uses the expression "Son of Man" is one of the most contentious and contended problems in New Testament scholarship,[40] but at least in the eschatological discourses and in certain other passages, such as the account of the trial before Caiphas, there can be no doubt that a direct allusion to the Danielic Son of Man

---

37. See Ashton, "Johannine Son of Man," 516–19, where this is argued in more detail.

38. Meeks, *Prophet-King*, 297.

39. Carston Colpe, ὁ υἱὸς τοῦ ἀνθρώπου, *Theological Dictionary of the New Testament,* ed. Gerhard Friedrich (Grand Rapids, MI: Eerdmans: 1972), 8:400–477.

40. On this question, see now especially the section "The Son of Man" in chapter 5 in Christopher Rowland and Christopher R. A. Morray-Jones, *The Mystery of God: Early Jewish Mysticism and the New Testament,* Compendia rerum iudaicarum ad Novum Testamentum, Section 3, Jewish Traditions in Early Christian Literature 12 (Leiden/Boston: Brill, 2009), 109–13.

is intended. In all of these passages, however, the Son of Man is already located in heaven: there can be no question of an ascent, and still less of a descent.

The difficulty for scholars wishing to explain the descent/ascent theme in John is that it is not found anywhere else, either in Daniel 7, the original source of the Son of Man motif, or in the Parables of Enoch, or in the other three Gospels. (The absence of the motif elsewhere is what accounts for the ill-considered appeal to Gnosticism.) John is unquestionably a powerful and imaginative thinker, so it is not unreasonable to inquire whether he could have come up with the idea himself. But if so how?

I believe that the answer to this question is to be found in an episode of the Gospel that has already occupied our attention more than once: the story of the blind beggar in John 9. Asked where the fourth evangelist places the most significant of his ideas concerning Jesus, most people would probably say that they come in the great controversy scenes in the first half of the Gospel, in the farewell discourse and prayer in the second half, and perhaps too in the great series of I-am sayings. But it is noteworthy how many of these sayings, and other little revelatory gems besides, occur in fragments of dialogue, scattered throughout the book, between Jesus and one or two individual interlocutors—Nathanael (chapter 1), Nicodemus (chapter 3), the Samaritan woman (chapter 4), Martha (chapter 11), Philip and Andrew (chapter 12), Thomas and Philip (chapter 14), and Pilate (chapter 19). In a number of these passages Jesus is seen to be freshly identifying himself, which is precisely what he does at the end of chapter 9, when he goes to look for the man he healed, who has just been thrown out of the synagogue. He questioned him directly, "Do you believe in the Son of Man?" "Who is that?" he asked. "You have seen him," said Jesus, "and he is speaking to you"; whereupon the man prostrated himself in worship (9:35-38).

In the great majority of the sayings in the other three Gospels the attribution of the title Son of Man, always in the third person, is indirect; and Jesus never actually says, "*I am* the Son of Man." In those sayings that include a clear or probable reference to the Danielic Son of Man, the usage is proleptic, anticipatory, eschatological, looking forward to a visionary future. In the Fourth Gospel too, for the most part, the evangelist follows the Synoptic convention in using the title indirectly, most notably in the three so-called passion predictions, where in all likelihood there is a direct dependence on the Synoptic sayings. But in this particular passage in chapter 9 he breaks this unwritten rule.

It is an extraordinary passage, prompting several questions, the most obvious of which concerns its connection with the preceding story. How are we to explain Jesus' deliberate introduction of himself as Son of Man at this point? The answer to this question is to be found in what he says next: "for judgment I have come into this world, that those who do not see may see, and that those who see may become blind" (9:39). This statement involves a dramatic reinterpretation of the original healing miracle. For the original purpose of the story was, first, to portray Jesus as a healer and, second, to show that his ability to heal proved that he was commissioned by God—that he was a prophet. But now, in the concluding paragraph of the chapter, the miracle is portrayed as an act of judgment (deliberately recalling the symbolism of sight and blindness), and judging was essentially the business of the Son of Man. This is stated quite clearly in chapter 5: "the Father . . . has given him [the Son] authority to execute judgment *because he is the Son of Man*" (5:27). So here is a claim far exceeding the authority to perform healing miracles: the claim that precisely *as Son of Man* Jesus was entitled to exercise *on earth* the kind of supreme authority that in Daniel's vision had been bestowed on the Son of Man *in heaven*. This means (and I cannot emphasize this too much) that *the evangelist himself had concluded that the heavenly figure of the Son of Man had come down to earth in the person of Jesus.*

With this in mind, we are in a position to return to one of the most puzzling sayings in the whole Gospel: "No one has ascended into heaven, but he who descended from heaven, the Son of Man" (3:13). What ascent is Jesus referring to here, when he is still on earth? What was the purpose of this saying? Whom did the evangelist have in his sights when he wrote this sentence? One answer to this last question, as we have already noted, was given long ago by the Swedish scholar Hugo Odeberg, who argued that the saying was directed against widespread Jewish traditions concerning the ascent into heaven of Jewish patriarchs or prophets such as Abraham and Elijah.[41] But it is equally likely that the target was Moses alone. We do not have to suppose that the evangelist had in mind a legend (attested only much later) according to which Moses was thought to have reascended into heaven to report to God that he had successfully carried out the mission he had been given to carry down the tablets of the law to the people of Israel. If that *was* the case, then we would have to see the saying as part of an ongoing polemic between the Jesus group in the synagogue and their conservative opponents, "the disciples of Moses." But this remains just a supposition.

Jan-Adolf Bühner sheds some additional light. In his conversation with Nicodemus in John 3, Jesus finds it necessary to correct Nicodemus's

---

41. Odeberg, *Fourth Gospel*, 72.

misunderstanding of something he had just said. He adds that he speaks of what he knows, including, apparently, heavenly things. What entitles him to speak of heavenly things? Why, his ascent into heaven (which can only mean his ascent as a visionary seer to receive revelations from God). Accordingly, basing his suggestion on a variety of evidence in Jewish sources, Bühner proposed that Jesus too was thought to have made an ascent into heaven to receive divine revelations, and then, *having undergone an angelic transformation*, to have descended as the Son of Man—the angelic being in Daniel's vision.[42] It is a bold suggestion, certainly, but it has the merit of providing a plausible solution to the puzzle of 3:13, at the same time suggesting an additional reason for the evangelist's belief in the descent of the Son of Man. Even more importantly, it enables us to understand how the evangelist thought of Jesus' career before he had read and digested what another member of his community had written concerning the preexistent Logos, before, that is, he had come to know, to value, and to adapt for his own use what we now call the Prologue to the Gospel.

In the second edition of the Gospel (which is where, as we have seen, chapter 6 belongs) he took the opportunity of correcting one assertion that occurs late in the hymn: "no one has ever seen God" (1:18): "Not that anyone has seen the Father"—no, wrong, there is one exception: "he who is from God: he has seen the Father" (6:46). Perhaps the evangelist was correcting a line that he had written himself (see p. 168n29 above), but when the Jesus whose story he was telling spoke of his own vision of God (as he did in 5:19, and again in 6:46), the evangelist was surely not making him refer to a vision that he was supposed to have had in a preexistent state before the Logos had taken flesh! That, of course, is what most exegetes assume, though without, I suspect, giving the matter much thought.

In the eschatological discourse in Matthew and Mark, where Jesus foretells that the Son of Man will be seen coming in clouds with great power and glory (Mark 13:26), he seems to imply that at the end of time he will assume the authority bestowed on the Son of Man in Daniel's vision. But here John is making a much stronger claim: that Jesus already had this authority while on earth. The Son of Man is an angelic figure—so Jesus, in the eyes of the fourth evangelist, is an angel!

---

42. Jan-Adolf Bühner, *Der Gesandte und sein Weg im vierten Evangelium: Die kultur- und religionsgeschichtliche Grundlagen der johanneischen Sendungschristologie sowie ihre traditionsgeschichtliche Entwicklung*, Wissenschaftliche Untersuchungen zum Neuen Testament 2/2 (Tübingen: J. C. B. Mohr, 1977), 341–73.

This is unquestionably a startling, even a shocking conclusion. John may well have read the book of Daniel attentively long before he was converted to the Jesus movement. There is already something shocking about seeing an angelic being enthroned beside God, even as a figure in a visionary dream; and we know that this figure came to seem worrisome and problematic in some rabbinical circles some time later.[43] But John's direct identification of Jesus as the Son of Man, however bold, was nevertheless limited. J. Louis Martyn says, quite unjustifiably, that there is in the Gospel "an emphasis on confessing Jesus as Son of Man."[44] Not so! There is nothing in the Gospel to warrant this assertion. The snatch of dialogue between Jesus and the man to whom he has just restored his sight is private, overheard by nobody except the one who tells the story. We are not told that the man born blind went back to the synagogue authorities to confront them with his new-found faith. Nor does Jesus' self-identification with the Son of Man ever figure among the accusations of blasphemy leveled against him by the Jews. There is no parallel in John's Gospel to the response given by Jesus in his trial before Caiaphas to the question, "Are you the Messiah, the son of the Blessed?" In Mark's version of this episode Jesus' reply is unambiguous: "I am, and you will see the Son of Man seated at the right hand of Power, and coming with the clouds of heaven" (13:62). It is not the claim to be the Messiah, but the claim to sit at the right hand of Power, as the Son of Man, that provokes the charge of blasphemy. But there is no hint of this in John's account of Jesus' interrogation by Annas (19:19-24). Neither here nor anywhere else in the Gospel does Jesus' claim to be the Son of Man figure among the many confrontations between him and the Jews. Yet it is unquestionably there and must be included in any estimate of the evangelist's picture of Jesus.

Study of the sonship and prophet motifs in the Gospel reveals that Jesus is sometimes seen as subordinate to God and sometimes as God's equal. In an earlier essay I had already argued that the consequent ambiguity was bridged by an angelic Christology,[45] suggesting too that the bridge was "probably connected with the more prominent bridge that leads back to the Danielic Son

43. Alan Segal quotes a passage from the *Mekhilta* (possibly as early as the second century CE) in which, directly after a quotation of Dan 7:9 ("As I looked, thrones were placed") a warning is given that no doctrine of "two powers in heaven" should be derived from this passage. See Alan F. Segal, *Two Powers in Heaven: Early Rabbinic Reports about Christianity and Gnosticism*, Studies in Judaism in Late Antiquity 25 (Leiden: Brill, 1977), 36; cf. 139.

44. J. Louis Martyn, *History and Theology in the Fourth Gospel*, 3rd ed. (Louisville: Westminster John Knox, 2003), 129 n. 195.

45. John Ashton, "Bridging Ambiguities," in *Studying John: Approaches to the Fourth Gospel* (Oxford: Clarendon, 1994), 71–89; see also *Understanding the Fourth Gospel*, 281–98.

of Man." I ended by saying that the purpose of the essay was "to inquire into certain possibilities of the new religion [i.e., of Christianity], not to offer a causal explanation of its actual genesis." After investigating the more prominent bridge, I have felt able to take this extra step.

CONCLUSION

The title of this chapter is "Human or Divine?" Perhaps, though, the "or" is misleading. I have pointed to three avenues in the Gospel, three different ways of seeing Jesus' entry into the world, three well-established Jewish traditions that have been exploited to good effect by the evangelist. The first is the prophetic tradition, whereby the prophet sent by God speaks the words of God—never, as Jesus says repeatedly throughout the Gospel, on his own account, but yet bringing him so close to the one who sent him that he can say, "I and the Father are one," and "he who has seen me has seen the Father." The second is the wisdom tradition absorbed into the Prologue: the Word was made flesh: God's divine plan for the world is embodied in the person of Jesus Christ. The third is the Danielic Son of Man tradition, whose use by the fourth evangelist is widely misunderstood, but probably depends on the concept of angelic transformation.

The evangelist's imaginative exploitation of all these traditions leaves his readers with the impression of a divine Christ, and before concluding his Gospel he reinforces that impression in a climactic scene, one of the most memorable episodes in the whole Bible. The second character in this episode (it is the last of those little dialogues in which Jesus freshly reveals himself) is universally known as "doubting Thomas." but the scene culminates in Thomas's fervent profession of faith: "my Lord and my God!" Deliberately placed where it is, as the Gospel is about to end, can one even conceive of a stronger declaration? Maybe not, but it is worth reflecting that what I have called Thomas's "profession of faith" depended in his case on his seeing Jesus physically present in front of him—as he is reminded: "Have you believed because you have seen me?"

This may prompt us to take a fresh look at some of the other passages in the Gospel in which the sight of God is in question, including the amazing opening, where after the Word has been identified as "the Light that enlightens every man," it is announced that he was himself an object of contemplation: "we have gazed upon his glory." But then follows the stern reminder: "no one has ever seen God"—except, of course, those who have gazed upon the Incarnate Word (who, as is asserted in the very first verse, was with God, and was God). So a few privileged people, among whom the writer includes himself ("we"), have actually witnessed God's theophanic appearance in the form of the Incarnate Word.

All this has somehow to be reconciled with certain of Jesus' declarations in the Gospel that follows, especially the passage in which an exception is made to the categorical denial that anyone has ever seen God: "Not that anyone has seen the Father *except him who is from God*; he has seen the Father" (6:46). The original denial (1:18) was almost certainly directed primarily against Moses, who was set over in the preceding verse against Jesus Christ. But although the new saying in which the exception is made must be given full value (no one at all except Jesus himself), this idea too had already been challenged in the first edition of the Gospel: "Philip said to him, 'Lord, show us the Father, and we shall be satisfied.' Jesus said to him, 'Have I been with you so long, and yet you do not know me, Philip? *He who has seen me has seen the Father*; how can you say, 'show us the Father'? Do you not believe that I am in the Father and the Father in me?' " (14:8-10). At one point he even says of the Jews (though without naming them) that "they have seen and hated both me and my Father" (15:24).

Earlier Jesus had told them: "if you knew me, you would know my Father also" (8:19). For the Jews to whom he addressed these words this was out of the question, because, as he told them immediately afterwards, "You are from below, I am from above; you are of this world, I am not of this world" (8:23). But the same was not true of Jesus' disciples: in his prayer to his Father he said of them that "they are not of the world, even as I am not of the world" (17:16). Wondering why Philip's long acquaintance with Jesus (he was after all one of the five very first disciples) did not bring with it the full knowledge required of him, we might think that Jesus was quite right to rebuke him. Yet this would be to forget the unvarying principle we discussed at length in chapter 3—that there is no full understanding of Jesus' words until he has risen from the dead.

When this full understanding comes, with the help of the Paraclete, it involves not just a knowledge of Jesus himself, but also of the Father. It will remain true that no one has seen the Father directly except Jesus himself. But indirectly, Philip and all the other disciples (though they are not yet aware of it) have already seen the Father, simply because they have seen Jesus. Indeed all that ever had been or could ever be seen of God had already been revealed in the words and deeds of Jesus (watched by his disciples from the beginning to the end of his public career), now enshrined in the Gospel—although the reader will soon learn that even more could have been told. Not an apocalyptic revelation in the strict sense but still a revealed truth, and one that superseded anything that had gone before.

In the final scene of the Gospel the situation has changed, because Jesus has now risen from the dead. Philip had asked to be shown the Father; Thomas had asked to be shown the print of the nails and expressed a wish to place his hand in Jesus' side (20:25). When he sees Jesus all his doubts fall away, because sight is now sufficient. Jesus, however, still has something to teach him, and rubs it in: "Put your finger here, and place your hand in my side." In his response Thomas shows that he has already learned Philip's lesson: seeing Jesus, he knows that in him he is also seeing the Father, and he bursts out: "My Lord and my God!" Into these few words the evangelist has compressed the essence of all he has come to think about Jesus' relationship with God. He nowhere uses the term εἰκών, "image," but few terms would be better suited to encapsulate his belief about the relationship between Jesus and the Father. Although any direct vision of the Father is now excluded, in this final scene the equivalent was there in the person of Jesus, as Thomas fully recognizes.

Yet there is one further lesson to be taught, and this concerns the crucial difference between vision and faith. Thomas, who, as one of the Twelve, is one of the last people to see the risen Jesus, believes because he has seen him physically present and has come close enough to put his hand in his side. Yet the very last words that Jesus addresses to him make it paradoxically plain that this unmediated vision is not to be thought of as a privilege: "Blessed are those who have *not* seen, and yet believe." *How* those who have not seen may come to believe is indicated in the closing sentence of the whole Gospel, addressed to the evangelist's readers. In a saying in which the reference of the word *signs* is extended to include the passion and resurrection stories he has just told, he announces that "these [signs] are written that you may believe." Scholars have argued endlessly whether all the prospective readers of the Gospel already stand within the circle of believers (in which case the Gospel must have been written to strengthen their already existing belief) or whether John was targeting others, pagans or Jews, in the hope that they too would come to believe. The evangelist unquestionably had the members of his own community in mind. So much is clear from the message of reassurance in the Farewell Discourse. Yet anyone who thinks, as I do, that he also hoped to reach other readers outside his own community, can hardly fail to be struck by the enormity of his ambitions. For these other readers, he appears to be saying, the path to faith is his own book! Powerful as his work undoubtedly is, is it compelling enough to persuade readers hitherto unfamiliar with the story of Jesus that in and through this little book they can find God?

The Gospel remains a puzzle full of mysteries. There are mysteries for the believer, and mysteries for the scholar too. For the scholar, I now think, the biggest mystery of all is the Johannine portrait of Jesus himself, sublimely confident and self-assured, constantly disclosing new and fascinating elements of a personality unlike any other in history or in literature. In the next and final chapter I will make some attempt to explain why this should be so.

9

The Johannine Christ

The Problem

I began the preceding chapter by highlighting the enormous differences between the Synoptic and the Johannine portrait of Christ, differences that have never been satisfactorily explained. Not that they have never been noticed: they were observed by F. C. Baur in 1847, in a book that greatly influenced Ernst Käsemann, who refers to it several times in his *Testament of Jesus* (1968).[1] For Baur the true essence of the Johannine Christ was divine: he speaks of "the absolute divinity of the person of Jesus."[2] Käsemann, as we noted in the previous chapter, pictures Jesus more imaginatively as "God striding (*schreitend*) over the earth," remarking that if comparisons between John and the Synoptics are drawn simply in order to demonstrate the closest possible approximation between them, "then the peculiar Johannine accents and stresses are shifted and the interpretation falls under the domination of apologetics."[3] Whatever one may think of Käsemann's quite extreme position, he was unquestionably correct to stress the singularity of the fourth evangelist's portrait of Christ. If the Christian church has nevertheless retained a strong memory of the human Jesus, this is due not to John, but to Matthew, Mark, and Luke.

So the puzzling question remains: why are the differences so great? If the question has not yet received a satisfactory answer, it must be partly at least because it ceased to be asked long ago. Käsemann himself paid it scant

1. See J. Louis Martyn, "Source Criticism and Religionsgeschichte in the Fourth Gospel," in *Jesus and Man's Hope*, ed. D. G. Buttrick, 2 vols. (Pittsburgh: Pittsburgh Theological Seminary, 1970), 1:248, where he remarks that one of Käsemann's numerous and distinct services has been "to renew and make potent in our time the voice of F. C. Baur."

2. Ferdinand Christian Baur, *Kritische Untersuchungen über die kanonischen Evangelien: Ihr Verhältniß zu einander, ihren Charakter und Ursprung* (Tübingen, Ludw. F, Fues, 1847), 193; cf. 97.

3. Ernst Käsemann, *The Testament of Jesus: A Study of the Gospel of John in the Light of Chapter 17* (London: SCM, 1968), 8.

attention. He promised in the preface to his book to "unfold the complex of theological problems [above all the problem of the glorious Christ] only so far as it can serve as a key for the historical question of the historical situation out of which this Gospel grew."[4] Yet his search for the historical situation is perfunctory at best. He concludes that the evangelist's doctrine of eternal life sprang from a conviction he shared with Paul's opponents in Corinth that they were already participating in the resurrection world and eternal life. "It is quite disturbing," he comments, "that the Evangelist, at the very centre of his proclamation, is dominated by a heritage of enthusiasm against which Paul had already struggled violently in his day and which in the post-apostolic age was branded as heretical."[5] Later on in the same chapter he reflects how important some of his speculations concerning subsequent interchurch struggles might turn out to be "*if* the origin of the Fourth Gospel in such circles of Hellenistic enthusiasm as are opposed both by I Cor. 15 and II Tim. 2.18 should prove to be correct."[6] Here he sounds rather less confident about the rightness of his theory (advanced earlier with no evidence and little argument).

This of course is the problem that preoccupied Rudolf Bultmann and convinced him of the need to find a single comprehensive answer to the first great riddle of the Gospel: What is the historical origin of the extraordinary conception that pervades and dominates the Gospel, Jesus' self-presentation of himself as the Revealer? At the beginning of chapter 7, following Wayne Meeks, I explained why the answer that Bultmann himself gave—the Mandaean hypothesis—had to be rejected, and why scholars came to concentrate instead on single strands in the complex christological web of the Fourth Gospel. And in the remainder of that chapter and in the next I pointed to what I prefer to call the three *streams* of Jewish tradition that I myself believe to be the most significant of all: prophet, wisdom, Son of Man.

Yet if we try to trace these streams as they keep surfacing throughout the Gospel, adding to the title of Prophet that of Son, which is also associated with the theme of mission, we find ourselves obliged to admit that the evangelist himself made little or no attempt to bring them together. One of them, in fact, the incarnation of wisdom, is restricted to the Prologue, and, as I argued, was originally somebody else's idea (although the story of wisdom is traceable in the body of the Gospel too).[7] Son of Man and Son of God (or rather Son) are

4. Käsemann, *Testament*, 3.

5. Käsemann, *Testament*, 15.

6. Käsemann, *Testament*, 24 (emphasis added).

7. See chapter 9 of *Understanding the Fourth Gospel,* 2rd ed (Oxford: Clarendon, 2007), 366–83, "The Story of Wisdom."

both prominent in chapter 3, but in adjacent paragraphs—in fact I can think of only one passage where they are inseparably linked: "For as the Father has life in himself, so he has granted the Son also to have life in himself, and has given him authority to execute judgment because he is the Son of Man" (5:26-27).

The conclusion is forced upon us that one consequence of the various shifts of focus that I discussed at the beginning of chapter 7, however significant they may have seemed at the time, was that students of the Gospel failed to realize that the response to Bultmann must be something other than a steady concentration on *narrow* aspects (Meeks's word) of Johannine Christology. Rather than a narrowing of focus, what is required is a broadening: rather than just a change of direction, we need a U-turn. So in this final chapter I will put forward a new and very different hypothesis, one that, I now see, I have been gradually approaching in the last two years, and which allows me at last to accept an idea that my friend Christopher Rowland has urged upon me more than once, specifically in his foreword to the second edition of *Understanding the Fourth Gospel*—by recognizing that what he calls "the basic theological presuppositions" of the Fourth Gospel "are remarkably similar" to those of the book of Revelation. Even so, having a residual reluctance to think in terms of theological presuppositions, I will propose that we should reflect instead on the *experience* of the two writers.[8]

In the opening section of the famous article in which he discussed the significance of some newly discovered Mandaean and Manichean sources for the comprehension of the Fourth Gospel, Bultmann briefly surveyed three alternative theories of the nature of the Fourth Gospel. This is the third:

> Is the author a mystic? . . . Possibly a mystic to whom the miracle-man [*Wundermann*] walking the earth would be a symbol of ineffable divinity? In fact the Farewell Discourse does contain some well-known mystical terminology: the formula of mutual mystical immanence: we in Jesus—Jesus in us; he dwelling in us and God too in us along with him; all one in one, the Father, the Son and "his own." But are these anything more than mere formulae? Is their purpose to describe an *experience* as distinct from *faith*?[9]

8. Responding to this concession, Rowland told me that for him the key resemblance lies in *the tabernacling of glory*, which in the eyes of the evangelist has already occurred (1:14) but is still awaited by the seer of Patmos and will not happen until the New Jerusalem comes down to earth.

9. Rudolf Bultmann, "Die Bedeutung der neuerschlossenen mandäischen und manichäischen Quellen für das Verständnis des Johannesevangeliums," *Zeitschrift für die neutestamentliche Wissenschaft* 24 (1925): 102–3. Bultmann's aversion to mysticism becomes more comprehensible if we know what he understood

Serenely confident of the rightness of his own view of the Gospel, Bultmann asked these questions only to dismiss them; but I now think that the answer must be yes. True, as he was quick to point out, John has "no mystical names for God, no anthropological dualism, no doctrine of the passage of souls." But I am less sure about the final item on his list: "no devotion based on experience [*Erlebnisfrömmigkeit*]." For besides the evidence from the Farewell Discourse that Bultmann himself brought up—not mere formulae but immediate reflections by the evangelist of an experience of an intimacy both with God and with his fellow believers—it is arguable that the image of the Shepherd ("I know my own and they know me") and the allegory of the vine ("I am the vine, you are the branches") also reflect a sense of union between Jesus and his followers best described as mystical.[10]

SOURCES

Scholars are inclined to think that the authors they study are no less interested than they themselves in seeking out sources and influences. Many indeed simply assume that the biblical authors had immediate access to any material that was not demonstrably composed after they were dead.[11] What is more, even the cautious Meeks devotes most of his fine monograph *The Prophet-King* to scrutinizing writings that were either much later than the Gospel or (as is the case of Philo and his fellow Alexandrian Ezekiel the Tragedian) probably unknown to the evangelist. Bultmann examined his Mandaean documents (centuries later) with scrupulous care, and C. H. Dodd was no less assiduous

by the term. Here is what he says about Jesus' words "I know my own and my own know me" (John 10:14): "the mutual relationship is not a circular process, as it is in mysticism, in which the mystic raises himself to equality with God, but a relationship which is established by God. And this relationship frees man from the circularity of the mystical relationship, in which in the end he can encounter only himself. The revelation unmasks the deception of the mystical relationship to God, in that it never loses its character as address and challenge; it unmasks the mystic's striving for God as a striving to turn God's address into his own human word, which he can hear in the depths of his own soul" (*The Gospel of John: A Commentary* [Oxford: Basil Blackwell, 1971], 382). This description of mystical experience would certainly not be recognized by genuine mystics, such as John of the Cross and Teresa of Avila.

10. This was recognized long ago by B. H. Streeter: "The starting-point of any profitable study of the Fourth Gospel is the recognition of the author as a mystic—perhaps the greatest of all mystics" (*The Four Gospels: A Study in Origins* (London: Macmillan, 1924), 365.

11. A moment's thought should be enough to make one see the unlikelihood of this supposition. This was not an age of printed books. Papyrus, though no doubt readily available, had to be imported from Egypt, and parchment was rare and expensive. Many copies will have been made of biblical books both in Hebrew and in Greek, certainly of the Torah and the Psalms, but most other religious works are likely to have had a much less widespread distribution. Copying demanded time, effort, and expertise.

in his perusal of the (rather earlier) *Hermetica*—even though he was careful not to call them sources. Many scholars today appear to be confident that the fourth evangelist was not only familiar with earlier Christian writings, Paul and the Synoptic Gospels, but eagerly sifted through them in the hope of finding confirmation of his own views of Christ or a stimulus to fresh thinking.

Despite my reservations about these widespread assumptions, I think that it may be nonetheless instructive to take a brief look at material with which we can be reasonably sure that John was acquainted. First of all, obviously, there is the Old Testament (or most of it), which he may have known in Hebrew as well as Greek. Then we have the stories that make up the missionary document generally known as the Signs Source. Third, I suggested earlier that besides the book of Daniel the evangelist had probably read the book of *1 Enoch* also, perhaps in a version that already included the Parables. Another apocalyptic writing in which an angelic figure with a divine name (Yaoel) plays a role vis-à-vis God similar to that of Jesus is the *Apocalypse of Abraham*,[12] and it is just possible that this work, now extant only in an Old Slavonic translation, was available to John. If he was a converted Essene, or even if he had ex-Essenes in his community, he may also have had access to certain Qumran documents. He must have known Mark, and he also probably knew an independent passion source. We should allow for the possibility of an indefinite number of Synoptic-type traditions. In any case there may well have been a few members of the Johannine group whose memories reached back to the time of Jesus.

Yet in the very act of compiling a list of possible sources, one becomes uneasily aware how little such a list accounts for the finished Gospel, and especially for the portrait of Christ that I have set out to explain in the present chapter. (On this at least Bultmann was right.) I am reminded of B. H. Streeter's sardonic comment on the source criticism of the Gospels: "If the sources have undergone anything like the amount of amplification, excision, rearrangement and adaptation which the theory postulates, then the critic's pretence that he can unravel the procedure is grotesque. As well hope to start with a string of sausages and reconstruct the pig."[13] The same strictures apply to the reverse procedure. Dodd comments, quite rightly, apropos of the Fourth Gospel, that "whatever influences may have been present have been masterfully controlled by a powerful and independent mind."[14] But this is not so much an answer to the problem as an alternative way of stating it.

---

12. See my *Understanding the Fourth Gospel*, 86–88.

13. Streeter, *Four Gospels*, 377.

14. C. H. Dodd, *The Interpretation of the Fourth Gospel* (Cambridge: University Press, 1953), 6.

CHANGES

A more profitable approach is to look for evidence of deliberate alterations to the material that John inherited. This is not hard to find. Two of his miracle stories (the healing of the cripple in chapter 5 and of the blind beggar in chapter 9), were probably based on the missionary document commonly known as the Signs Source. According to this, Jesus was charged by his adversaries with infringing the Sabbath legislation. In both stories this objection is retained, but the evangelist had other things in mind. More important, however, for our purposes, is his deliberate decision to eliminate from his sources any impression they might give of weakness on Jesus' part or any sense that his adversaries, either Jews or Romans, had control over him. In the presence of the Roman governor Jesus' behavior is literally majestic. He organizes his own passion. He is not humiliated by being spit upon and stripped, and his death on the cross is seen as an elevation. (On the three occasions when he prophesies his passion he uses the verb ὑψοῦν, "to exalt.") When he says "I thirst," it is to fulfill Scripture (19:28), and his only other recorded request for water (4:7) prefaces an assertion that he himself can provide the water or life. Most significantly, for Mark's cry of desolation, amounting to an accusation that God has abandoned him, John substitutes a cry of triumph: "It is accomplished" (19:30). Earlier, in a scene reminiscent of the agony in the garden, Jesus decides against asking his Father to save him from this hour, knowing that it is for this hour that he has come (12:27).[15]

Obvious though it is that John has made these changes in order to portray a Jesus free from ordinary human weakness, it is far from obvious why he wished to do so. The changes themselves are a large part of the problem. Käsemann offers the explanation that John has gone the way of the Corinthian "enthusiasts," being convinced like them that he and his fellow Christians are already enjoying the benefits of the resurrection. He thinks that the passion story was an embarrassment to the evangelist, who made things easier for himself by imprinting the features of Christ's victory upon it.[16] He is right to say that this Gospel "knows Jesus only as the Risen One and the power of the

---

15. In his review of Käsemann's book, Meeks attempts to refute the charge of docetism by highlighting the passion story. In his response Käsemann, quite justifiably in my view, sticks to his guns (*Jesu Letzte Wille nach Johannes 17*, 3rd ed. [Tübingen: J. C. B. Mohr, 1980], 23 n. 7a). Though wrong to call the passion narrative "a mere postscript" (*Testament*, 7), Käsemann is right, against both Günther Bornkamm ("Zur Interpretation des Johannesevangeliums: Eine Auslegung von Ernst Käsemanns *Jesu Letzter Wille*," *Evangelische Theologie* 28 [1968]: 8–25) and Meeks, to insist that John has no theology of the cross as such and that he sees Jesus' death as a path to glory.

16. Käsemann, *Testament*, 23.

resurrection is the sign [*Merkmal*] of his presence";[17] but we shall see that his is not the only possible explanation.

CONTROVERSY

So let us take a different tack, following the lead of J. Louis Martyn, who advanced Johannine scholarship by inquiring into "the actual circumstances in which John wrote his Gospel." Martyn recognized how much greater an insight we could gain into the meaning of the Gospel if we could find in its pages evidence of the fraught relationship between the traditionalists in the synagogue and the followers of Jesus. This led him to focus on *controversy* or debate. As narrated in the Gospel, Jesus' whole public career was dogged by controversy, but we know now, thanks largely to Martyn's little book, that all the debates recorded in the Gospel must be interpreted in the light of the antagonism between the two opposing parties in the synagogue.[18]

Yet we must not stop there. Martyn goes on to ask: "How are we to picture daily life in John's church? Have elements of its peculiar daily experiences left their stamp on the Gospel penned by one of its members?"[19] Good questions, but the answer cannot be that the members of the community spent most of their waking hours fending off accusations that they were harboring un-Jewish or even anti-Jewish sentiments. Having quoted on the first page of his book Jesus' famous assertion that "the truth shall make you free," Martyn goes on to remark that to single this saying out from its present context in chapter 8 of the Gospel would be to "pick the flowers from among the thorns." In performing the immense service of drawing our attention to the community's experience of the hostility of their fellow Jews, he fails to observe that they must have had many other experiences besides. He cannot really be blamed for this, since it was not part of his purpose to give a comprehensive account of the life of the community: he is focusing on *some elements* of its peculiar daily experiences (the thorns rather than the flowers), not on all. Had he wished to do so, he could no doubt have underlined other features of the community's experience, especially perhaps their sense of the overwhelming revelation of the truth that was Jesus, and all that this implied.

---

17. Käsemann, *Testament*, 40.

18. I have given close attention to particular examples of controversy, as of riddle and prophecy, in a chapter entitled "The Community and Its Book," *Understanding the Fourth Gospel*, 115–35.

19. J. Louis Martyn, *History and Theology in the Fourth Gospel* (New York/Evanston: Harper & Row, 1968), xviii.

Besides the abundant evidence of controversy we must recognize two further elements of the community's experience that find expression in the pages of the Gospel. Both of these, in fact, are illustrated by Jesus' assertion that "the truth shall make you free." "We are descendants of Abraham," respond the Jews, "and have never been in bondage to anyone. How is it that you say, 'You will be made free?'" (8:33). Rightly understood, as it would have been by the members of the community, the word *truth* indicates the new revelation that, having replaced the Torah, was God's special gift to them. But to the Jews it was not a revelation but a *riddle*. As Jesus goes on to say to them in this very passage, "Why do you not understand what I say? It is because you cannot bear to hear my word. . . . If I tell the truth, why do you not believe me? He who is of God hears the words of God; the reason why you do not hear them is that you are not of God" (8:43, 46-47). Here, then, contained somehow in this single saying, are two other kinds of discourse, riddling and revelatory, that have to be noticed if we are to do justice to the literary riches of the Gospel.

RIDDLE

We observed in chapter 2 the importance of the distinction between enigmatic and plain speech (ἐν παροιμίαις and παρρησίᾳ) in the understanding of the disciples of Jesus before and after the resurrection. This was one function of riddling discourse in the Gospel. A second function, equally important, was to erect a cognitive barrier between the members of the community and their adversaries, "the Jews," thus enhancing their sense of privilege vis-à-vis those who were incapable of comprehending the truth, and fostering a conviction that they, not the traditionalists whom they had left behind, were in the right—that they were the ones who had the truth. (As social theorists have shown, this is a regular response on the part of any group that has become isolated from the parent body. We have already seen an example of just such a response from the Essenes at Qumran.) In certain passages in the Gospel the claim to possess the truth is exploited to good effect by making the word *truth* itself into a riddle. As we have just noticed, when he said to the Jews, "the truth will set you free" (8:32), they failed to understand. How could they, when a condition of understanding was to "remain in his word" and to become his disciples? Instead they rejected the one who is the truth, and he responded by drawing further and further away from them. In fact, another example of the Gospel's riddling language is the actual word *withdraw* (ὑπάγειν), misunderstood by the Jews to mean simply "depart," when in its special sense it signified the whole process whereby Jesus was to leave the world, to which he did not really belong, and rejoin his Father in heaven. So the use of riddling language contributes to the strangeness of the portrait of Jesus given in the Gospel.

REVELATION

Commenting, in *Understanding the Fourth Gospel*, on the fact that three literary styles or modes of discourse are to be found in John's Gospel—revelation, riddle, and debate—I laid particular emphasis on the first of these, remarking that even the few scholars who do acknowledge the presence of prophecy in the Gospel do not seek examples in the text of the Gospel itself. Yet if Jesus himself did not actually pronounce more than a small faction of the words attributed to him in the Gospel, it is fair to ask who did. There is no obvious answer available unless we are prepared to recognize that the Johannine community was a prophetic community in the Pauline sense—by which I mean the kind of community we know of through Paul's correspondence with the Corinthians. The Gospel is full of individual sayings and also of extended discourses that deserve to be called prophetic in the broad sense of the term. Paul leaves us in no doubt how high a value he attached to the gift of prophecy, a gift that enabled certain members of the community, as Paul puts it, to speak to the others for their upbuilding, or as some translations quaintly put it, for their edification (1 Cor. 8:1, 10; 10:23; 14:4, 17).[20] Just as the Old Testament tells us of many men, and women too, who spoke with the voice of God, there were some in the Johannine community who spoke with the voice of Jesus. [21]

When they did so speak, they testified to the continuing presence of the risen Jesus among them. Nowhere does the sense of his presence and of the new kind of life that he brought with him find more eloquent expression than in the *I-am* sayings. In the Gospel all of these are put in the mouth of Jesus, but since he cannot have uttered them in his earthly existence, we may reasonably ask who did. The obvious answer is the Johannine prophet, but one passage in the Gospel suggests that more than one person was involved. Chapter 10 records two *I-am* sayings in quick succession: "I am the door" and "I am the shepherd" (10:9, 14). These two claims are clearly incompatible: no one individual could perform both roles at the same time. Various explanations have been offered, but the most plausible is that they were made by two different voices in a

---

20. Greek οἰκοδομεῖν; Latin *aedificare*.

21. As Streeter observed, the evangelist's claim that his interpretation of the person and work of Christ is a revelation of the spirit "must be set side by side with that of the Old Testament prophets that their message was in the same way derived direct from God" (*Four Gospels*, 373).

prophetic gathering, responding antiphonally to one another.[22] Likewise, we cannot simply assume of all the other sayings that they proceeded from a single source. If they too were uttered in a prophetic gathering, anyone with the gift might feel inspired to use it. Here is the Spirit in action, taking what belongs to Jesus and proclaiming it (see 16:14).

All of the *I-am* sayings contain a promise of life, and they all allude to the source of life, Jesus himself. They are either followed or preceded by an explanation or justification, stating directly or indirectly the purpose of his coming—that they may have life (10:10). All the sayings are miniature Gospels, inasmuch as they affirm simply and graphically the purpose for which the Gospel was written—that you may believe, and believing, have life in his name (20:31). In the most succinct examples of this affirmation—"I am the resurrection and the life" (11:25), "I am the way, the truth, and the life" (14:6)—both the purpose and the consequence of Jesus' coming are drawn back into his self-proclamation—self-proclamation because all these sayings come from members of the community with the gift of prophecy speaking with his voice.[23] Among these sayings we find what is perhaps the fullest expression of what Jesus came to mean to his followers: "Abide in me and I in you. . . . I am the vine, you are the branches. He who abides in me and I in him, he it is that bears much fruit, for apart from me you can do nothing" (15:4-5), words crying out, as we can now see, for gender-inclusive language. The vine is indistinguishable from its branches, so in their harmonious intertwining the members of the community *are* Jesus: he lives anew in and through his followers, most of whom never knew him in person. *Pace* Bultmann (see n. 9 above) the best explanation of this and similar phrases, no doubt spoken in the context of a prophetic gathering, is that it expressed the mystical intimacy between Jesus and his followers that was explicitly promised in terms of dwelling or abiding. It is no doubt largely through the imaginative power of this and other sayings attributed to Jesus in this Gospel that many other Christians in the centuries that followed have come to enjoy the same sense of close intimacy.

THE NEW REVELATION

Although we have come some way to answering our question we have not yet got to the heart of it. From the first page of this book I have argued that

---

22. See John Ashton, "The Shepherd," in *Studying John: Approaches to the Fourth Gospel* (Oxford: Clarendon, 1994), 126–27.

23. See *Understanding the Fourth Gospel*, 2nd ed., 125.

resonating through the Gospel, and most emphatically in the Prologue, is the insistence that the truth, the real revelation of God, is not the law but the self-revelation of Jesus, who represents in his own person God's plan for his people, and indeed for all humankind. For he now replaces both the law and the great figure of Moses through whom the law was given.

If, accordingly, we ask for the best explanation of this dramatic change, we may look for clues, as Wayne Meeks did, in the Samaritan and rabbinic traditions concerning the exaltation of Moses. These might well have led, as Meeks suggests, to counter-speculations on the part of the evangelist, causing him to promote the figure of Jesus ahead of Moses. Such counter- speculations, which cannot but have alarmed the Jewish establishment, will have fully accounted for the eventual breakup of the opposing parties in the synagogue. In this way, by combining the insights of two great American scholars, Meeks and Martyn, we could get behind the scenes of the synagogue disputes and so arrive at some understanding of John's shift in allegiance from Judaism to Christianity.

Alternatively, however, as Christopher Rowland has suggested to me, the speculations may actually have begun among the followers of Jesus. If he was more than the Messiah, more even than the awaited Moses–like prophet, if his new revelation was possible only because he had ascended into heaven and had been enabled to convey "heavenly things" as a consequence of his ascent, then he would somehow have shouldered past Moses into an intimacy with God beyond anything that the Bible claimed for Moses. The later Samaritan and rabbinic speculations could then be explained as a reaction to the claims made on behalf of Jesus, and not the other way around. Such an explanation would relieve the interpreter of the need to assume that traditions first evidenced in sources dating from the second and third centuries CE (and in the case of the Samaritans as late as the fourth century) must have originated long before, in sources now lost. Similar assumptions had proved an embarrassment to the theories of both Bultmann (the Mandaeans) and Dodd (the *Hermetica*).

This fresh perspective opens the way for a new interpretation not only of the puzzling 3:13, with its challenge to claims made on behalf of a number of Jewish seers,[24] but also of the occasional references in the Gospel to Jesus' vision of God. Many if not most interpreters of the Prologue assume an exception in the final verse, reading "no one has ever seen God" as "no one except the Logos" or "no one except the (preexistent) Son." I have suggested that, although there is no reason to read the Prologue in this way, the evangelist corrects it later: "Not

---

24. See Hugo Odeberg, *The Fourth Gospel: Interpreted in Its Relation to Contemporaneous Religious Currents in Palestine and the Hellenistic-Oriental World* (Uppsala: Almqvist & Wiksell, 1929).

that anyone has seen God [as was said in 1:18] *except* him who is from God; he has seen the Father" (6:46). But "he who is from God" is not the preexistent Son but the one who is addressing these words to the Jews who have just challenged him. Earlier in the Gospel Jesus had confronted his adversaries directly. After asserting that he himself was the object of the Father's witness, he went on: "His voice you have never heard, his form you have never seen" (5:37), echoing but going beyond Moses' own confession in Deut. 4:12, that when God spoke to the Israelites from the midst of the fire "you heard the sound of words, but saw no form; there was only a voice." When he states that he does "only what he sees the Father doing" (5:19) he is referring to the miracle he has just performed. This is undoubtedly difficult, but to my mind not nearly as difficult as the idea of a preexistent vision that was somehow recalled by Jesus when on earth. For we should remember that there is nothing in the body of the Gospel (except in chapter 17, added later) to suggest that Jesus had some kind of earlier existence before he was born as a son to Joseph—whose father and mother were known to the Jews (6:42).

SUFFERING AND GLORY

We have already observed that in his narration of the passion the evangelist elides all the humiliating aspects (spitting and stripping) and any suggestion that Jesus is not in control of the action throughout. He tackles the predictions of the passion in a similar way, for he portrays Jesus' approaching crucifixion as a raising-up or an elevation. His chosen word ὑψοῦν has often been commented upon. Meeks, for instance, speaks of an "ironic pun" and "a jarring bit of gallows humor,"[25] but there is no joke intended here. We should ask ourselves how John imagined the crucifixion. If he had ever actually witnessed a man dying in agony on the cross, one might suppose that a memory of this appalling torture would lead him to picture a scene something like, to take a well-known example, the terrifying portrayal of the crucifixion by Mathias Grünewald. This tormented image would surely have blocked out altogether any awareness of a man raised up, exalted, ascending up to heaven. The deliberate choice of a word meaning "exalt" (reinforced by an avoidance of the words *cross* and *crucifixion*, *suffering*, *death*, and *dying*) is surely something other than a clever verbal device. The third passion prediction exhibits an even more remarkable modulation, when Jesus declares that "the hour has come for the Son of Man to be glorified" (12:23). Although the predictions in all four Gospels refer to the same event, the

25. Wayne A. Meeks, "The Man from Heaven in Johannine Sectariansim," *Journal of Biblical Literature* 91 (1972): 58, 62.

contrast between John and, say, Mark, is striking. Where Mark's Jesus, in the first prediction (8:31), speaks of suffering and death, John's Jesus (3:14) speaks of lifting up or exaltation; and where in the third prediction Mark's Jesus (10:34) says that he is about to be mocked, spat upon, and scourged, John's Jesus talks of glorification! The crowd's response to this prediction is "How can you say that the Son of Man must be lifted up?" (12:34), interpreting what Jesus has just said about glorification as a reference to the exaltation (on the cross) of the Son of Man. Lifting up or exaltation, on the one hand, and glorification, on the other, are alternative ways of speaking of the same event. The evangelist is inviting his readers to *see past* their own memory or knowledge of Jesus' agonizing death to his triumph over the forces of evil: "Now is the judgment of this world, now shall the ruler of this world be cast out" (12:31), words spoken in the context of the third and last passion prediction—an invitation that can best be accounted for if we suppose that John himself had a vision overwhelming enough to eliminate the painful and humiliating aspects of Jesus' passion and to replace them with signs of exaltation and glory, so as to compress the events of Good Friday and Easter Sunday unto a single momentous happening, the defeat of the prince of this world and the victory of Christ.

A similar capacity to contemplate Jesus' suffering in the course of a vision of glory is to be found in an early Christian apocalypse called the *Ascension of Isaiah* (dated by Rowland at the end of the first or the beginning of the second century CE).[26] Already in the seventh heaven, and seeing there "all the righteous from the time of Adam," Isaiah asks his accompanying angel why they have not yet received their crowns. The angel replies that they must wait until "*the Beloved* has descended and become like you in form," when they (unspecified) "will hang him on a tree and will kill him" (9:6-14). Nils Dahl suggests that this apocryphon is taking over earlier traditions concerning Isaiah, one of which is the interpretation of Isaiah's great vision (in Isaiah 6) as a vision of Christ: Isaiah "saw his glory and spoke of him" (John 12:41). The basic idea in 12:41, adds Dahl, is akin to that of the *Ascension of Isaiah*: "the prophet is supposed to have seen . . . the glory of Christ incarnate and crucified."[27] Paradoxical as it sounds, "the glory of Christ crucified" is an accurate summary of John's own vision.

26. Christopher Rowland, *The Open Heaven: A Study of Apocalyptic in Judaism and Early Christianity* (London: SPCK, 1982), 386.

27. Nils Alstrup Dahl, "The Johannine Church in History," in *The Interpretation of John,* ed. John Ashton, Studies in New Testament Interpretation (Edinburgh: T&T Clark), 154–55.

AGENCY AND VISION

Pursuing this theme further, we should take a careful look at the epilogue to the Book of Signs (12:44-50) one of the rare points in the Gospel where the evangelist, like a Victorian novelist, pauses to comment on the significance of his narrative. He has just told us that Jesus had spoken for the very last time to the Jews, after which "he departed and hid himself from them" (12:36). So these additional words, emphasized by the unusual manner of utterance—crying out loud (ἔκραξεν)—demand our particular attention, delivered as they are not to Jesus' audience but to John's readers. I cite here the first two verses: "He who believes in me, believes not in me but in him who sent me. And he who sees me sees him who sent me."

Rudolf Bultmann, who downplays the epilogue by removing it from its proper place at the climactic end of the Book of Signs, says of these two sentences that their content is the same.[28] The truth is that the second makes an important advance on the first, which is itself a significant variant of the familiar law of agency, the equivalence or virtual identity of the sender and the sent. Worth noting is one of the earliest occurrences of this principle, where Jesus instructs the twelve by taking a child in his arms, and telling them, "whoever receives one such child in my name receives me; and whoever receives me, receives not me, but him who sent me" (Mark 9:37). Matthew, saying nothing about the child here (though he reworks the same tradition later, 18:1-5), repeats the principle but alters its focus by adding a word about prophets: "He who receives a prophet because he is a prophet shall receive a prophet's reward" (Matt. 10:40-41). John too repeats the principle word for word (13:20), but only after he had introduced a particularly interesting variant as a lesson to be learned from his washing of his disciples' feet: "Amen, amen I say to you, a slave is not greater than his master, nor is an agent [ἀπόστολος] greater than the one who sent him" (13:16; cf. Matt. 10:24).

In the opening of his epilogue, the evangelist adds a new twist to the principle by changing the verb from "receive" to "believe." This enables him to insert into the ending of the first half of the Gospel the lesson of faith with which he concludes the second half. Even more significant, however, is the extra twist in the next verse ("And he who sees me sees him who sent me"). For the new variant adds a vertical dimension to the strong horizontal axis of the original principle of agency. Seeing Jesus in his earthly existence, John suggests, is equivalent to seeing the Father up above. Here again, in an epilogue carefully composed to round off the first part of his Gospel, the evangelist is

---

28. Bultmann, *Gospel*, 345.

emphasizing a lesson of particular importance to him, one that he will resume at the beginning of the Farewell Discourse in his reply to Philip: ". . . you do not know me, Philip? He who has seen me has seen the Father" (14:9).

POINTS AND STARS

The dominant themes of the Farewell Discourse, which is modeled on the form of a final testament, are departure and return. But there is also a pervasive sense of presence. No longer physically present, Jesus is present to the community in a new way: "You heard me say to you, 'I go away and I will come to you.' . . . And now I have told you before it takes place, so that when it does take place, you will believe" (14:28-29). So when he does return his presence will now be a spiritual presence, assured by the gift of the Spirit. Previously I have emphasized that one of the roles of the Spirit was to enable the community to understand properly for the first time the significance of Jesus' words and deeds. These remained incomprehensible in Jesus' lifetime. But now the Spirit will lead them into the truth, thus fulfilling the promise of the concluding beatitude: "Blessed are those who have not seen and yet believe" (20:29).

One of the Paraclete sayings illustrates the experience of the community: "But when the Paraclete comes, whom I shall send to you from the Father, even the Spirit of truth, who proceeds from the Father, he will bear witness to me; and you also are witnesses because you have been with me from the beginning" (15:26-27). "The community's preaching," remarks Bultmann, "is to be none other than witness to Jesus"—a comment that must also hold good for its *prophecy*. "Their witness," Bultmann continues, "is not a historical account of that which was, but—however much it is based on that which was—it is 'repetition,' 'a calling to mind' [14:26], in the light of their present relationship with him. It is perfectly clear that their witness and that of the Spirit are identical. The Gospel is itself evidence of the kind of witness this is, and of how that which was is taken up again"—and here Bultmann quotes some famous lines spoken by the dying evangelist in Robert Browning's "A Death in the Desert":

Since much that at the first, in deed and word,
Lay simply and sufficiently exposed,
Had grown. . .
Of new significance and fresh result
What first were guessed as points, I now knew stars,
And named them in the Gospel I have writ. (lines 169–75).[29]

Bultmann, of course, did not believe that the Gospel was written by one of Jesus' disciples. And although the vast majority of researchers into the Gospel have rejected Bultmann's own account of its origins, almost all of them have shared this disbelief.[30] Aware of the huge difference between the stars and the points—the words and deeds of the historical Jesus—they have simply taken for granted that whoever found new significance in earlier memories or records concerning Jesus cannot have been one of his actual followers. But it is worth asking ourselves whether Browning, himself a poet of considerable power, may not have displayed real insight when he attributed the evangelist's ability to form stars out of points to his poetic and/or his religious genius. For many great poets and writers do just that: looking back on, reimagining, and reliving their experiences, they realize that these have grown "of new significance and fresh result."[31]

GLORY

Let us remain a little longer with the dying evangelist in Browning's desert. We first see him in a coma, as his few remaining companions are trying to revive him: "He is not so far gone but he might speak." One of his followers, called simply "the Boy," "stung by the splendour of a sudden thought," fetches "a plate of graven lead" and reads from it, as if proclaiming for the first time, the words "I am the Resurrection and the Life" / "Whereat he opened his eyes wide

---

29. Bultmann, *Gospel*, 554–55.

30. One of them being Martin Hengel, who nevertheless puts the following searching question: "If Paul, who became a Christian a few years after the ministry of Jesus, had earlier received his education as a pupil of learned Pharisees in Jerusalem, and after his conversion, between about 33 and 50 CE, was surely several times in personal contact with eyewitnesses, including the physical brother of Jesus, could develop his quite specific high christology, are we to deny it to a disciple of Jesus who had grown old, some fifty, sixty or even seventy years later?" (*The Johannine Question* [Philadelphia: Trinity Press International, 1989], 131).

31. The first example must be Augustine's *Confessions*, which contains some profound reflections on human memory and greatly influenced Dante, whose *Commedia* may be the supreme example of the magical transformation of knowledge and experience into poetry. Further examples that spring to mind are William Wordsworth's "The Prelude" and Marcel Proust's *A la recherche du temps perdu*, T. S. Eliot's *Four Quartets*, and Wallace Stevens's "Notes Toward a Supreme Fiction," all works imbued with a self-consciousness comparable to that of the Fourth Gospel. And artists do the same: I think in particular of Van Gogh and of Cézanne. The latter, who said of his contemporary Monet that he was "just an eye," added, "but what an eye!" (*Ce n'est qu'un oeuil. Mais, bon Dieu, quel oeuil!*). His comment shows that he thought of himself as more than just an eye, and that the truth he sought untiringly in his own paintings but with a restless uncertainty (it was said of him that he was *inquiet de vérité*), was different from that sought by the Impressionists (a school he was once prepared to be associated with but later abandoned).

at once, / And sat up of himself, and looked at us; / And thenceforth nobody pronounced a word." Nobody, that is, except John himself, who carried on talking for more than five hundred lines, giving Browning the opportunity to exercise his special gift—what a French critic called his *introspection d'autrui*, his knack of getting inside other people's skins.

This John is far from being an old man rummaging among his memories. He reflects that of all Jesus' closest disciples he is the only one left:

> And I am only he, your brother John,
> Who saw and heard, and could remember all:
> Remember all! It is not much to say.
> What if the truth broke on me from above
> As once and oft-times? Such might hap again.

John proceeds by running through all his writings, first Revelation, when the message came to him "in Patmos isle," where he had to set down all that he was told, "with nothing left to my arbitrament to choose or change," then the Letters, and finally the Gospel, speaking of it in the famous words already quoted. But he does not stop there: "To me that story," he reflects, "ay, that Life and Death of which I wrote 'it was'—to me, it is; —is, here and now: I apprehend nought else." Going on to consider how his friends and followers might share his vision, he finds a way of enabling them to see the past "reduced to plain historic fact, / diminished into clearness." But this done, he urges them to "stand before that fact, that Life and Death, / stay there at gaze, till it dispart, dispread, / as though a star should open out, all sides, / grow the world on you, as it is my world." He himself had known stars, and now his friends too could see the truth—as a single star.

I venture to suggest that Robert Browning, equipped with none of the gleaming tools of scholarly exegesis, and with only his poet's imagination and a tentative faith to assist him, realized, as scholars have never quite managed to do, that to account for the Fourth Gospel we have to accord to its author a quite exceptional *vision*. For the object of that vision Browning chose the word *stars*. The evangelist's word was *glory*.

Not incidentally, this was the word selected by Ernst Käsemann. In *The Testament of Jesus* he built on an important article, written as early as 1957, that focused on John 1:14, "And the Word became flesh and dwelt among us, full of grace and truth; and we have beheld [perhaps *gazed upon*] his glory."[32] In this article, Käsemann had placed all the weight on the conclusion of the verse, "and we have beheld his glory." It should cause us no surprise, then, that when he came to give a more extended discussion of the Gospel he turned for inspiration to John 17, Jesus' long prayer to the Father at the end of his life. In fact the subtitle of the new book reads, in English, *A Study of the Gospel of John in the Light of Chapter 17*.

Scholars who accept the hypothesis that there were at least two editions of the Gospel of John are agreed that chapter 17 belongs to the second edition. The Prologue too belongs to the second edition, so there are no echoes of it in the first; but the prayer that opens John 17 does, I think, hark back to it: "glorify me in your own presence with the glory I had with you before the existence of the world (πρὸ τοῦ τὸν κόσμον εἶναι)" (17:5). And there is another reference toward the end of the prayer, where the disciples are also included: "Father, I desire that these whom you have given me may also be with me where I am, to behold my glory which you have given me in your love for me before the foundation of the world" (17:24). Käsemann does not actually quote either of these verses, because he is more interested in the glory Christ displayed on earth than his preexistent glory in heaven. What he does say is this: "The beginning of John 17 is dominated by the key word 'glorification' of Jesus. With this key word, the message of the whole Gospel is taken up once more in our chapter. The prologue in 1.14 has already summarized the content of the Gospel with 'We beheld his glory.'"[33] Perhaps Käsemann should rather have said that the phrase "We beheld his glory" summarizes his own interpretation of the Gospel; but in any event it must be admitted that almost from the start of Gospel the figure of Christ is bathed in glory: he manifested his glory at the wedding feast of Cana (2:11), and his glory never left him, even though it was to be manifested more particularly in his death (13:31-32).

Conscious as they were of the continuing presence in their midst of the Glorified One, no wonder the community, or rather the evangelist who was its chief spokesman, smoothed out the rough edges of the traditions of the historical Jesus and expanded the points into stars. Here we have the most likely explanation of the extraordinary difference between his portrait of Jesus and that of the Synoptics. It had nothing to do with a decision to present a docetic Christ, but arose from his constant awareness, which he shared with the members of his community, that they were living in the presence of the Glorified One. So dazzling was this glory that any memory of a less-than-glorious Christ was altogether eclipsed. Here is the true explanation of the

---

32. Ernst Käsemann, "Aufbau und Anliegen des johanneischen Prolog," in *Libertas Christiana: Friedrich Delekat zum 65. Geburtstag*, ed. Walter Matthias and Ernst Wolf, Beiträge zur evangelischen Theologie 26 (Munich: Kaiser, 1957), 75–99.

33. Käsemann, *Testament*, 6. Here Käsemann refers in a footnote to his earlier article on the Prologue.

transformation of a fully human Christ into one who was virtually divine—not a divine man in the sense of a Greek superman but a man who manifested for those who knew him the glory of God. The Johannine community, and the evangelist in particular, realized that the truth that they prized as the source of their new life was to be identified not with the Jesus of history but with the risen and glorious Christ, and that this was a Christ free from all human weakness. The claims they made for him were at the heart of the new religion that soon came to be called Christianity.

Conclusion

More than once in the course of this book I have observed that despite what seems to be a general consensus among Johannine scholars the fourth evangelist was not a theologian, at least if we understand by this term a person mainly occupied with rational reflection about God. He did not spend most of his time endeavoring to work out a consistent and satisfactory Christology. Nor of course was he a biblical scholar, hunting for sources, either Jewish or Christian, to be used in complementing or supplementing his own ideas. And although he was certainly familiar with at least one of the Synoptic Gospels, so that the *gospel form* (sayings, stories, and a passion narrative) supplied him with a framework for his own composition, and although too he must have inherited many treasured memories of Jesus' words and deeds, his use of these was incidental rather than systematic.

Like Paul, he had received a revelation, and that revelation, again like Paul's, concerned Christ. Paul, brought up as a Pharisee, did think theologically; but I have argued at length elsewhere that what was primary for Paul was not theology but religious experience;[1] and the same is surely true of John. In the last chapter I suggested that the evangelist's thrice-repeated statement concerning Jesus' exaltation on the cross is better explained as stemming from a visionary experience than as a clever piece of wordplay. And what of the assertion in the Prologue that "we have seen (or gazed upon) his glory"? Rudolf Bultmann actually notes that "Δόξα in the LXX, the NT and in the literature of magic, the mysteries, and related Hellenistic literature, refers to the epiphany and the manifestation of the Godhead."[2] But then he immediately asserts that "the revelation clearly does not occur, as some might naively wish to imagine, in a divine demonstration, visible to the natural eye of the body or the soul," and goes on to speak instead of "the vision of faith,"[3] an expression neither argued for nor explained: Bultmann is stating a theological conviction. Would it not have been better, methodologically speaking, to turn for assistance to other statements in the Gospel that refer to the manifestation of Christ's glory? The difference between John's portrait of Christ and that of the Synoptists is best accounted for by the *experience* of the glorious Christ, constantly present to

1. John Ashton, *The Religion of Paul the Apostle* (New Haven: Yale University Press, 2000).

2. Rudolf Bultmann, *The Gospel of John: A Commentary* (Oxford: Basil Blackwell, 1971), 67 n. 2.

3. Bultmann, *Gospel*, 68–69.

him and to his community, that has all but obliterated the memory of a human Jesus subject to the weaknesses of ordinary mortals—so that, above all else, his uncertainty about his own fate and, in his dying moments, his failure of faith, were completely forgotten.

Why is it then, it might reasonably be asked, that there is no mention of this in the commentaries? Why is it that one scholar after another speaks of John's theology rather than of his religious experience? There are two, complementary, answers to the question. The first answer must be the crushing weight of a tradition that has been piling up ever since the patristic era, when the Greek church gave John the honorable title of *Theologian*—largely because the great doctrines of the Incarnation and Trinity were elaborated mostly on the basis of texts drawn from the Fourth Gospel. In the modern era other great figures emerged—first Friedrich Schleiermacher and then, towering above all the rest, Ferdinand Christian Baur, whose unremitting emphasis on the theological achievement of John paved the way for what was to follow. In the twentieth century no one could match the astonishing learning and insight of the great Bultmann, to whom we owe the clear perception, put forward in the "Bedeutung" article I mentioned earlier, that the basic theme of the Gospel, its *Grundkonzeption*, was revelation: "Precisely what though," he asked, "does the Jesus of John's Gospel reveal? One thing only, though put in different ways: *that he has been sent as the revealer.*"[4]

The commentators who succeeded Bultmann, also men of considerable learning, could not but stand in his shadow. In Britain, C. H. Dodd and C. K. Barrett did their best, without admitting it, to confront Bultmann; but they too were equally convinced that the Fourth Gospel was the work of a theologian.

Raymond E. Brown, whose large two-volume Anchor Bible commentary earned him justifiable acclaim, advanced the study of the Gospel by judiciously employing the Dead Sea Scrolls to situate it firmly in the context of Second Temple Judaism. Yet it was J. Louis Martyn, Brown's friend and fellow American, who made the biggest step forward—with his imaginative reconstruction of the situation of the members of the Johannine group as they confronted the more traditionally minded Jews who worshiped alongside them in the synagogue. Martyn's study was perhaps the first ever to require some consideration of the *experience* of believers in Jesus as they confronted the hostile

---

4. Rudolf Bultmann, "Die Bedeutung der neuerschlossenen mandäischen und manichäischen Quellen für das Verständnis des Johannesevangeliums," *Zeitschrift für die neutestamentliche Wissenschaft* 24 (1925): 103. This was Bultmann's answer to what he called the second riddle (*Rätsel*) of the Gospel. His answer to the first riddle, concerning the historical origin of the Gospel, enmeshed him in the toils of his Mandaean hypothesis.

questioning of people who, according to the Gospel, called themselves "disciples of Moses."[5]

Critical as I have been of Martyn's little book, I believe that its novel insights help us to understand the second reason why Johannine scholars had hitherto focused exclusively on what they call the evangelist's theology instead of on his experience: they had not been venturesome or imaginative enough to try to picture, as Martyn did, the life of the Johannine community in its synagogal setting. Although, in my opinion, he sometimes goes too far, he does not proceed without evidence. His achievement was to furnish a life setting, a *Sitz im Leben*, for the controversies with the Jews that crowd the pages of the Fourth Gospel.

Building on Martyn's work in my own book, *Understanding the Fourth Gospel*, I was also able to investigate, though briefly, two other areas of the community's experience: first the quarrel over the truth that prompted John's riddling discourse, and, second, the revelatory experiences of the risen Jesus that found expression in the *Amen* sayings and the *I-am* sayings, which, if I am right, exemplified the charismatic prophecy that characterized the religious life of the community.[6] Neither the riddles nor these prophetic sayings were the work of a theologian. The riddles, like the controversies, were fashioned by the evangelist while he was busy defending his beliefs in Jesus against hostile questioning on the part of his adversaries; and he also used them to bolster the confidence of the community by suggesting to them that they alone were the privileged possessors of the truth. As for the prophetic sayings, I proposed that they were probably uttered at times of communal worship.

The final question must concern the evangelist's own revelatory experience. In chapter 6 of this book I systematically dismantled the case I myself had made earlier for the Gospel's affinity with apocalyptic, while nevertheless maintaining that it is right to call the Gospel an apocalypse in reverse. What the evangelist perceived as a new revelation was, of course, Jesus himself, revealing, as Bultmann put it, that he was the revealer. What Bultmann failed to see was that the revelation was also the gospel story, a truth cryptically expressed in the Prologue, where God's plan for the world—for humankind—is identified with the person of Jesus Christ, who glorified God in his life, death, and resurrection. It is hard to express this insight without drawing on the actual

5. The title of Martyn's work, *History and Theology in the Fourth Gospel*, is misleading, for Martyn's sole interest was in the *history* of the community: the theology in this book is confined to the challenge-and-response debates between the two groups in the synagogue.

6. These brief studies, labeled *controversy*, *riddle*, and *revelation*, take up nineteen pages of the chapter entitled "The Community and Its Book."

words of the Gospel—the way, the truth, and the life. How it came to John himself we cannot say with any precision. But like the seer of Revelation and like the great Jewish seers, Ezekiel, Enoch, Ezra, and Baruch, it must have come to him as revealed wisdom.

Both Johns—for despite a long-standing tradition, the authors of the Gospel and of the book of Revelation can hardly have been the same person—were uncompromising in their conviction that the revelation they were recording superseded all that had gone before.

> The essence of Christianity is the revelation of the glory of God in the only Son of the Father, the fullness of his grace and truth disclosed in him who was made flesh—wherein all the imperfections, limits, and negativity of the law given by Moses are absolutely transcended.

Thus, in his stately, unhurried German prose, Ferdinand Christian Baur concludes a sentence that he had begun by stating what the essence of Christianity *is not*:

> What is primary and essential about Christianity is not that self-fulfilling process which, viewed objectively, is the reconciling death [of Christ], viewed subjectively the belief in its reconciling power, a process which, though conditioned by the forces of sin and of the law, nevertheless continues to surmount all obstacles put in its way; rather . . . the essence of Christianity *is* . . . .[7]

Here Baur is summarizing a conviction central to his theology, that Paul's message concerning the ultimate defeat of sin and of the law is transcended by the Johannine revelation (in the Prologue) of the glory of God, as this is exhibited in the incarnate Christ. (It is important to note that Baur's sonorous sentence ends with a form of the verb *aufheben*, the Hegelian term for the final synthetic movement that both brings together and transcends two earlier truths [thesis and antithesis] that began in opposition.)

I leave it to others more competent than myself to decide whether Baur is right about the essence of Christianity; but I have reached the surprising conclusion (surprising to me at least) that he was right about John, and consequently that Ernst Käsemann, who learned from him, was right too. Yet

---

7. Ferdinand Christian Baur, *Kritische Untersuchungen über die kanonischen Evangelien: Ihr Verhältniß zu einander, ihren Charakter und Ursprung* (Tübingen: Ludw. Fr. Fues, 1847), 313.

Bultmann, whose emphasis on "the Word was made flesh" was what provoked Käsemann in the first place into placing the emphasis instead upon "we have seen his glory," was no less right in his insistence that the fundamental concept (*Grundkonzeption*) of the Gospel is *revelation*. It is just that his Lutheran prejudice for the preeminence of the word made it impossible for him to realize that the revelation of the Word is equally *a revelation of glory*.

Bibliography

Aberle, Moriz von. "Über den Zweck des Johannesevangeliums." *Theologische Quartalschrift* 42 (1861): 37–94.

Aland, Kurt. "Eine Untersuchung zu Joh I 3, 4: Über die Bedeutung eines Punktes." *Zeitschrift für die neutestamentliche Wissenschaft* 59 (1968): 174–209.

Ashton, John. "Bridging Ambiguities." In John Ashton, *Studying John: Approaches to the Fourth Gospel*, 36–70. Oxford: Clarendon, 1994.

———. "Intimations of Apocalyptic: Looking Back and Looking Forward." In *John's Gospel and Intimations of Apocalyptic*, edited by Christopher Rowland and Catrin H. Williams. London: T & T Clark, 2013.

———. "The Jews in John." In John Ashton, *Studying John: Approaches to the Fourth Gospel,* 71–89. Oxford: Clarendon, 1994.

———. "The Johannine Son of Man: A New Proposal." *New Testament Studies* 57 (2011): 508–29.

———. "'Mystery' in the Dead Sea Scrolls and the Fourth Gospel." In *John, Qumran and the Dead Sea Scrolls: Sixty Years of Discovery and Debate*, ed. Mary L. Coloe and Tom Thatcher. 53–58. Society of Biblical Literature Early Judaism and Its Literature 32. Atlanta: Society of Biblical Literature, 2011.

———. "Reflections on a Footnote." In *Engaging with C. H. Dodd on the Gospel of John: Sixty Years of Tradition and Interpretation*, ed. Tom Thatcher and Catrin H. Williams, 203–15. Cambridge: Cambridge University Press, 2013.

———. "The Shepherd." In John Ashton, *Studying John: Approaches to the Fourth Gospel*, 11440. Oxford: Clarendon, 1994.

———. "The Transformation of Wisdom: A Study of the Prologue of John's Gospel." *New Testament Studies* 32 (1986): 161–86.

———. *Understanding the Fourth Gospel.* Oxford: Clarendon, 1991. 2nd ed., 2007.

Aune, David E. *The New Testament in Its Literary Environment.* Philadelphia: Westminster, 1987.

Bammel, Ernst. "'John did no miracle': John 10: 41." In *Miracles: Cambridge Studies in Their Philosophy and History*, ed. C. F. D. Moule, 175–202. London: Mowbray, 1965.

———. "Die Tempelreinigung bei den Synoptikern und im Johannessevangelium." In *John and the Synoptics*, ed. Adelbert Denaux,

507–13. Bibliotheca ephemeridum theologicarum lovaniensium 101. Leuven: University Press, 1992.

Barclay, John M. G. *Jews in the Mediterranean Diaspora: From Alexander to Trajan (323 BCE– 117 CE)*. Edinburgh: T&T Clark, 1996.

Barrett, C. K. *The Gospel according to St. John: An Introduction with Commentary and Notes on the Greek Text*. 2nd ed. London: SPCK, 1978.

———. *The Prologue of John's Gospel*. London: Athlone, 1971.

Bauckham, Richard. "The Audience of the Fourth Gospel." in *Jesus in Johannine Tradition*, ed. Robert T. Fortna and Tom Thatcher, 101–11. Louisville: Westminster John Knox, 2001.

———. "The Beloved Disciple as Ideal Author." *Journal for the Study of the New Testament* 49 (1993): 21–44.

———. "For Whom Were the Gospels Written?" In *The Gospels for All Christians: Rethinking the Gospel Audiences*, ed. Richard Bauckham, 9–49. Grand Rapids: Eerdmans, 1998.

Baur, Ferdinand Christian. *Kritische Untersuchungen über die kanonischen Evangelien: Ihr Verhältniß zu einander, ihren Charakter und Ursprung*. Tübingen: Ludw. Fr. Fues, 1847.

Bernard, J. H. *A Critical and Exegetical Commentary on the Gospel according to St. John*, ed. A. H. McNeale. International Critical Commentary. Edinburgh: T&T Clark, 1928.

Bieler, Ludwig. Θεῖος ἀνήρ, *das Bild des "göttlichen Menschen" in Spätantike und Frühchristentum*, vol. 1. Vienna: O Höfels, 1935.

Blenkinsopp, Joseph. "Interpretation and the Tendency to Sectarianism: An Aspect of Second Temple History." In *Jewish and Christian Self-Definition: Aspects of Judaism in the Greco-Roman Period*, ed. E. P. Sanders et al., 1:1–26. 3 vols. London: SCM, 1981.

Borgen, Peder. "God's Agent in the Fourth Gospel." In *Religions in Antiquity: Essays in Memory of Erwin Ramsdell Goodenough*, ed. Jacob Neusner, 137–48. Supplements to Numen 14. Leiden: Brill, 1968.

———. "Observations on the Midrashic Character of John 6." *Zeitschrift für die neutestamentliche Wissenschaft* 54 (1963): 232–40.

Bornkamm, Günther. "Zur Interpretation des Johannesevangeliums: Eine Auslegung von Ernst Käsemanns *Jesu Letzter Wille*." *Evangelische Theologie* 28 (1968): 8–25.

Bousset, Wilhelm. *Kyrios Christos: Geschichte des Christusglaubens von den Anfängen des Christentums bis Irenaeus*. Göttingen: Vandenhoeck & Ruprecht, 1913.

Boyarin, Daniel. "The Ioudaioi in John and the Prehistory of 'Judaism.'" In *Pauline Conversations in Context: Essays in Honor of Calvin J. Roetzel*, ed. Janice Capel Anderson, Philip Sellew, and Claudia Setzer, 216–29. Journal for the Study of the New Testament: Supplement Series 221. Sheffield: Sheffield Academic Press, 2002.

———. *The Jewish Gospels: The Story of the Jewish Christ*. New York: New Press, 2012.

Box, G. A., ed. *The Ezra-Apocalypse*. London: Sir Isaac Pitman & Sons, 1912.

Bretschneider, Karl Gottlieb. *Probabilia de evangelii et epistularum Joannis apostoli, indole et origine eruditorum judiciis modeste subjecit*. Leipzig: Jo. Ambros. Barth, 1820.

Brown, Raymond E. *The Community of the Beloved Disciple: The Life, Loves, and Hates of an Individual Church in New Testament Times*. New York: Paulist, 1979.

———. *The Gospel according to John: Introduction, Translation, and Notes*. 2 vols. Anchor Bible 29, 29A. New York: Doubleday, 1966, 1970.

———. "The Qumran Scrolls and the Johannine Gospel and Epistles." In *The Scrolls and the New Testament*, ed. Krister Stendahl, 183–207. New York: Harper, 1958.

Browning, Robert. "A Death in the Desert." In Robert Browning, *Poetical Works 1833–1864*, ed. Ian Jack, 818–36. Oxford: Oxford University Press, 1970.

Bühner, Jan-Adolf. *Der Gesandte und sein Weg im vierten Evangelium: Die kultur- und religionsgeschichtliche Grundlagen der johanneischen Sendungschristologie sowie ihre traditionsgeschichtliche Entwicklung*. Wissenschaftliche Untersuchungen zum Neuen Testament 2/2. Tübingen: Mohr Siebeck, 1977.

Bultmann, Rudolf. "Die Bedeutung der neuerschlossenen mandäischen und manichäischen Quellen für das Verständnis des Johanesevangeliums." *Zeitschrift für die neutestamentliche Wissenschaft* 24 (1925): 100–146.

———. *The Gospel of John: A Commentary*. Oxford: Basil Blackwell, 1971. German, *Das Evangelium des Johannes*. Göttingen: Vandenhoeck & Ruprecht, 1941, with the Supplement of 1966.

———. "Hirsch's Auslegung des Johannesevangeliums." *Evangelische Theologie* 4 (1937): 115–42.

———. "The New Approach to the Synoptic Problem." *Journal of Religion* 6 (1926): 337–62.

————. "Untersuchungen zum Johannesevangelium A: Ἀλήθεια.": *Zeitschrift für die neutestamentliche Wissenschaft* 27 (1928): 113–63.

————. "Untersuchungen zum Johannesevangelium B: Θεὸν οὐδεὶς ἑώρακεν πώποτε (Joh 1,18)." *Zeitschrift für die neutestamentliche Wissenschaft* 29 (1930): 134–92.

Burkitt, F. C., ed., *Evangelion da-Mepharreshe: The Curetonian Version of the Four Gospels.* 2 vols. Cambridge: University Press, 1904.

Burridge, Richard A. "About People, by People, for People: Gospel Genre and Audiences." In *The Gospels for All Christians: Rethinking the Gospel Audiences,* ed. Richard Bauckham, 113–45. Grand Rapids: Eerdmans, 1998.

————. *What Are the Gospels? A Comparison with Graeco-Roman Biography.* Cambridge: Cambridge University Press, 1992. 2nd ed., Grand Rapids: Eerdmans, 2004.

Capper, Brian J. "John, Qumran, and Virtuoso Religion." In *John, Qumran, and the Dead Sea Scrolls: Sixty Years of Discovery and Debate,* ed. Mary L. Coloe and Tom Thatcher, 93–116. Society of Biblical Literature Early Judaism and Its Literature 32. Atlanta: Society of Biblical Literature, 2011.

Collins, John J. *The Apocalyptic Imagination: An Introduction to the Jewish Matrix of Christianity.* New York: Crossroad, 1984.

————. *Daniel: A Commentary on the Book of Daniel.* Hermeneia. Minneapolis: Fortress Press, 1993.

————. *The Scepter and the Star: The Messiahs of the Dead Sea Scrolls and Other Ancient Literature.* Anchor Bible Reference Library. New York: Doubleday, 1995.

Colpe, Carsten, "ὁ υἱὸς τοῦ ἀνθρώπου." *Theological Dictionary of the New Testament,* ed. G. Kittel and G. Friedrich, 8:403–81. Grand Rapids: Eerdmans, 1968.

————. *Die religionsgeschichtliche Schule: Darstellung und Kritik ihres Bildes vom gnostischen Erlösermythus.* Forschungen zur Religion und Literatur des Neuen Testament 78. Göttingen: Vandenhoeck & Ruprecht, 1961.

Cox, Patricia. *Biography in Late Antiquity: A Quest for Holy Men.* Transformation of the Classical Heritage 5. Berkeley: University of California Press, 1983.

Culpepper, R. Alan. *Anatomy of the Fourth Gospel: A Study in Literary Design.* Minneapolis: Fortress Press, 1983.

Dahl, Nils Alstrup. "The Johannine Church in History." in *The Interpretation of John,* ed. John Ashton, 147–67. Studies in New Testament Interpretation. Edinburgh: T&T Clark, 1997.

Davies, Philip R. *The Damascus Covenant: An Interpretation of the Damascus Document.* Journal for the Study of the Old Testament: Supplement Series 25. Sheffield: JSOT Press, 1982.

Dodd, C. H. *Historical Traditions in the Fourth Gospel.* Cambridge: Cambridge University Press, 1963.

———. *The Interpretation of the Fourth Gospel.* Cambridge: Cambridge University Press, 1953.

Esler, Philip F. *The First Christians in Their Social Worlds: Social-scientific Approaches to New Testament Interpretation.* London: Routledge, 1994.

Evans, Craig A. *Word and Glory: On the Exegetical and Theological Background of John's Prologue.* Journal for the Study of the New Testament: Supplement Series 89. Sheffield: Sheffield Academic Press, 1993.

Flint, Peter W. "The Daniel Tradition at Qumran." In *Eschatology, Messianism and the Dead Sea Scrolls,* ed. Craig A. Evans and Peter W. Flint, 41–60. Studies in the Dead Sea Scrolls and Related Literature 1. Grand Rapids: Eerdmans, 1997.

Harnack, Adolf. *History of Dogma,* vol. 1. New York: Russell & Russell, 1958. First German ed., 1886.

Hengel, Martin. "The Four Gospels and the One Gospel of Jesus Christ." In *The Earliest Gospels: The Origins and Transmission of the Earliest Christian Gospels. The Contribution of the Chester Beatty Gospel Codex P^{45},* ed. Barbara Aland and Charles Horton, 13–26. Journal for the Study of the New Testament: Supplement Series 258. London: T&T Clark, 2004.

———. *The Johannine Question.* Philadelphia: Trinity Press International, 1989.

Holladay, Carl. *Theios Aner in Hellenistic Judaism: A Critique of the Use of This Category in New Testament Christology.* Society of Biblical Literature Dissertation Series 40. Missoula, Mont.: Scholars Press, 1977.

Käsemann, Ernst. "Aufbau und Anliegen des johanneischen Prolog." In *Libertas Christiana: Friedrich Delekat zum 65. Geburtstag,* ed. Walter Matthias and Ernst Wolf, 75–99. Beiträge zur evangelischen Theologie 26. Munich: Kaiser, 1957.

———. *Jesu letzter Wille nach Johannes 17.* 3rd ed. Tübingen: Mohr Siebeck, 1971.

———. *The Testament of Jesus: A Study of the Gospel of John in the Light of Chapter 17.* London: SCM, 1968.

Keener, Craig S. *The Gospel of John: A Commentary.* 2 vols. Peabody, Mass.: Hendrickson, 2003.

Klink, Edward W., III. *The Sheep of the Fold: The Audience and Origin of the Gospel of John.* Society for New Testament Studies Monograph Series 141. Cambridge: Cambridge University Press, 2007.

Kovacs, Judith. "'Now Shall the Ruler of This World Be Driven Out': Jesus' Death as Cosmic Battle in John 12:20-26." *Journal of Biblical Literature* 114 (1995): 227–47.

Lamarche, Paul. "The Prologue of John." In *The Interpretation of John*, ed. John Ashton, 36–52. Studies in New Testament Interpretation. London: SPCK, 1986.

La Potterie, Ignace de. *La vérité dans saint Jean.* 2 vols. Analecta biblica 73, 74. Rome: Biblical Institute Press, 1977.

Lenski, Gerhard E. *Power and Privilege: A Theory of Social Stratification.* New York: McGraw-Hill, 1966.

Léon-Dufour, Xavier. "Le signe du Temple selon saint Jean." *Recherches de science religieuse* 39 (1951–52): 155–75.

Lincoln, Andrew T. *The Gospel according to St. John.* Black's New Testament Commentaries 4. Peabody, Mass.: Hendrickson, 2005.

Lindars, Barnabas, *Behind the Fourth Gospel.* Studies in Creative Criticism 3. London: SPCK, 1971.

———. *The Gospel of John.* London: Marshall, Morgan & Scott, 1972.

Martyn, J. Louis. "A Gentile Mission That Replaced an Earlier Jewish Mission?" In *Exploring the Gospel of John: In Honor of D. Moody Smith*, ed. R. Alan Culpepper and C. Clifton Black, 124–44. Louisville: Westminster John Knox, 1996.

———. "Glimpses into the History of the Johannine Community." In *The Gospel of John in Christian History: Essays for Interpreters,* 90–121. New York: Paulist, 1979.

———. *History and Theology in the Fourth Gospel.* New York: Harper & Row, 1968. 2nd ed., revised and enlarged, Nashville: Abingdon, 1979. 3rd ed., Louisville/London: Westminster John Knox, 2003.

———. "Source Criticism and Religionsgeschichte in the Fourth Gospel." In *Jesus and Man's Hope*, ed. D. G. Buttrick, 1:247–73. 2 vols. Pittsburgh: Pittsburgh Theological Seminary, 1970.

Marxsen, Willi. *Der Evangelist Markus: Studien zum Redaktionsgeschichte des Evangeliums.* Forschungen zur Religion und Literatur des Alten und Neuen Testaments 67. Göttingen: Vandenhoeck & Ruprecht, 1956.

Meeks, Wayne A. "Breaking Away: Three New Testament Pictures of Christianity's Separation from the Jewish Communities." In *"To See Ourselves*

As Others See Us": Christians, Jews, "Others" in Late Antiquity, ed. Jacob Neusner and Ernest S. Frerichs, 93–115. Chico, Calif.: Scholars Press, 1985.

———. "The Man from Heaven in Johannine Sectarianism." *Journal of Biblical Literature* 91 (1972): 44–72.

———. *The Prophet-King. Moses Traditions and the Johannine Christology*. Supplements to Novum Testamentum 14. Leiden: Brill, 1967.

———. Review of *The Testament of Jesus*, by Ernst Käsemann. *Union Seminary Quarterly Review* 24 (1969): 414–20.

Mowinckel, Sigmund. "Some Remarks on Hodayot 39.5-20." *Journal of Biblical Literature* 75 (1956): 265–76.

Newsom, Carol A. *The Self as Symbolic Space: Constructing Identity and Community at Qumran*. Studies on the Texts of the Desert of Judah 52. Leiden: Brill, 2004.

Nickelsburg, George W. E. *1 Enoch 1: A Commentary on the Book of 1 Enoch, Chapters 1–36; 81–108*. Hermeneia. Minneapolis: Fortress Press, 2001.

———. "Revealed Wisdom as a Criterion for Inclusion and Exclusion: From Jewish Sectarianism to Early Christianity." In *"To See Ourselves As Others See Us": Christians, Jews, "Others" in Late Antiquity*, ed. Jacob Neusner and Ernest S. Frerichs, 73–81. Chico, Calif.: Scholars Press, 1985.

Odeberg, Hugo. *The Fourth Gospel: Interpreted in Its Relation to Contemporaneous Religious Currents in Palestine and the Hellenistic-Oriental World*. Uppsala: Almqvist & Wiksell, 1929.

Portier-Young, Anthea E. *Apocalypse against Empire: Theologies of Resistance in Early Judaism*. Grand Rapids: Eerdmans, 2011.

Phillips Peter M. *The Prologue of the Fourth Gospel: A Sequential Reading*. Library of New Testament Studies 294. London/New York: T&T Clark, 2006.

Roberts, Colin H., and T. C. Skeat. *The Birth of the Codex*. London: Oxford University Press for the British Academy, 1983.

Rowland, Christopher. *The Open Heaven: A Study of Apocalyptic in Judaism and Early Christianity*. London: SPCK, 1982.

———, and Christopher R. A. Morray-Jones. *The Mystery of God: Early Jewish Mysticism and the New Testament*. Compendia rerum iudaicarum ad Novum Testamentum, Section 3, Jewish Traditions in Early Christian Literature 12. Leiden/Boston: Brill, 2009.

Saldarini, Anthony J. *Pharisees, Scribes and Sadduccees in Palestinian Society: A Sociological Approach*. Wilmington, Del.: Michael Glazier, 1988.

Schnackenburg, Rudolf. "Die Erwartung des 'Propheten' nach dem neuen Testament und den Qumran Texten." *Studia Evangelica 1* (Berlin: Akademie-Verlag, 1959.

Schürer, Emil. *The History of the Jewish People in the Age of Jesus Christ (175 B.C.–A.D. 135).* A New English Version revised and edited by Geza Vermes, Fergus Millar, and Martin Goodman. 3 vols. in 4. Edinburgh: T&T Clark, 1973–87.

Schwartz, Eduard. "Aporien im vierten Evangelium." In *Nachrichten von der Königlichen Gesellschaft der Wissenschaft zu Göttingen: Philologisch-historische Klasse* (1907): 342–72; (1909): 115–48, 497–650.

Segal, Alan F. "Heavenly Ascent in Hellenistic Judaism, Early Christianity and Their Environment." In *Aufstieg und Niedergang der römischen Welt* 23.2 (Berlin/New York: de Gruyter, 1980), 1333–94.

———. *Two Powers in Heaven: Early Rabbinic Reports about Christianity and Gnosticism.* Studies in Judaism in Late Antiquity 25. Leiden: Brill, 1977.

Segovia, Ferdinand F. "The Tradition History of the Fourth Gospel." In *Exploring the Gospel of John: In Honor of D. Moody Smith,* ed. R. Alan Culpepper and C. Clifton Black, 179–89. Louisville: Westminster John Knox, 1996.

Smith, Dwight Moody. "The Contribution of J. Louis Martyn to the Understanding of the Gospel of John." In *The Conversation Continues: Studies in Paul and John in Honor of J. Louis Martyn,* ed. Robert T, Fortna and Beverly R. Gaventa, 275–94. Nashville: Abingdon, 1990.

———. "The Johannine Miracle Source: A Proposal." In *Jews, Greeks and Christians: Religious Cultures in Late Antiquity. Essays in Honor of William David Davies,* ed. Robert Hamerton-Kelly and Robin Scroggs, 164–80. Leiden: Brill, 1976.

Smith, Jonathan Z. "Good News Is No News: Aretology and Gospel." In Jonathan Z. Smith, *Map Is Not Territory: Studies in the History of Religions,* 190–207. Studies in Judaism in Late Antiquity. Leiden: Brill, 1978. Reprint, Chicago: University of Chicago Press, 1993..

Smith, Morton. *Palestinian Parties and Politics That Shaped the Old Testament.* 2nd ed. London: SCM, 1987.

———. "Prolegomena to a Discussion of Aretologies, Divine Men, the Gospels and Jesus." *Journal of Biblical Literature* 90 (1971): 174–99.

Stibbe, Mark. *The Gospel of John: An Anthology of Twentieth-Century Perspectives.* New Testament Tools and Studies 17. Leiden: Brill, 1993.

Stone, Michael Edward. *Fourth Ezra: A Commentary on the Book of Fourth Ezra.* Hermeneia. Minneapolis: Fortress Press, 1990.

Streeter, Burnett Hillman. *The Four Gospels: A Study in Origins.* London: Macmillan, 1924.

Strugnell, J., D. J. Harrington, and T. Elgvin, in consultation with J. A. Fitzmyer. *Qumran Cave 4.XXIV: 4QInstruction (Musar leMevin): 4Q415 ff.* Discoveries in the Judaean Desert 34. Oxford: Clarendon, 1999.

Talmon, Shemaryahu. "The Emergence of Jewish Sectarianism in the Early Second Temple Period." In *Ancient Israelite Religion: Essays in Honor of Frank Moore Cross,* ed. Patrick D. Miller et al., 587–616. Philadelphia: Fortress Press, 1987.

Teeple, Howard M. *The Mosaic Eschatological Prophet.* Journal of Biblical Literature Monograph Series 10. Philadelphia: Society of Biblical Literature, 1957.

Theobald, Michael. *Das Evangelium nach Johannes Kapitel 1–12.* Regensburger Neues Testament. Regensburg: Pustet, 2009.

Thomas, Samuel I. *The "Mysteries" of Qumran: Mystery, Secrecy, and Esotericism in the Dead Sea Scrolls.* Society of Biblical Literature Early Judaism and Its Literature 25. Atlanta: Society of Biblical Literature, 2009.

Trebolle-Barrera, Julio. "Qumran Evidence for a Biblical Standard Text and for Non-Standard and Parabiblical Texts." In *The Dead Sea Scrolls in Their Historical Context,* ed. Timothy H. Lim et al., 89–106. Edinburgh: T&T Clark, 2000.

VanderKam, James C. "Apocalyptic Tradition in the Dead Sea Scrolls and the Religion of Qumran." In *Religion in the Dead Sea Scrolls,* ed. John J. Collins and Robert A. Kugler, 113–34. Studies in the Dead Sea Scrolls and Related Literature. Grand Rapids: Eerdmans, 2000.

Vermes, Geza. *The Complete Dead Sea Scrolls in English.* London: Penguin, 1997.

———. *The Story of the Scrolls: The Miraculous Discovery and True Significance of the Dead Sea Scrolls.* London: Penguin, 2010.

———, and Martin Goodman, eds. *The Essenes according to the Classical Sources.* Oxford Centre Textbooks 1. Sheffield: JSOT Press, 1989.

Wellhausen, Julius. *Erweiterungen und Änderungen im vierten Evangelium.* Berlin: Georg Reimer, 1907.

Wetter, Gillis Petersson. *Der Sohn Gottes: Eine Untersuchung über den Charakter und die Tendenz des Johannes Evangeliums. Zugleich ein Beitrag zur Kenntnis der Heilandsgestalten der Antike.* Forschungen zur Religion und Literatur des

Alten und Neuen Testaments 26. Göttingen: Vandenhoeck & Ruprecht, 1916.

Wilson, Brian R. *Magic and the Millennium: A Sociological Study of Religious Movements of Protest among Tribal and Third World Peoples.* London: Paladin, 1975.

Wrede, William. *Charakter und Tendenz des Johannesevangelium.* Tübingen: Mohr Siebeck, 1903.

———. *The Messianic Secret.* Cambridge: James Clarke, 1971.

Index of Ancient Sources

RABBINICAL LITERATURE

Index of Names and Subjects

2015.12.30   49.95 (44.65)